D0908369

Beyond Desegregation

New Frontiers in Urban Education
Kofi Lomotey, Series Editor

Beyond Desegregation

The Politics of Quality in African American Schooling

Editor
Mwalimu J. Shujaa

CORWIN PRESS, INC.
A Sage Publications Company
Thousand Oaks, California

Copyright © 1996 by Corwin Press, Inc.

For information address:

 Corwin Press, Inc.
A Sage Publications Company
2455 Teller Road
Thousand Oaks, California 91320
E-mail: order@corwin.sagepub.com

SAGE Publications Ltd.
6 Bonhill Street
London EC2A 4PU
United Kingdom

SAGE Publications India Pvt. Ltd.
M-32 Market
Greater Kailash I
New Delhi 110 048 India

Printed in the United States of America

Library of Congress Cataloging-in-Publication Data

Main entry under title:

Beyond desegregation: The politics of quality in African American
schooling / editor, Mwalimu J. Shujaa.
    p.   cm. — (New frontiers in urban education; v. 1)
    Includes bibliographical references and index.
    ISBN 0-8039-6262-2 (acid-free paper).—ISBN 0-8039-6263-0 (pbk.:
acid-free paper)
    1. Afro-Americans—Education—United States. 2. Politics and
education—United States. 3. School integration—United States.
4. Segregation in education—United States. I. Shujaa, Mwalimu J.
II. Series.
LC2717.B49   1996
371.97'96'073—dc20   95-50166

This book is printed on acid-free paper.

96 97 98 99 00 01 02 10 9 8 7 6 5 4 3 2 1

Corwin Production Editor: Diana E. Axelsen
Corwin Typesetter: Andrea D. Swanson

Contents

Preface

This book focuses on the politics of quality schooling for African Americans. School desegregation strategies are examined in political contexts. Through this approach, racialized uses of power in white self-interest are shown to influence policy making and policy implementation related to the schooling of African Americans. Also examined in these pages are some of the uses of power by African Americans to (re)define schooling and education in forming patterns of resistance to oppressive social relations.

Quality schooling has been a human rights issue among people of African descent since long before the so-called modern Civil Rights Movement. Anderson (1988) describes some of the efforts by formerly enslaved Africans to develop universal public schooling following the U.S. Civil War. In many instances, these schools were subverted by whites, who used private financial resources, ostensibly for philanthropic purposes, to manipulate the policies of these schools. The emergence of tax-supported, racially segregated public schools for African Americans provided the local white elites who controlled taxation an effective means of control over African American schooling.

Growing up in the 1950s, I saw my own schooling manipulated by white self-interest articulated by the local board of education. My first 3 years of schooling were spent at Frederick Douglass School in Parsons, Kansas. In Parsons, Douglass was the school designated for children of African descent from its founding in 1908 until it was closed in 1958. I loved Douglass School. I have never been able to say that about any school I have attended since. I visit my family and friends in Parsons at least once a year. Over the years, I have used some of my time during those visits to learn more about Douglass School. I interviewed the last principal to serve at Douglass and an African American minister who served on the local human relations commission during the period of school desegregation in Parsons. I also spent a few days poring over the Parsons Board of Education's minutes and local newspaper files from the Douglass School era. These inquiries have led me to believe that Douglass School was essentially dismantled as a community institution from 1951 to 1958.

The Parsons Board of Education's minutes of March 16, 1951, report that a letter from the superintendent of the Topeka, Kansas, school system had been received regarding a suit brought by the NAACP against the Topeka Board of Education. The letter asked if Parsons would participate in the suit as a friend of court "since the Parsons system also maintained separate schools for colored people" (Parsons Board of Education, 1951, p. 315). The board voted not to participate in the suit. The *Parsons Sun*, the city's daily newspaper, usually reported on Board of Education meetings in the next day's issue. There was no mention of the board's action in the *Sun* or of the letter from Topeka.

At a July 25, 1951, special meeting, the Parsons Board of Education voted to discontinue the upper 2 years (Grades 9 and 10) of junior high school at Douglass. It was noted that "in the last few years a trend had developed whereby many of the eighth grade graduates did not return to Douglass, but enrolled in other junior high schools" (Parsons Board of Education, 1951, p. 327). The board's report indicates that, at least as early as 1947, African American students were not totally restricted to attending Douglass School. The issue for whites in Parsons, many in the African American community believe, was not desegregating students. The real problem was putting African American teachers in classrooms to teach white students. Consider that on March 9, 1954, at a special meeting, the board voted to eliminate the seventh and eighth grades at Douglass and directed that "the Superintendent was to be instructed to notify those teachers whose services would not be needed because of this change" (Parsons Board of Education, 1954, p. 387). This pattern of eliminating grades at Douglass and dismissing African American teachers was repeated again on February 7, 1956, when the fifth and sixth grades were eliminated and another teacher was "notified that her services will be terminated at the end of the contract year" (Parsons Board of Education, 1956, p. 423).

Further credence is lent to the Douglass dismantlement theory by the board's decision on June 8, 1954, to negotiate the sale of a portion of the

Douglass School property to Powell Awbry, a local manufacturer, whose plant sat adjacent to the school. The final blow for Douglass came on July 10, 1957, when the board met for the "primary purpose of further discussion of integration in the Parsons public schools" (Parsons Board of Education, 1957, p. 440). At that meeting it was decided to eliminate the Douglass kindergarten for the 1957-1958 school year and to discontinue the school for the 1958-1959 school year. Ironically, the person who made the motion was none other than Powell Awbry, now a board member.

To accommodate the increased enrollment at the elementary school, whose attendance area included a large portion of the African American community on the west side of Parsons, a temporary K-3 elementary school was created in a wing of the West Junior High. As for the remaining Douglass teachers, the board's minutes state that it was "the present intention of the board to retain all Douglass personnel that can be used in the school system" (Parsons Board of Education, 1957, p. 441). Two Douglass teachers were retained; neither was assigned to a classroom. One, the former Douglass School principal, was hired as an itinerant music teacher; the other, who taught third grade when Douglass was closed, was hired as a librarian. A woman who had retired as principal of McKinley elementary school was brought out of retirement to teach third grade at the new temporary school. She was my first white teacher. The first words she said to me were, "Shut up. I don't know what you people were used to doing at Douglass, but things are going to be different here."

Douglass School was unquestionably the center of African American community life in Parsons, and it left an indelible impression on my life. I have always felt that African American people in Parsons lost something of great cultural value when Douglass School closed. This feeling has been exacerbated by the fact that the event certainly did not mean the end of racial segregation in Parsons. The local economy was controlled entirely by whites. We lived in distinct racial communities. The municipal government had no African American representation. In fact, when Parsons' schools were said to be desegregated, most of my Douglass classmates were resegregated by curriculum tracking when they reached the city's junior and senior high schools. My experiences have made me understand the importance of looking beyond school desegregation for ways to resolve what Kofi Lomotey (1990) has described as the persistent, pervasive, and disproportional failure of public schooling in the United States to meet the needs of African American students.

School desegregation crystallized as a legal strategy in 1950. Earlier litigation against segregated public schooling focused on making the funding and facilities provided African American students equal to that available to white students. In 1950, however, Thurgood Marshall, James Nabrit, and other legal scholars decided to abandon the strategy of challenging segregated schools on the basis of the separate but equal doctrine set forth in *Plessy v. Ferguson* (1896). The strategy they adopted challenged the constitutionality of the very concept of racial segregation in school systems. This shift in approach ultimately led to the 1954 decision by the Supreme Court in *Brown v. Topeka Board of Education* (Williams, 1987).

Although school desegregation's initial focus was on the quality of schooling afforded African Americans, since 1954 the pursuit of racial balance strategies emphasizing the physical reassignment of pupils in public school districts has increasingly dominated discussions about African American education (National Alliance of Black School Educators, 1984). Nonetheless, the majority of African American students live in large urban centers and attend schools that are predominantly African American (National Alliance of Black School Educators, 1984; Wilson, 1991-1992). African American students are not faring well in these schools. Moreover, recent increases in private school enrollments (Benson, 1991) suggest that many African Americans are choosing to put desegregation commitments aside, at least temporarily, to obtain quality schooling for their children in safe, antiracist, culturally affirming environments (Ratteray & Shujaa, 1987).

Scholars have expressed different views about whether school desegregation is, in fact, a necessary condition for quality schooling. Willie (1987) argues that African Americans have benefited overall from school desegregation but he points out that, although African Americans tend nationally to support desegregated schooling, there is resistance to the way desegregation has been implemented. Yeakey (1993) contends that African Americans have unfairly carried the burden for school desegregation. Hilliard (1988) points out that school desegregation strategies have left the substance of interrelated inequity functions in U.S. society unaddressed, or addressed only at a minimal level. Carruthers's (1994) view is that school desegregation became a strategy to diffuse intellectual resistance in African American communities where schools, although segregated, were important meeting places.

This book emanates from a project conceived during a series of discussions between the late Gail P. Kelly, Kofi Lomotey, and myself during 1990. A scholar-activist herself, Gail was intrigued that Kofi and I had been consistently involved in the independent African-centered schools movement since the early to mid-1970s. We discussed the implications of indicators suggesting that enrollments in these and other types of African

American independent schools were increasing while faith in public schools was waning. Our interpretation of these phenomena was that growing numbers of African American families were making critical distinctions between the imperatives associated with desegregating schools and those associated with obtaining quality schooling for their children. The fact that these African American families were looking at strategies beyond the desegregation of public schools in order to obtain quality schooling for their children led us to propose discussions about this phenomenon among scholars (Institute for Independent Education, 1990). The first of these discussions took the form of a conference at the State University of New York at Buffalo in November 1991. The second was a special issue of the journal, *Educational Policy*, which I edited in 1993. In these pages, we continue and expand this discussion among scholars.

I have divided the 12 chapters of this book into four parts:

I. Rethinking School Desegregation: Historical and Philosophical Contexts
II. Politics of Implementation and School Desegregation
III. School Desegregation's Impact on African American Community Life and Life in Schools
IV. Quality Schooling for African Americans: Visions Beyond Desegregation

A brief introduction is provided for each part.

References

Anderson, J. D. (1988). *The education of blacks in the South, 1865-1935.* Chapel Hill: University of North Carolina Press.

Benson, P. L. (1991). *Private schools in the United States: A statistical profile, with comparisons to public schools.* Washington, DC: U.S. Department of Education.

Carruthers, J. H. (1994). Black intellectuals and the crisis in Black education. In M. Shujaa (Ed.), *Too much schooling, too little education: A paradox of black life in white societies* (pp. 37-56). Trenton, NJ: Africa World Press.

Hilliard, A. G., III. (1988). Conceptual confusion and the persistence of group oppression through education. *Equity & Excellence, 24*(2), 36-42.

Institute for Independent Education. (1990). *African-American enrollment in independent schools* (Research notes on education). Washington, DC: Author.

Lomotey, K. (1990). Introduction. In *Going to school: The African-American experience* (pp. 1-9). Albany: State University of New York Press.

National Alliance of Black School Educators. (1984). *Saving the African American child.* Washington, DC: Author.

Parsons, Kansas, Board of Education. (1951-1957). Minutes. Unpublished.

Ratteray, J. D., & Shujaa, M. (1987). *Dare to choose: Parental choice at independent neighborhood schools.* Washington, DC: U.S. Department of Education.

Williams, J. (1987). *Eyes on the prize: America's civil rights years 1954-1965.* New York: Viking Penguin.

Willie, C. V. (1987). The future of school desegregation. In *The state of Black America, 1987.* New York: National Urban League.

Wilson, F. H. (1991-1992). The changing distribution of the African American population in the United States, 1980-1990. *The Urban League Review, 15*(2), 53-74.

Yeakey, C. C. (1993). The social consequences of public policy. *The Journal of Negro Education, 62*(2), 125-143.

Acknowledgments

This book would not have been possible without the support of Corwin Press. I especially want to thank Gracia Alkema, President of Corwin Press, for her faith in and patience with this project. Thanks also to the "point people" who worked with me at Corwin Press, Diana Axelsen, Ann McMartin, and Penny Domenico, for their calm guidance and assistance throughout the project.

I thank my fellow editors of *Educational Policy*—Philip Altbach, Edith Hoshino, Gail P. Kelly, Hugh G. Petrie, and Lois Weis—for their support and encouragement on the book and for letting it be my project.

There are many people at the State University of New York at Buffalo to whom I am grateful. To Patricia Maloney, I offer my sincere thanks for her assistance with the administration, organization, and editing of the manuscript. I also thank Sally Claydon for all the time she managed to find to clean up manuscripts in the midst of all the other things she had to do. Thanks to Nancy Myers for converting all those Mac diskettes to IBM format and to Brenda Myers for keeping my accounts in order. I am especially indebted to Austin Swanson, chair of the Department of Educational Organization, Administration, and Policy, for making departmental resources available during the course of this project.

I extend thanks to the following people who helped in an assortment of ways, ranging from proofreading to making comments about various chapters: Jennifer Beaumont, Mary Beth Boger, Nah Dove, Mark Garrison, and Barbara Shircliffe. Also, thanks to the copy editor, Jacqueline Tasch. In addition, I greatly appreciate the assistance of Thomas Barone and Rini Wahyuningsih, graduate students at SUNY-Buffalo, for their help with indexing this book.

I am grateful to Mr. Luther Dale and the Rev. G. E. Lakes for permitting me to interview them about the closing of Douglass School.

Finally, this project was supported in part by funding received from two State University of New York grants: Conversations in the Disciplines, sponsored by the Research Foundation of SUNY through the SUNY Faculty Senate, and Conferences in the Disciplines, sponsored by SUNY-Buffalo through the Office of the Provost. I also benefited from a Nuala McGann Drescher Affirmative Action Award and Leave provided jointly by New York State United University Profession Affirmative Action Committee and SUNY.

About the Authors

Hannibal T. Afrik is the National Public Relations Officer for the Council of Independent Black Institutions (CIBI). He has been an activist, writer, administrator, and educator in the movement for independent African-centered education for more than 20 years. He cofounded and served as administrator of Shule Ya Watoto (School for Children) in Chicago. He founded School Tech Services in 1989 and serves as an educational consultant. He has also been an instructor of biology at Northeastern Illinois University since 1986. Afrik's column, "For Black Education," has been a regular feature in the *Chicago Defender* since 1983.

Jennifer J. Beaumont is an Assistant Professor of Educational Administration at the State University of New York at Buffalo. Her research interests include the leadership of schools in urban systems, the superintendency, the role of central office administration in educational policy development and implementation, and the politics of education. She is completing a book for SUNY Press entitled *Urban School Leadership: The Politics of Involuntary Superintendency.*

Van Dempsey is an Assistant Professor of Educational Foundations at West Virginia University. His scholarly interests include education and morality, Appalachian culture and education, and school reform and restructuring. He and George Noblit were co-researchers in a school oral history project that provided the basis for the work presented here. A fuller presentation of that research is contained in their forthcoming book, *The Social Construction of Virtue: The Moral Life of Schools.*

Patricia A. Edwards is a Professor of Reading and a Senior Researcher at the National Center for Teacher Learning at Michigan State University. She is also the author of two nationally acclaimed family literacy programs, *Parents as Partners in Reading: A Family Literacy Training Program* and *Parents Prepare Their Children for Reading.* Her research interests include family/intergenerational literacy and emergent literacy, with a special focus on semiliterate and illiterate parents and children.

Judith L. Failer is an Assistant Professor of Political Science at Indiana University, Bloomington. She did her undergraduate work at Wesleyan University and her graduate studies at Princeton University. Her research interests include rights, legal status, homelessness, and mental illness.

Christine J. Faltz is Director of Precollege Programs at Marquette University in Milwaukee, Wisconsin. She is a former high school teacher for the Milwaukee Public Schools (MPS). In 1990, she was appointed to the African American Male Task Force of the MPS, served as one of the technical writers of the African American Immersion School Proposal, and currently chairs the personnel subcommittee of the African American Immersion School Implementation Committee. Her research interests, in addition to school desegregation, include the motivation and learning of African American students, culture-based and multicultural curricula, and systemic urban school district reform efforts. Currently she serves as a consultant for SRI International, as a member of the independent assessment team for Milwaukee's School-to-Work Initiative.

Carl A. Grant is Hoefs-Bascom Professor of Teacher Education in the Department of Curriculum and Instruction and a Professor in the Department of Afro-American Studies at the University of Wisconsin-Madison. He has written or edited 15 books or monographs in multicultural education and/or teacher education. These include *Research and Multicultural Education* (1993); *Making Choices for Multicultural Education* (with Christine Sleeter, 1994); *After the School Bell Rings* (with Christine Sleeter, 1986); *Bringing Teaching to Life* (1983); and *Community Participation in Education* (1979). He has also written more than 100 articles, chapters in books, and reviews. In 1993, Grant became president of the National Association for Multicultural Education (NAME).

Nancy M. Greenberg is a Researcher, Policy Analyst, and Pollster with the National Education Association. She is a member of the American Educational Research Association and the American Association for Public Opinion Research.

Anna Harvey is an Assistant Professor of Politics at New York University. Her research to date has investigated the effects of institutional structures on political outcomes. Her current project involves a book-length study of the effects of prior disfranchisement on political outcomes for women after passage of constitutional suffrage in the United States. She worked as a consultant on *Yonkers v. State of New York* (1995).

Ronald D. Henderson is presently Director of Research at the National Education Association (NEA). He was research manager at the National Institute of Education (now the Office of Educational Research and Improvement) and the U.S. Commission on Civil Rights and was manager of surveys at the NEA. His research activities as a writer or project manager have resulted in publications and presentations in areas of equity, desegregation, quality education, health insurance, underemployment and unemployment, aging, feminization of poverty, public opinion polls on education, and teacher opinion polls on a variety of topics.

Jennifer Hochschild is a Professor of Politics and Public Affairs at Princeton University, with a joint appointment in the Department of Politics and the Woodrow Wilson School of Public and International Affairs. She has been a Fellow at the Center for Advanced Study in the Behavioral Sciences and a visitor at the Institute for Advanced Study. She has served as a consultant or expert witness in several school desegregation cases, most recently *Yonkers Board of Education v. New York State.* She is the author of *Facing Up to the American Dream: Race, Class, and the Soul of the Nation* (1995); *The New American Dilemma: Liberal Democracy and School Desegregation* (1984); *What's Fair: American Beliefs About Distributive Justice* (1981); and a coauthor of *Equalities* (1981). She is a coeditor of *Social Policies for Children* (1996). She is currently writing a book on lessons to be learned from the history of school and housing desegregation in Yonkers, New York.

Gloria Ladson-Billings is an Associate Professor of Curriculum and Instruction at the University of Wisconsin-Madison, specializing in issues of multicultural education and culturally relevant pedagogy. She has written extensively on successful teachers for African American students. She is a 1989 recipient of the National Academy of Education's Spencer Postdoctoral Fellowship, the 1995 recipient of the National Association of Multicultural Education's Outstanding Research Award, and the 1995 recipient of the American Educational Research Association's Committee on the Role and Status of Minorities Early Career Contribution Award. Her latest research interest is critical race theory and its application to education.

Donald O. Leake is an Associate Professor of Educational Administration at Trenton State College in New Jersey. He cochaired the African American Immersion School Implementation Committee for the Milwaukee Public Schools. His areas of interest and expertise include urban schools, motivation of African American students, teacher effectiveness, and educational administration. His professional participation includes membership on the review board for the *Journal of Research in Middle Level Education.* He is coauthor of *Marginal Teachers* (1993) and has contributed articles to several educational journals including *Educational Policy, The Journal of Negro Education, Phi Delta Kappan, The National Association of Secondary Schools Bulletin,* and *Schools in the Middle.*

George Noblit is a Professor of Social Foundations of Education in the School of Education at the University of North Carolina at Chapel Hill. He is coeditor of *The Urban Review,* as well as a book series, *Understanding Education and Policy,* for Hampton Press. He received his Ph.D. in sociology from the University of Oregon and is an elected Fellow of the American Anthropological Association. Noblit studied school desegregation for over 20 years and was a Senior Fellow at the National Institute on Education on the Desegregation Studies Team in the mid-1970s. His current work is on the social construction of difference, focusing on both race and gender.

Janet W. Schofield is a Professor of Psychology and a Senior Scientist in the Learning Research and Development Center at the University of Pittsburgh. She is a social psychologist whose major research interest for over 20 years has been social processes in desegregated schools. She has authored or coauthored over 30 papers in this area and has written three books. One of these, *Black and White in School: Trust, Tension, or Tolerance?* was awarded the Society for the Psychological Study of Social Issues's Gordon Allport Intergroup Relations Prize.

Jeffrey M. Schneider is a Senior Policy Analyst in the National Center for Innovation at the National Education Association. He has written many papers and articles on methodological and substantive issues related to organizational characteristics, productivity, public policy, academic tracking, the inclusion of special needs students in regular classrooms, and student achievement. He was a member of the research team that established the fundamental principles of effective schooling. He also developed the NEA Team Approach to Better Schools (TABS) site-based decision making project and is currently a principal investigator of Keys to Excellence for Your Schools (KEYS), studying how school organizations influence the quality of educational outcomes for all types of students.

Mwalimu J. Shujaa is an Associate Professor of Social Foundations of Education at the State University of New York at Buffalo. He is executive officer of the Council of Independent Black Institutions (CIBI), an editor of *Educational Policy,* and a member of the editorial board of *Urban Education.* Shujaa edited *Too Much Schooling, Too Little Education: A Paradox of Black Life in White Societies,* Africa World Press (1994).

William F. Tate is an Assistant Professor in the Department of Curriculum and Instruction at the University of Wisconsin-Madison. He is also a senior researcher at the National Institute on Science Education sponsored by the National Science Foundation. His research interests include educational equity and the political and cultural dimensions of mathematics and mathematics education. He is a member of the editorial review boards of the *Journal for Research in Mathematics Education* and *Readings on Equal Education.* He has published recent articles on the political dimensions of African American education.

Carolyn J. Thompson is an Assistant Professor of Higher Education at the State University of New York at Buffalo. Prior to her SUNY appointment, she worked on state-level policy reform issues at the Education Commission for the States. Her research interests include higher education policy, college student leadership and development, and African American faculty issues. She is a member of the SUNY Press editorial board and the advisory board of the ASHE-ERIC Higher Education Reports.

Oscar Uribe, Jr., is Program Manager at the National Education Association's National Center for Innovation, where he provides leadership to professional and administrative personnel responsible for conceptualizing, designing, and implementing national programs in support of NEA's strategic objectives. His areas of interest include school reform, school restructuring, site-based

decision making, strategic planning, practice issues and trends, higher education, and information management.

Richard R. Verdugo is a Senior Policy Analyst in the Human and Civil Rights
Division of the National Education Association. His previous experiences were
with the National Council of La Raza, the Congressional Research Service
(Library of Congress), and the U.S. Department of Education. His areas of
expertise are the sociology of labor markets, sociology of education, racial
stratification, and survey methods. He is a reviewer for *The Hispanic Journal of
Behavioral Sciences, Social Science Quarterly, Journal of Human Resources,* and
Sociological Perspectives.

Emilie V. Siddle Walker is an Assistant Professor at Emory University in the
Division of Educational Studies. She is a former Spencer Post Doctoral Fellow
and recipient of the Young Scholars Award from the Conference of Southern
Graduate Schools. In addition to numerous talks and articles on the subject of
the segregated schooling of African American students, she is also coauthor of the
edited volume, *Facing Racism in American Education* (1990) and author of *Their
Highest Potential: A Case Study of African American Schooling in the Segregated
South* (1996).

William H. Watkins is an Associate Professor of Education at the University
of Illinois at Chicago. A veteran of the civil rights and antiwar movements, he
has committed his life, teaching, and scholarship to the causes of racial,
economic, and political justice. He is active in professional, political, and
community organizations. He has published recently in the *International Encyclopedia of Education, the International Encyclopedia of Curriculum, Harvard Educational Review,* and *Educational Theory.* Watkins is currently working on a
book entitled *The Architects of Black Education.*

This book is dedicated to Frederick Douglass School, Parsons, Kansas, 1908-1958

▨ PART I ▨

Rethinking School Desegregation
Historical and Philosophical Contexts

INTRODUCTION

Mwalimu J. Shujaa

In Chapter 1, William H. Watkins reconnects contemporary discourse about quality schooling and education with the work of early 20th-century intellectuals of African descent. Watkins reminds us that we have decontextualized and separated much of the contemporary dialogue about the quality of African American schooling from the African American intellectual tradition. The thinking of W. E. B. DuBois, Carter G. Woodson, Kelly Miller, Alexander Crummell, and others forms an essential part of that rich tradition. Our professional training has grounded many of us within the disciplinary boundaries that demarcate the social sciences. Part of learning the histories of these disciplines and their subdisciplines is learning in genealogical-like fashion which white men have laid claim to or been assigned paternity—the father of functionalism, the father of progressivism, and so on.

Many of us have struggled to gain recognition for intellectuals of African descent as contributors to the development of these disciplines. It must be quickly recognized, however, that these disciplinary distinctions are often products of internecine conflicts among whites for ideological dominance in the canon of Western thought. The overlapping

1

histories of sociology and anthropology as disciplines provide numerous illustrations of having been influenced by the pursuit of grand
theories of hierarchical ordering among human groups essentially to
justify white supremacy ideology and capitalist industrialization. A
hundred years ago and earlier, intellectuals of African descent were
exposing and writing in opposition to the ideas that were at the heart of
these power struggles within white supremacist scholarship. The structuring of knowledge within disciplines and subdisciplines has made
icons of racists and left the impact of white supremacy on the foundations of the disciplines unexamined.

Watkins points out that because the academy itself was segregated,
many people of African descent who today would be termed sociologists
were identified instead as journalists, as clergy, and often simply as
"professors" of unspecified disciplines. Yet, these are the people whose
written legacies offer us critical insights to the theoretical and conceptual foundations that contextualize much of the contemporary discourse about the schooling of people of African descent all over the
planet. Watkins calls on the contemporary African American scholar,
in particular, and all scholars, generally, to pay serious attention to the
work of late 19th- and early 20th-century intellectuals of African descent. The thinking of these intellectuals has to be revisited, connected
with, and built upon. Of particular concern for this volume are the
lessons that can be learned from this intellectual base that will contribute to our contemporary analyses of the role of schooling in African
American development and the relationship of the types of schooling
supported for African Americans to U.S. racial politics.

In Chapter 2, William F. Tate, Gloria Ladson-Billings, and Carl A.
Grant argue that the *Brown* decision was an attempt by the U.S. Supreme
Court to apply an essentially mathematical solution to a social problem.
The fact that the court failed to provide a verbal interpretation of the
mathematical model it developed allowed individual school districts to
implement peculiar responses that did not address the needs of African
American students. Tate and colleagues also put forth the idea that the
socially constructed definition of equality applied to the schooling of
African Americans is restrictive. These authors propose a shift to an
expansive vision of equality in schooling that reconsiders student diversity, curriculum, instruction, and parent-community involvement. They
point out that the Supreme Court's failure to make a clear statement

about how desegregation was to be carried out virtually ensured that the quality of the schooling afforded African American students would be a function of local power relations.

Tate and colleagues' expansive vision of equality has as its goal equal schooling outcomes regardless of students' physical placement. Although they acknowledge the significance of *Brown*, they argue that its implementation has not provided quality schooling for African American students. The primary reason for *Brown*'s failure, they argue, has been the influence of white self-interest on its implementation.

The United States was established as a nation-state for white people. In their historical analysis, Tate, Ladson-Billings, and Grant argue that people of African descent were objectified in such a way that they were thought of by the white architects of the society in mathematical rather than in human/social terms. This mathematical objectification was codified in the U.S. Constitution as the Three-Fifths Compromise. The authors connect this mathematical thinking to the *Brown* decision and the prevailing sociopolitical climate. They reason that the *Brown* decision, when broadly interpreted, potentially threatened existing U.S. social relations and the structuring of power. The courts left the existing white power structures to deal with mathematical tests of desegregation as they saw fit.

The mathematical model of equality constructed in the United States equates quality schools and schooling for African Americans with school desegregation. However, as Tate et al. also point out, the success of this model is and always has been contingent upon its ability to adapt to a cultural ethos of white self-interest. Thus, in the desegregation equals quality schooling for African Americans model, social laws of white self-interest that govern the desegregation process somehow become analogous to the natural laws that govern the universe.

We gain from Tate et al. a way of interpreting the logic upon which the strategy of equating school desegregation with quality schooling for African Americans rests. They show the logic to be faulty. If we accept their arguments, we are compelled to rethink our strategies for achieving quality schooling and the contribution that schooling might ultimately make to the education of African Americans.

Together, these two opening chapters provide a context for examining the historical and political construction of school desegregation as a strategy for achieving quality schooling for African Americans. We have invested much over the years in this strategy. Although it is often easy to ascertain how collective white self-interest has been protected in the way that the scenario has been played out, we must also open our minds to the ways in which *individual* black self-interests have also been served by the continuing investment in this strategy at the expense of African American students. Standards for quality schooling are needed that are grounded on principles of *collective* African American self-interest. Watkins directs us toward the black intellectual tradition for grounding and guidance; Tate, Ladson-Billings, and Grant encourage us to deconstruct the school desegregation model and to construct an expansive vision that commits us to equal schooling outcomes.

1

Reclaiming Historical
Visions of Quality Schooling
The Legacy of Early
20th-Century Black Intellectuals

WILLIAM H. WATKINS

Among the most disturbing phenomena in today's debates on the quality of African American schooling is that we seem to have lost sight of our history. Reforms such as multicultural education and the Afrocentric curriculum are presented and discussed as if they only recently fell from the sky. Our collective amnesia has decontextualized and separated much of the current dialogue from any historical antecedents. We have all but ignored the rich intellectual tradition of theory and practice in the protracted battle to provide, reform, and improve the schooling and education of African Americans.

The long history of slavery and segregation prevents us from explaining African American education in the same terms as the white community does. By the turn of the 20th century, the prevailing mode of intellectual inquiry was to compartmentalize. In the social sciences, for example, specialization was becoming the watchword. Psychology, sociology, political science, and even social studies were being defined as discrete pursuits that would ultimately locate them as separate subject-area curricula in

schools. The African American intellectual, educational, and reform tradition, however, developed differently.

Owing to the exclusion of enslaved Africans from most schooling, a
substantial African American scholarship did not congeal until the mid-
1890s. Although early black scholars were often trained in discrete disciplines, the realities of black life forced them to become generalists. It was
not uncommon to find African American sociologists identified as journalists, clergymen, and often simply as professors. Although a few scholars,
such as Alain Locke, were trained specifically in pedagogy, the majority of
African-descended educational thinkers, such as W. E. B. DuBois, Kelly
Miller, Carter G. Woodson, and bibliophile Arthur Schomberg, came from
other disciplines.

As white educational theorists of the period were linked to the likes of
the Eliot humanists, the Herbartians, the child study movement, and so on
(Kliebard, 1987), African-descended educators were tied more to general
sociological inquiry. With this understanding, we can locate and contextualize the early African American educational literature. Beyond locating
early 20th-century African American educational scholars and scholarship,
much needs to be said about how we currently understand nearly two
centuries of African American education and related reform movements.

The schooling or miseducation of African Americans has been inextricably connected to the politics of colonialism, slavery, and the subsistence
labor practices of the corporate-industrial United States (Watkins, 1989,
1994). Racial discrimination must be understood within the realm of
politics, not reduced to the level of aberrant human behavior or ethnocen-
trism. U.S. racial politics is the product of a desire for free and cheap labor
spanning nearly 400 years. Racism and exclusion belong within the category
of power, hegemony, and the economic arrangements of U.S. society.

Given the special political/racial development of the United States, it
is virtually impossible to examine African American education and educational reform purely from the standpoint of pedagogy. African American
education must be approached from the circumstances of politics and
power. It cannot be separated from the harsh and barbaric conditions under
which African Americans existed. Thus, in most cases for African Americans, educational reform has been wedded to social and political reform.

The examination of African American educational reform and reformers may best be approached from the knowledge bases of history, economics, and political sociology. This approach should situate African American
education within the social, economic, and racial order. Moreover, we
should not lose sight of formal and informal efforts to educate African

Americans prior to the mid-19th century. The task of this inquiry is to explore the theories, ideologies, and practices that have preceded and influenced current discourse. The intention is not to unearth the names and activities of every African American educational reformer, although some individuals will be highlighted as representatives of particular outlooks. The intent is, rather, to seek out trends and categories that are tied to the social and educational history of African Americans. A central objective is to identify the *ideological* nature of African American educational reform. Moreover, the chapter will briefly exhibit several early 20th-century giants of African American education who have been obscured in the public debate.

This chapter is divided into three sections. The first part (re)introduces the American Negro Academy (ANA), focusing on its role in assembling the emergent African American intelligentsia of the period. The discussion situates the Academy within the broad protest discourse that influenced the early thinking on African American educational reform. The second section presents a categorization or typology of the ideological nature of varying outlooks around the century's turn. Nationalist-separatist, Reconstructionist, Christian-Humanist, and Progressive-Liberal outlooks are presented for consideration. The third and concluding section reflects on a century of African American educational reform efforts. In so doing, the discussion strives to identify continuity and linkages between early outlooks and the contemporary discourse. The chapter closes with critical suggestions for further inquiry.

The American Negro Academy: Toward a Black Intelligentsia

Historians of African American education, such as Bond (1966), Bullock (1967), and Anderson (1988), have done an excellent job of describing the impact of the missionary societies, historically black colleges, philanthropic organizations, and other forces involved in the shaping of education and reform efforts. Although the American Negro Academy has not been overlooked, the full impact of its formation, outlooks, and membership has not found its way into the popular dialogue.

Beyond its obvious importance in formally assembling the outstanding African American social thinkers of the day, the Academy has importance in the educational discourse. With both social scientists and educators among them, Academy scholars devoted significant attention to matters of black education, its delivery, its ideological posture, and the prospects for its refinement and expansion.

Founded March 5, 1897, in Washington, D.C., the Academy has been called "the first major black American learned society" (Moss, 1981, p. 1). Its constitution defined the ANA as "an organization of authors, scholars, artists, and those distinguished in other walks of life, men of African descent, for the promotion of Letters, Science, and Art" (Moss, 1981, p. 1). The charge of the Academy was to publish, disseminate information on the harsh conditions of African American life, build a black intellectual community, encourage the intellectual development of black youth, and issue the truth about black life in America.

Its founding members included Alexander Crummell, an Episcopal minister educated in England, who became the Academy's first president; Francis Grimké, a Presbyterian minister and descendant of the famous abolitionist Grimkés; W. E. B. DuBois, then professor of history and economics at Atlanta University; William Crogman, professor of classics at Clark University; William Scarborough, professor of classics at Wilberforce University; and John Cromwell, a lawyer, politician, and journalist from Washington, D.C. Within a few years, that illustrious group would be joined by the likes of John Hope, president of Morehouse College and later Atlanta University; Alain Locke, philosopher, writer, and social critic; Carter G. Woodson, the so-called father of Black History; and James Weldon Johnson, writer and activist.

This all-star gathering of intellectuals of African descent restricted membership as individuals set about their tasks. Perhaps judged elitist or conservative by today's standards, the ANA became committed to the building of black civilization. In the Academy's framework, civilization meant the (re)construction of a literature, identity, art, music, and an education. Much of its early work was polemical in nature, taking on the dogma of the Social Darwinists and the scientific racists.

Among the noteworthy examples was Kelly Miller's (1897) attack on Hoffman's *Race Traits and Tendencies of the American Negro*. Hoffman argued in this work that blacks were degenerate and on the verge of extinction. Miller's critique was an articulate and scholarly defense of his people. It would join the many essays written by DuBois, Crummell, T. Thomas Fortune, and others, which contested racist explanations of societal and human development.

Education and educational reform were ever-present items in the platform of the ANA. Although perspectives differed, it is clear that Academy members favored expanding educational opportunities for African Americans. This expansion meant a full academic curriculum for the elementary grades and especially more higher education.

Academy members reacted strongly to Booker T. Washington and the Hampton-Tuskegee accommodationist model of education. Most of them, having received classical university training, had little sympathy for a program that highlighted vocational and agricultural training. Needless to say, Washington was not invited to join their ranks, nor did he have much sympathy for their efforts.

In the spirit of reconstructionism and reform, Academy members insisted that educated African Americans be situated to uplift their people. In one of its early Occasional Papers (number 8), the Academy articulated its educational position. Entitled "The Educated Negro and His Mission,"[1] the paper spoke of the urgent need for African American college graduates to shape the social, economic, and political development of the African American population.

The notion of the "talented tenth" popularly attributed to DuBois found sympathetic ears within the Academy among members such as the Rev. Crummell. In fact, it was not DuBois who developed the concept (see Anderson, 1988, p. 243). Generally, the Rev. Crummell and other Academy members believed that African Americans would have to be educated broadly in history, the classics, the humanities, mathematics, and the sciences. They understood that participation in the new U.S. social order would require intellectual as well as occupational skills.

The historical significance of the Academy for schooling and education and school and educational reform should not be overlooked. The Academy assembled the nation's top scholars and activists of African descent in the cause of the uplift of the race. It highlighted education as central to that uplift. It uniformly opposed accommodationist educational and political practices. Finally, within its ranks were articulated a variety of political and ideological strategies that would help shape a century of African American protest dialogue.

A Typology of African American Ideas About Educational Reform

The central purpose of this inquiry is to begin developing a typology of African American education reform ideology in the early 20th century. Several issues and questions surround that task. First, it can be argued that this period, approximately 1896 to World War I, was the crucial period in African American education. It ran from the end of Reconstruction through the key period in the corporate-industrial reordering of U.S. society. Questions about the place of African Americans in the social order were more urgent than ever. Could they integrate? Should they return to Africa? What would be their continuing economic and political role in the United States? What educational agenda would best suit their status? Who would decide?

Second, it has to be understood how African American educational reformers could overcome, or at least contest, the accommodationist educational program introduced by Samuel Armstrong, expanded by Thomas Jesse Jones, and practiced by Booker T. Washington. More important than Washington's popularity among the African American masses was his financial and personal support from white corporate foundations (Watkins, 1989). His notion of black people adapting themselves to the racial climate of the South was ideally suited to white corporate hegemonic objectives of maintaining blacks as semiskilled and subservient labor. Combating Washington's influence would be no easy task.

Third is the issue of ideological unity among the reformers themselves. Although African American intellectual and social theorizing was relatively nascent, distinct philosophical and political outlooks were discernible. The circumstances of slavery and sharecropping had created varied forms of resistance and opposition. By the turn of the century, black nationalists, separatists, and emigrationists were to be joined by different strains of socialists,[2] progressives, and assorted liberals. Challenges to U.S. capitalism would become a part of the dialogue on educational reform (Woodson, 1933).

Last, and of most contemporary concern, questions need to be raised about today's reform movement(s), including school desegregation. Afrocentrism, multiculturalism, and the like are rooted in early 20th-century (and earlier) black educational reform ideology. What is that legacy? How have the various separatist, liberal, and revolutionary outlooks shaped today's discourse? Perhaps most important, we should recognize today's political context in which reform efforts operate. Black educational reform outlooks had their roots in the protest ideology that first emerged in the early 19th century. The assortment of nationalist and Africanist outlooks took on new meaning in the early 20th century.

Black Nationalists, Pan-Africanists, and Separatists

European colonialism and the international slave trade scattered African people throughout the Western hemisphere. Nationalists, Pan-Africanists, and separatists emerged in response to the debasement of Africa and the shameless and humiliating exploitation of her scattered people. Wilson

Moses (1978) discusses the origins of these outlooks. He points to the emergence of *macro-nationalist* theories evident in the emergence of Pan-Germanism and Pan-Slavinism, where the objective was to unite various independent ethnic groups under the banner of collective nationalism. He traces the historical development of Pan-Africanism especially to the maroon revolutions of Haiti, Jamaica, and Surinam during the 17th and 18th centuries. Within the United States, he believes the slave rebellions, especially the Vesey and Turner insurrections, were important factors in nationalist, Africanist, and separatist concept formation.

Colonialism became so profitable to the Western industrial nations that its continuation was much desired. All political, social, and educational policy was designed to exploit cheap labor, repatriate profits to Western corporations, and maintain a level of acquiescence or social control. The southern United States and much of Africa were to become linked as objects and subjects of colonial educational practices. Southern accommodationist educational practices were to be exported to Africa via the missionary associations and corporate foundations (King, 1971; Watkins, 1989, 1994). Thomas Jesse Jones, former Hampton social science professor and educational director at the powerful Phelps-Stokes Fund for nearly three decades, was among the important white architects and administrators of these colonial education programs (Watkins, 1990b).

The curriculum of colonial schooling called for manual labor training, character building, patriotism, piety, and healthful living. The Hampton social studies encouraged acceptance of racial evolutionism, support for U.S. capitalism, and disdain for socialist and communist economic systems (Jones, 1906). Intellectual training for participation in the emergent industrial democratic society was mostly absent from accommodationist schooling.

Nationalist, Africanist, and miscellaneous separatist ideologies in America date to the early 19th century.[3] Although these ideas and their advocates were hardly in complete ideological agreement, they nevertheless had much in common.

Strains of Pan-Africanist and black nationalist thought covered a wide range of outlooks and activities. They may be described as identificationist, emigrationist, culturalist, separatist, and so on. Over time, their activities have ranged from polemics to armed movements for national liberation. In the broadest terms, these views have stood against colonialism, for a united Africa, for the revitalization and promotion of African or black cultural ideals, and for the betterment and uplift of black people.

Until the turn of the 20th century, black nationalist and separatist educators were scattered among the literary societies, Freedmen's Bureaus, independent schools, Sabbath schools, and similar institutions. Black education in the Reconstruction-era South was active. About one in four black children attended some kind of school during this period (Anderson, 1988). These schools, typically funded by missionary societies, favored a classical curriculum aimed to prepare formerly enslaved people for participation in the new order.

By the early 20th century, the more militant nationalist ideology fueled by emigrationist sentiment had taken shape in the African American political community. Stirred by Bishop Turner, now under the leadership of Marcus Garvey, the emigrationist movement became a significant mass movement with tens of thousands of adherents.

Within education, the program of the nationalists has always reflected their ideology. Separatism, racial and cultural unity, and uplift have served as general themes. For two centuries, the separatists and nationalists have longed for a curriculum where the interests of Africans and African Americans could take precedence over the Eurocentric models of civilization and culture. These outlooks have provided a long legacy of African schools, free schools, civil rights schools, Black Muslim schools, alternative schools, and many others committed to the black race.

Because nationalist, Pan-Africanist, and separatist sentiments have been so overlapping, broad, and inclusive, it is far beyond the scope of this chapter to tag certain individuals with precise labels. Certainly DuBois, various Academy members, and a variety of African American educational thinkers at different times fit these general descriptions. However, DuBois, by virtue of his broad economic and political outlooks, deserves further scrutiny as a reconstructionist theorist.

W. E. B. DuBois: Black Social Reconstructionist Reformer

The reconstructionist orientation is one not often associated with African American education. The social reconstructionist movement usually brings to mind George S. Counts, the Rugg brothers, Sidney Hook, and their colleagues. They are most often seen as the radical progressives who embraced leftist outlooks during the late 1920s and early 1930s. Having interests beyond education, they advocated the involvement of schools in challenging and changing the political and economic arrangements of society (Counts, 1932). Embracing collectivism, democratic socialism, and other varieties of egalitarianism, these so-called radicals contributed a historical foundation to many of today's radical reformers and critical theorists.

Woodson (1933) and others[4] spoke of the growing popularity of socialistic ideas among African Americans in the early 20th century. A. Philip Randolph is often cited among this group. Socialistic and reconstructionistic outlooks were noted in the Academy as well. There can be little doubt that DuBois, in no small way, is linked to this general category of thought. It has been argued (Watkins, 1990a) that DuBois, by virtue of his outlook and activities, must be associated with this group. DuBois's linkages to the social reconstructionists help to explain both his and their views, as they emerged in the polemics of Booker T. Washington. DuBois's influence was so powerful he merits our attention.

DuBois personally explored nearly every strain of radical thought that surfaced in the 19th and 20th centuries. However, it can be said that the progressives were of particular interest to DuBois. As the progressives and reconstructionists advanced the cause of social reform, they called attention to the emerging problems of the U. S. corporate-industrial state and issues related to it. In this effort, education came under increased scrutiny.

The progressives[5] advanced a new examination and critique of the dynamics of schooling. They began to look at school as a social and political construct. The more radical progressives[6] began to explain schooling in terms of power and ideology. They viewed schools as linked to dominant political and economic ideologies, that is, the corporate state and its narrow objectives. It was at this chronological and political juncture that the interests of DuBois very definitely overlap the progressive educational community in general and the social reconstructionists in particular.

Although the social reconstructionists never claimed DuBois, nor did he claim them, they were undeniably linked by virtue of their views on the nature of society, socialism, school curriculum, and reform. As segregationism dominated the sociopolitical processes, racial politics also influenced radical social theory. Notions of nationalism frequently confronted views of internationalism.

Societal reform represented the common historical thread between DuBois and the reconstructionists. The democratic-socialist views of the left wing of the movement were consistent with DuBois's views between 1910 and 1930. A collectivist economic order without revolution is what DuBois had long advocated. Consistently supporting and being supported by such progressives as Walter Lippmann, Jane Addams, and many others, DuBois was comfortable with this company. Also, he was an unyielding supporter of educational reform, the suffrage movement, and trade unionism—all of which were reform issues. Marable (1986) said of DuBois:

He sought to advance theoretical concepts on the meaning of each
movement to the reconstruction of American democracy. But as a Negro,
DuBois was always aware of the veil of color that inhibited many white
radicals from pursuing creative reform strategies challenging racial inequality. He believed that the central contradiction in democratic society
was the burden of racism, and that if left unchallenged, racial prejudice
would compromise the goals of social reformers. (p. 84)

Because of DuBois's intense concern with questions of race, class, and
politics, his views on education are often overshadowed. It will be argued
that DuBois's views on the purposes of education are closely connected with
those of George S. Counts, Harold Rugg, Sidney Hook, and others associated with the heyday of social reconstructionism during the 1930s.

Because he focused on race and they did not, three points of emphasis
obscure DuBois's kinship to the social reconstructionists. DuBois was
convinced that a differentiated system of education existed for the mostly
southern and rural African American population. The educational system
for African Americans, he repeatedly argued, was a product of the politics
of control. He pointed to the unholy alliance of the white North and
reactionary South as responsible for the segregated, underfunded, and
inferior schooling of African Americans.

Second, we must consider DuBois's demand for rigor within this
context. Often funded and controlled by private agencies, such as corporate
philanthropies, black schools and colleges in many cases had a curriculum
that placed socialization ahead of academic training. As he railed against
differentiated education, DuBois demanded rigorous study as imperative
to understanding the complexities of an ever-changing world. Although he
is sometimes branded as an elitist, DuBois recognized that only those widely
read in the social sciences and humanities would be capable of offering
intelligent leadership for the tasks of liberation.

Finally, the black college, in DuBois's view, should teach about social
problems. Their curriculum should be infused with the problems of race,
caste, and the socioeconomic order. The black college should mercilessly
critique every manifestation of injustice. Opposing the traditional view of
the academy, DuBois felt the black college could not separate itself from
politics and social reform. Speaking on the cultural mission of Atlanta
University, DuBois suggested that a primary social objective of the black
college should be to uplift the civilization.

In this area, DuBois becomes the consummate social reconstructionist.
Beyond cognitive development, the reconstructionists saw a special role for

schooling. That role was to assist the evolution of a new enlightenment and even a new social order. By virtue of its positioning in society, its confrontation with ideas, its dynamic nature, and the perceived leadership role of teachers, schools were to be viewed as having revolutionary possibilities (Watkins, 1990a).

DuBois consistently upheld the notion that schooling was both personally and socially emancipatory. He noted that education should "give to our youth a training designed above all to make them men of power" (p. 14) DuBois often said that education must prepare one to do the "world's work." What was the world's work? DuBois (1973) answers:

> The world compels us today as never before to examine and reexamine the problem of democracy. In theory we know it by heart: all men are equal and should have equal voice in their own government. This dictum has been vigorously attacked. All men are not equal. Ignorance cannot speak logically or clearly even when given voice. If sloth, dullness, and mediocrity hold power, civilization is diluted and lowered, and government approaches anarchy. The mob cannot rule itself and will not choose the wise and able and give them the power to rule. (p. 118)

Education, for DuBois (1973), becomes social capital that can be used to influence society. In an eloquent summary of his views on the power of education, DuBois noted in 1930 that people of African descent would have to force themselves into the modern world by "outthinking and outflanking the owners of the world who are too drunk with their own arrogance and power to oppose us successfully" (p. 77).

Ultimately the social reconstructionism of DuBois rests with his political and social philosophy. Like his radical counterparts in the 1930s, DuBois advocated a (collectivist) democratic socialist organization of society's wealth, resources, and knowledge. He argued in 1942:

> In the period between 1860 and 1914, capitalism had come to its highest development in the European world, and its development meant the control of economic life and with that the domination of political life by the great aggregation of capital. It became, therefore, increasingly clear, as Karl Marx emphasized at the beginning of the era, that there could be no real democracy unless there was greater economic equality. (cited in Weinberg, 1970, p. 196)

DuBois the socialist looked for a vehicle of social reform. Like many others, he concluded that the dynamic nature of ideas and ideology could prompt change. For DuBois, there was an undying belief that ideas, when adopted by people, became a force in the real world. That belief continues to point reformers and radicals to the schools in search of change.

Although DuBois embraced reconstructionist outlooks, many of his colleagues, contemporaries, and fellow reformers were bound by more traditional views within the African American sociohistorical experience. Christian humanism was such an outlook.

The Christian Humanists

The Christian humanists were among the most significant educational reformers of the early 20th century. Christian humanism was rooted in a century of abolitionist/missionary society thought. Just as many missionary societies campaigned vigorously for the end of chattel slavery, their fundamental belief in God and human righteousness shaped their continued advocacy of human justice for African Americans.

Despite their humanism, missionary outlooks were problematic, as their ideology lacked political focus. Driven to do God's work, missionaries often did not distinguish between Christianizing and civilizing. Anderson (1988) describes this phenomenon:

> Most northern missionaries went south with the preconceived idea that the slave regime was so brutal and dehumanizing that blacks were little more than uncivilized victims who needed to be taught the values and rules of civil society. They were bent on treating the freedmen almost wholly as objects. Many missionaries were astonished and later chagrined, however, to discover ex-slaves had established their own educational collectives and associations, staffed schools entirely with black teachers, and were unwilling to allow the educational movement to be controlled. (p. 6)

For missionaries, there was little distinction between Christianizing, civilizing, and educating. These were seen as inextricably connected. Although the missionary curriculum varied, for the most part it looked to training in literature, the humanities, and the natural sciences. Vocational training was viewed by many missionary societies as perpetuating black people's status as beasts of burden. Missionary education was, for the most part, classical or liberal education.

Christian humanist, missionary-influenced education had a profound impact on African American educational theorizing. First, Africans saw that the roots of the abolitionist movement were missionary-connected. Second, Christian humanism was consistent with the sociospiritual outlook already engendered in the African masses in the United States. Last, people of African descent in the United States unanimously believed that formal education was the path to a better life.

Alexander Crummell offers an example of the Christian humanist influence in educational reform. Crummell, born a free African man in the United States, was educated at the Quaker-operated African Free School in New York City in the early 1820s. This school was noted for its Lancasterian or Monitorial format, which employed parent participation, rigid discipline, regular inspection, and oral work. The subject matter focus was on astronomy, geography, grammar, spelling, reading, arithmetic, elocution, and penmanship (Rigsby, 1987). Crummell frequently recalled how the school's emphasis on group effort in place of competition gave him a love for learning.

He continued his classical-liberal education at Oneida Institute (in New York), where he studied Greek, Roman history, English history, modern languages, and classical English poetry. This European classical education in the midst of African enslavement not only forged his educational outlooks but also helped point him to the ministry as a vocation. Crummell, as the senior and most respected African American scholar of his time, would profoundly influence educators in the Academy and beyond.

It can be argued that the philosophical and ideological thought of Crummell was representative of the Christian humanist tradition, which influenced not only his period but perhaps a century of ideology. Rigsby (1987), a biographer of Crummell, presents an exhaustive study of his intellectual, educational, social, and world outlook. Several points attract our attention.

Crummell believed people are creatures of reason who possess intellectual and moral powers that must be cultivated. Education is to prepare the intellectual power, whereas religion works toward moral development. Development was essential to Crummell as he saw an incomplete world. Crummell's world was imperfect and in a state of becoming. Intellectual and moral education was to assist in that unfolding process. Man's responsibility to God is to complete the world.

Brotherhood was an important notion in Crummell's philosophic scheme. The liberation of the African race thus became a sacred cause. Black people were thus admonished to use all energy in this cause.

Regarding the talented tenth, Crummell believed this select group of people could and should accept the responsibility to lead their people. Sometimes criticized as elitist, Crummell (1992) defended his outlook in an essay entitled "Civilization the Primal Need of the Race": "If the academic scholars are not inspired with the notion of leadership and duty, then with all their Latin and Greek and science they are but pedants, trimmers, opportunists" (p. 287). Talented African Americans, for Crummell, were not those who enjoyed privilege, but rather those who would commit their talent and capabilities to the mission of their people's uplift.

Truth was central to Crummell's Christian humanism. It is God's will that human beings educate themselves to seek truth. Truth seeking is thus a duty of humanity. Education then becomes elevated to a commitment. Choosing ignorance could not be tolerated. Not to educate oneself is to thwart the plan of God.

Christian humanism was deeply imbedded in the African American experience. However, perhaps the most popular ideological approach among African American educational reformers was the progressive-liberal approach. This outlook seemed well-suited for a people seeking a place in the new democratic industrial order.

The Progressive-Liberal Outlook

The progressive-liberal reform outlook probably represents the most mainstream and consensus viewpoint. It can be argued that this outlook is rooted in the notion of the liberal democratic state. The liberal democratic state tolerates reform. Reform is viewed as the way to correct past inequities. It is assumed that the political state responds to exclusion and injustice and accepts the democratic process as the optimum vehicle for change. A large number of African American educators—perhaps a majority—at the century's turn believed change could be made within the established political and educational bureaucracy.

Progressive liberalism might be illustrated by profiling four black educators of this period. Two, Woodson and Locke, are well-known in the popular literature. The other two, Cromwell and Miller, are unknown in the various mainstream literatures, but were highly regarded in their field.

Carter G. Woodson: Historian/Educator

Carter Woodson was among the best-schooled African Americans of his time. Obtaining his A.B. and M.A. from the University of Chicago, he later took his Ph.D. from Harvard. Popularly known as the father of black history, Woodson was founder and director of the Association for the Study of Negro Life and History (ASNLH) in 1915 and editor of its organ, *The Journal of Negro History*.

Like many of his peers, Woodson cut his intellectual teeth during the Progressive era. He became a member of the American Negro Academy and was credited by some with preventing a significant rivalry between it and the ASNLH—the two preeminent African American scholarly organizations of the day—by working actively in both. Others thought he favored his own ASNLH.

As with his contemporaries in the ANA, Woodson was drawn to matters of education and curriculum. After much reflection, he completed his *The Mis-Education of the Negro* in 1933. It is Woodson the curricularist who captures our attention here.

Woodson's work is an angry one. He believed the prevailing educational system had failed the cause of African Americans. He believed the curriculum was creating accommodating, accepting, conforming people rather than dynamic, socially and politically conscious individuals who would step forward in the cause of their people. Although not a treatise on progressive education, Woodson's themes sound much like Dewey's. Education should foster civic participation. For Dewey, it was for the ideals of democratic society, whereas for Woodson, it was for the cause of equality in the democratic society.

In the true spirit of progressive education, Woodson was appalled at the political education of the African American. Political participation should force a new dialogue on justice and equality and public policy. Instead, Woodson observed the political silencing of a people. The processes of schooling and the curriculum were complicit in that silencing process. The depoliticizing of African Americans, Woodson noted, had led to their exclusion from the political processes.

Beyond civic participation, Woodson believed blacks unwittingly contributed to prolonging their oppression by not putting education to the service of equality. Speaking of mis-education, Woodson's (1933) oft-quoted assertion reads,

The problem of holding the Negro down therefore is easily solved. When you control a man's thinking, you do not have to worry about his actions. You do not have to tell him not to stand here or go yonder. He will find his "proper place" and will stay in it. You do not need to send him to the back door. He will go without being told. In fact, if

there is no back door, he will cut one for his special benefit. His
education makes it necessary. (p. xxxiii)

Woodson was concerned about the Eurocentric nature of the curriculum. He lamented that the culture and civilization of the European was
promoted to the exclusion of any other. In this process the African became
a nonentity deserving of no scholarly attention.

Having witnessed the great debates between advocates of industrial
education versus the European classical or liberal outlook, Woodson criticized both. He understood that the corporate philanthropies were invested
in the continuation of African American subservience, and he held out little
hope that their brand of industrial education would equip black people for
the new social order. On the other hand, he saw no great gains coming from
European classical education. He observed that lack of opportunity in the
social order prevented African Americans schooled in the European classical sense from applying their intellectual skills.

Among Woodson's most stinging indictments was that highly schooled
and mostly middle-class African Americans were being estranged from their
own people. He lamented that the formally educated were abandoning the
African American church and other institutions where their talents could be
put to use. Christian agency for Woodson was important to foster the kind of
altruistic uplift needed for the African American masses. Instead, he felt that
formally educated African Americans were being drawn to a misguided degenerate theology that justified inequality and the inhumane social order.

Woodson suggested that schooling left African Americans in a state of
moral surrender. Confused and dispirited African Americans were resigned
to segregation and long-term inequality. He wrote, "At one moment Negroes fight for the principles of democracy, and at the very next moment,
they barter it away for some temporary advantage" (Woodson, 1933, p. 3).
For Woodson, hopeless, helpless, and hapless formally educated African
Americans, seeing no hope for alteration in their social circumstances,
succumb to the system and reach for small crumbs. In so doing, they join
in the exploitation of their own people.

Woodson found miseducated African Americans not only dispirited
but corrupt as well. Abandoning hope, the twisted African American intellectual seeks to lead rather than serve. Blacks in responsible positions
become irresponsible, trading on power and privilege. Those designated to
serve end up trying to fleece the flock.

Woodson was particularly discouraged by the exclusion of the African
and African American experiences from the general curriculum. The con-

sequences were that both the larger society and African American people themselves were deprived of much human knowledge. The story of African enslavement, among the greatest of human dramas, would not be properly told. Woodson deeply believed that a race separated from its history could never find itself.

John W. Cromwell: Journalist/Educator

Among the little-known Progressive era African American educators and curricularists was John Wesley Cromwell. Known in African American literature as a founding member of the ANA (1896) and as a confidant of the Rev. Alexander Crummell, Cromwell was a figure of considerable importance.

Not unlike other African American scholars of his time, Cromwell was drawn in many directions. Considered an accomplished amateur historian, with extensive collections of books and art from the African experience, Cromwell was a public school teacher in Washington, D.C., as well as the publisher of a newspaper for which he was the principal journalist. As a young man, Cromwell had been involved in the Reconstruction politics of Virginia (Moss, 1981). Upon receipt of a law degree from Howard University, he accepted a clerkship in the U.S. Treasury Department. He understood early the African American community's need for information from an African American perspective. His paper, *The Washington Record*, was well-regarded.

That same drive to inform compelled Cromwell during the Progressive era. He believed it imperative that African American educators, as well as the larger community, have access to the dialogues and debates surrounding slavery, Reconstruction, and the general plight of the African American community. Reconstruction was a pet issue for Cromwell. He was disturbed that white scholars falsely conjured up its horrors, thus calling black self-government into question. Thus, in April 1910, the first publications of the American Negro Monograph Company appeared with Cromwell its editor-in-chief. The advertisement for the Monographs read,

There are many rare historical documents of especial interest to the American Negro that are not accessible outside of the great libraries or special collections. In this day of rapid movements and stirring events, there are frequently facts of far-reaching import that deserve the widest circulation and which should be brought within the reach of educators, professional men and women, scholars and thinkers, in the smallest hamlet. (Cromwell to John Edward Bruce, personal communication, February 3, 1912, quoted in Moss, 1981, p. 197)

Although short-lived—it was published for only 11 months—the Monographs were clearly aimed at providing African American educators with curriculum materials for progressive education. Cromwell lamented the cessation of publication: "We have not one educational magazine in the land that can reach our large body of teachers" (Cromwell to Bruce, personal communication, February 3, 1912, quoted in Moss, 1981, p. 197).

Cromwell, finally, can be considered among the important black educator-curricularists of the Progressive era. As an educator, his commitment to the learning of black history and the promotion of social justice was unswerving. He spent a good portion of his professional life trying to rally black educators to that cause. His election as president of the ANA in December 1919 was the capstone to his long life and career-long commitment to the education of his people.

Kelly Miller: Mathematician/Educator

Although he received little attention in mainstream educational and curriculum scholarship in the United States during the Progressive era or since, Kelly Miller was an acknowledged giant among African American educators. Earning an A.B. degree from Howard University, Miller spent 2 years as a graduate student at Johns Hopkins University, studying both mathematics and physics. He would later return to Howard University as a professor of mathematics and, more important, as one of the most hailed educators of his time.

Early on, Miller advocated for the assembling of the African American learned community. Like Crummell, DuBois, and others, he believed that scholars of African descent had a special responsibility to history and their people. He would quickly join with the founders of the ANA in calling for an intellectual clearinghouse.

As mentioned earlier, Miller announced his presence to the academic world in 1897 in his polemic against Hoffman. He distinguished himself as an educator in a talk to the American Social Science Association (ASSA) in 1900. Charles Warner, president of ASSA, had lectured that higher education was wasted on black people. Instead of bringing about personal and social elevation, Warner argued that it "bred ideas, indisposition to work, and vaporous ambition in politics, and that sort of conceit of gentility of which the world has already enough" (quoted in Moss, 1981, p. 86). Miller defended black higher education in his talk to the ASSA and continued that theme throughout many of his later essays and activities. Like his intellectual colleagues, he viewed higher education as a central agent in reclaiming and promoting the greatness of his people.

Miller's educational and curricular views were elaborated in his widely circulated essay on his beloved Howard University. Entitled "Howard: The National Negro University," the article by Miller (1925) integrated his views on racial uplift, politics, and education. In that essay, Miller acknowledged that Howard, and the African American academy in general, had to restore formal education to African Americans. He wrote of the need to

> develop a body of Negro men and women with disciplined faculties and liberalized powers with the hope and expectation that they would quickly assume their place as leaders of the life of the masses by virtue of the rightful claim and authority of the higher culture. (p. 316)

He acknowledged that the emergent industrial order placed new demands on the black academy, and that "its new objective as the old is to develop leaders for the wise guidance and direction of the masses of the Negro race" (p. 316). For Miller, the black college had both vocational and social mandates.

Acknowledging the need for race consciousness, Miller (1925) called for a curriculum whose "philosophy must be based upon the fundamental principles of democracy and human brotherhood" (p. 321). Miller's notion was that the curriculum should go beyond professional training into preparation for societal participation. He wrote,

> The fundamental aim of education, therefore, should be manhood rather than mechanism. The ideal is not a working man, but a man working, not a business man, but a man doing business; not a school man, but a man teaching school, not a statesman, but a man handling the affairs of state, not a medicine man, but a man practicing medicine, not a clergyman, but a man devoted to the things of the soul. (pp. 317-318)

Alain L. Locke: Philosopher/Educator

Alain LeRoy Locke was born in Philadelphia in 1886. He studied at the Philadelphia School of Pedagogy and later attended Harvard, where he received three degrees, including a Ph.D. A Phi Beta Kappa at Harvard,

Locke was the first African American to win the prestigious Rhodes Scholarship. After study at Oxford and the University of Berlin, Locke received his initial academic appointment as professor of education and English at Howard University. He later moved to the department of philosophy, where he remained as professor and chair for the next 40 years.

Locke rapidly gained notoriety for his many published books and articles. He eventually published more than a dozen books on black culture, art, literature, and race relations. On the strength of his work and respect within the black intellectual community, Locke was quickly invited to join the ANA, where he rose to positions of leadership.

Locke's most acclaimed book, published in 1925, originally was entitled *The New Negro: An Interpretation.* The progressive liberal influence can be discerned in this work, which examines the changing cultural and social life of African Americans in the new order. He speaks of the "dynamic phase," the "spiritual emancipation," and the new promise of "self-expression" in the modern period. Locke sees the new industrial democracy providing hopes for a break with the stultifying past. Locke observed both a physical and cultural transformation in the early 20th century. He wrote, "In the very process of being transplanted, the Negro is becoming transformed" (p. 6). He spoke of black people having, for the first time, a "democratic chance."

Locke was hopeful that the new order would protect African Americans. If democracy was to be the watchword, then certainly it would protect all who fell under its domain. He wrote,

> Democracy itself is obstructed and stagnated to the extent that any of its channels are closed. Indeed they cannot be selectively closed. So the choice is not between one way for the Negro and another way for the rest, but between American institutions frustrated on the one hand and American ideals progressively fulfilled and realized on the other. (1925, p. 12)

Locke's deep connection to progressive education and educators is revealed in a little-known article he wrote for *Frontiers of Democracy* (1940/ 1971). Entitled "With Science as His Shield: The Educator Must Bridge Our 'Great Divides,' " Locke revealed his curriculum platform. Here he argues for intercultural, akin to today's multicultural, education. His rationale is drawn directly from Progressive era thought: that is, the curriculum should prepare students for participation in the democratic, in this case pluralistic, society.

This essay reflects Locke's outlook that the school has a social purpose. That purpose is to contribute to democratic societal development. He warns of looming totalitarianism, as well as the absolutism of the past. Locke's words are drawn directly from the progressive liberal tradition.

> This is apparently the most reliable and constructive contribution education can make to democracy, for it should further enlightened and functional citizenship. . . . The school, after all, cannot alone create democracy or be primarily responsible for it. At the same time, it has an obligation to contribute vitally toward it and a critical, progressive, and unprejudiced social understanding sure would seem to be the most appropriate and valuable contribution to democracy the school could possibly make. (1925, p. 210)

Locke, like his kindred progressive liberals, held out hope that educational reform was possible in the liberal democratic state. Reform for him was both quantitative and qualitative. Insisting that education be expanded among the African American population, he also wanted his people to be prepared for full participation in economics, politics, and culture.

Reflections on a Century of African American Thought on Educational Reform

Reforming African American education is hardly a new enterprise. For the last century (and more), the African American educational community has been critical of colonial practices in both the form and content of schooling and education. The various strains of protest and critique are deeply rooted in the social, economic, political, racial, and religious experiences of an oppressed and long-suffering people. Views on education reform are not dissimilar to the broader reform views within the African experience in the United States.

Christian humanism is deep within the marrow of black folk. It is a reflection of both their piety and their hope for all people to be treated decently. Black nationalist, Pan-Africanist, and separatist views are a reaction to the harshness of racism and discrimination. Their evolution over two centuries has witnessed hope for the revitalization of an African culture capable of uplifting its people on the continent and in the diaspora. The reconstructionist thread represents the radical and revolutionary restlessness of a dominated people. This outlook wishes to rebuild a new world, perhaps upon the ashes of the old. Finally, the progressive liberals represented a centrist commitment to the viability of the democratic state. This outlook is most consistent with the prevailing views of the Democratic Party and the hope for reform within the existing system.

These conceptual frameworks for educational reform are neither exclusively political nor exclusively educational. They are, in fact, socioeducational ideas and worldviews. It can be argued that these views are both consistent and persistent. How then can knowledge of early 20th-century ideas about African American education reforms and reformers be instructive to us in today's climate, where the demand for educational reform is ubiquitous?

First, such knowledge provides a historical referent. African American educational reform must acknowledge and evaluate past efforts in light of colonial politics and colonial education. Present-day reformers too often separate education from the social and political life of African Americans.

Second, the question of ideology emerges as a crucial one. The well-meaning educational reformer must ask the tough questions. What is this reform really about? Who benefits? What ideas and world outlooks are supported in this reform? Reformers must consider that change is substantive, not simply organizational. What do any changes in education mean to the political and racial status of this people?

Finally, and perhaps most important, reformers must consider the impact of their proposals. Afrocentrists and multiculturalists must ask what their proposals mean in today's world. What exactly is a pluralistic society? Can ethnic groups have equal representation without equal power?

Few among us would not agree that public schooling has done little to create egalitarianism and equal opportunity in our society. Reformers must turn to the long history of theory and practice among African American educators for a sober assessment of possibility and reality.

Notes

1. This document was originally presented by William S. Scarborough at the December 1899 meeting of the American Negro Academy under the title "Higher Education: Its Relation to the Future of the Negro." For additional discussion, see Moss (1981), pp. 102-104.

2. For extensive discussion of the emergence of black socialists and communists, please see Haywood, 1976; Kelley, 1987; Record, 1951; Robinson, 1983.

3. For a complete discussion, please see Moses, 1978.

4. Please see readings in Note 2 for that discussion.

5. *Progressive* here refers to the general progress movement that so greatly affected education. John Dewey is generally considered its ideological leader. Its organized expression was the Progressive Education Association.

6. Here we are referring to the group identified with Counts, the Ruggses, Hook, and others who were separated from the Progressive Education Association in the early 1930s. For a full discussion of the social reconstructionists, please see Watkins, 1990a.

References

Anderson, J. A. (1988). *The education of blacks in the South, 1860-1935*. Chapel Hill: University of North Carolina Press.

Bond, H. M. (1966). *The education of the Negro in the American social order*. New York: Octagon.

Bullock, H. (1967). *A history of negro education in the south: From 1619 to present*. Cambridge, MA: Harvard University Press.

Counts, G. S. (1932). *Dare the schools build a new social order*. New York: John Day.

Crummell, A. (1992). *Destiny and race: Selected writings, 1840-1848* (W. J. Moses, Ed.). Amherst: University of Massachusetts Press.

DuBois, W. E. B. (1969). *The souls of black folk*. New York: New American Library. (Original work published 1903)

DuBois, W. E. B. (1973). *The education of black people: Ten critiques, 1906-1960 by W. E. B. DuBois* (H. Aptheker, Ed.). New York: Monthly Review Press.

Haywood, H. (1976). *Black bolshevik: Autobiography of an African American communist*. Chicago: Liberator Press.

Jones, T. J. (1906). *The Hampton social studies*. Hampton, VA: Hampton University Press.

Jones, T. J. (1929). *Essentials of civilization: A study in social values*. New York: Henry Holt.

Kelley, R. D. G. (1987). *Black radicalism and the Communist Party in Alabama 1929-1941*. Unpublished Ph.D. dissertation, University of California at Los Angeles.

King, K. (1971). *Pan-Africanism and education: A study of race philanthropy and education in the southern states of America and East Africa*. Oxford: Clarendon.

Kliebard, H. (1987). *The struggle for the American curriculum 1983-1958*. New York: Routledge Kegan Paul.

Locke, A. (Ed). (1925). *The new Negro: An interpretation*. New York: Albert & Charles Boni.

Locke, A. (1971). With science as his shield. *Frontiers of Democracy* (Vols. 5-6, pp. 208-210). New York: Arno Press, New York Times. (Original work published April 15, 1940)

Marable, M. (1986). *W. E. B. DuBois: African American radical democrat*. Boston: Twayne.

Miller, K. (1897). Review of Hoffman's *Race Traits and Tendencies of the American Negro. ANA Occasional Papers*, No. 112897.

Miller, K. (1925). Howard: The national Negro university. In A. Locke (Ed.), *The new Negro: An interpretation* (pp. 312-322). New York: Albert & Charles Boni.

Moses, W. (1978). *The golden age of African American nationalism: 1850-1925*. New York: Oxford University Press.

Moss, A. A., Jr. (1981). *The American Negro Academy: Voice of the talented tenth.* Baton Rouge: Louisiana State University Press.

Record, W. (1951). *The Negro and the Communist party.* Chapel Hill: University of North Carolina Press.

Rigsby, G. U. (1987). *Alexander Crummell: Pioneer in nineteenth-century pan-African thought.* New York: Greenwood.

Robinson, C. J. (1983). *Black Marxism: The making of the black radical tradition.* London: Zed Press.

Watkins, W. H. (1989). On accommodationist education: Booker T. Washington goes to Africa. *International Third World Studies Journal and Review, 1*(1), 137-143.

Watkins, W. H. (1990a). The social reconstructionists. In T. Husen & T. N. Postelthwaite (Eds.), *The international encyclopedia of education* (Supplementary Vol. 2, pp. 589-592). London: Pergamon.

Watkins, W. H. (1990b). W. E. B. DuBois vs. Thomas Jesse Jones: The forgotten skirmishes. *Journal of the Midwest History of Education Society, 18,* 305-328.

Watkins, W. H. (1994). Curriculum for immigrant and minority children. In T. Husen & T. N. Postelthwaite (Eds.), *The international encyclopedia of education* (pp. 3840-3848). London: Pergamon.

Weinberg, M. (1970). *W. E. B. DuBois: A reader.* New York: Harper Torchbook.

Woodson, C. G. (1933). *The mis-education of the negro.* Washington, DC: Associated Publishers.

2

The *Brown* Decision Revisited
Mathematizing a Social Problem

WILLIAM F. TATE
GLORIA LADSON-BILLINGS
CARL A. GRANT

White Americans today don't know what in the world to do because they put us behind them; that's where they made their mistake. If they had put us in the front, they wouldn't have let us look back. But they put us behind them, and we watched every move they made.

Fannie Lou Hamer,
1991 speech to the NAACP
Legal Defense Funding Institute

They had for more than a century before been regarded as . . . so far inferior . . . that the negro might justly and lawfully be reduced to slavery for his benefit. . . . This opinion was at that time fixed and universal in the civilized portion of the white race. It was regarded as an axiom of morals as well as in politics, which no one thought of disputing . . . and men in every grade and position in society daily and habitually acted upon it without doubting for a moment the correctness of this opinion.

Dred Scott v. Stanford, 1857

T he sentiments expressed in the above quotation from the *Dred Scott v. Stanford* decision of 1857 reflect the prevailing cultural ethos of America

This chapter is adapted from an article in *Educational Policy* (September, 1993); © 1993 by Corwin Press.

at the time the Supreme Court justices were called on to render a decision
in the 1896 case of *Plessy v. Ferguson.* In their decision to uphold Louisiana's
separate railroad cars, the court was rendering a decision that was consistent
with the social and cultural mores of the nation. These beliefs had been
firmly established from the creation of the republic. They are reflected not
just in the Three-Fifths Compromise, but in the very beliefs expressed by
founders such as Thomas Jefferson. In Jefferson's (1784/1954) *Notes on the
State of Virginia,* he suggested that

> deep rooted prejudices entertained by the whites; ten thousand rec-
> ollections, by the blacks, of the injuries they have sustained; new
> provocations; the real distinction that nature has made; and many
> other circumstances, will divide us into parties, and produce convul-
> sions which will probably never end but in the extermination of the
> one or the other race. (p. 138)

As he further explained the "real distinction that nature has made,"
Jefferson made it clear that he believed the African person to be an inferior
being. He suggested that whites, by virtue of their fairer skin, flowing hair,
and "a more elegant symmetry of form," were more beautiful. Jefferson also
commented that Africans "secrete less by the kidnies [sic], and more by the
glands of the skin, which gives them a very strong and disagreeable odour"
(p. 139). He felt that African people required less sleep, as evidenced by his
observation that they had the ability to work all day and engage in merry-
making through the night. Jefferson regarded African people as lusty and
less capable of deep emotional feelings. The African person described by
Jefferson was less capable of reason and imagination.

Peters (1982) suggests that Jefferson's beliefs about the African's blackness "took on moral overtones. Humanity to [Jefferson] was white, and this
whiteness carried a sanctity about it which meant that any deviation from
whiteness was neither true nor right, an aberration from the true likeness
of humanity" (p. 24). Peters further posits that the Jeffersonian view of
African people helped lay the foundation for segregation. Because of these
perceived differences and inferior qualities, Jefferson (1784/1954) argued
that the African, when emancipated, must be "removed beyond the reach
of mixture" (p. 143), that is, segregated from whites. At the time of this
writing, Jefferson's sentiments were not seen as scandalous or absurd. They
accurately reflected the common thinking of the time. With this thinking
as a backdrop, the opinion handed down in *Plessy v. Ferguson* made perfect
sense to the general public. The belief in the inherent inferiority of African

Americans made it impossible for white Americans to see themselves sharing public spaces with them as equals.

In addition to reflecting the prevailing cultural ethos, the laws that laid the groundwork for the relationship between citizens (i.e., white male property owners) and noncitizens (i.e., blacks) in the United States were based on a mathematical notion of equality[1] that we will explore in greater detail in a subsequent section of this chapter. Simply put, the objectification of Africans, and later African Americans, made it possible to think of them purely in mathematical terms and almost never in human/social terms. The slave trade provides a graphic illustration of this objectification:

> The price of slaves in the domestic trade reflected all the forces operating to create supply and demand. In the early nineteenth century, the prices of prime field hands were modest, ranging from $350 in Virginia to about $500 in Louisiana. Later, as the demand increased in the lower South, the prices on both the Northern and Southern markets tended to rise. . . . In order to convince themselves and the abolitionists that slavery was a moral and economic good and to convince their neighbors of their affluence, planters continued to purchase all the slaves offered on the market. Prices skyrocketed, and by 1860 prime field hands were selling for $1,000 in Virginia and for $1,500 in New Orleans. (Franklin & Moss, 1988, p. 108)

This objectification and reduction to a mathematical quantity was codified in the Three-Fifths Compromise that was inserted into Article I, Section 2, of the Constitution and reads as follows:

> Representatives and direct Taxes shall be apportioned among the several States which may be included within this Union, according to their respective Numbers, which shall be determined by adding to the whole Number of free Persons, including those bound to Service for a Term of Years, and excluding Indians not taxed, three fifths of all other persons.

Both the economy (e.g., the slave trade) and the constitutional philosophy of the United States reinforced the notion that African Americans were devoid of humanity and could be considered in strictly mathematical terms. Unfortunately, these mathematical conceptions continued into 20th-century thinking and provided a backdrop for the historic *Brown v. Board of Education* (1954) decision.

Understanding *Plessy* and *Brown*

Plessy v. Ferguson (1896) was handed down in an era that had seen racial and voter violence in Louisiana; the Coushatta Massacre of more than 60 African Americans, also in Louisiana; the refusal of the U.S. attorney general to send troops to Mississippi to protect African American voters; the enactment of the first Jim Crow law, providing for segregated railroad cars in Tennessee; and the repeal of the Civil Rights Act of 1875, which had given African Americans equal access to public accommodations and public amusement (Carson, Garrow, Harding, & Hine, 1987). *Plessy v. Ferguson* represented a good cultural fit between what was happening in the nation, the ways in which many white people thought and felt about African Americans, and the current state and local laws and ordinances. It was not seen as a particularly significant ruling among whites because it merely reinforced the prevailing sentiment.

On the other hand, although *Brown v. Board of Education* was handed down after a number of other rulings had chipped away at the foundation of segregation (e.g., *Henderson v. United States,* 1950; *McLaurin v. Oklahoma State Regents for Higher Education,* 1950; *Sipuel v. Board of Regents of the University of Oklahoma,* 1948; *Sweatt v. Painter,* 1950), the cultural ethos and sociopolitical climate had not changed radically from the time of *Plessy v. Ferguson.* In 1948, Clarendon County, South Carolina, was paying the cost of busing white children to school but refused to do the same for African American children (Carson et al., 1987). In 1951, in Cicero, Illinois, Governor Adlai Stevenson had to call out the National Guard to quell rioting when 3,500 whites tried to prevent an African American family from moving into an all-white city. And, just one year after *Brown* was handed down, the African American community was shaken by the kidnapping and brutal lynching of Emmett Till, a teenager accused of whistling at a white woman. Despite the eyewitness testimony of Till's uncle, the accused were found not guilty.

Brown was perceived as a threat because of its widespread social and cultural implications. Throughout the nation and in the South in particular, the *Brown* decision was seen as the Supreme Court's attempt not only to interpret the law but also to shape the sociocultural conscience of the nation. The Supreme Court seemed to see *Brown* as an opportunity to institutionalize the cultural assimilation function of the public schools. In a section of the decision, the justices wrote,

> Today, it [education] is a principal instrument in awaking the child to cultural values, in preparing him for later professional training, and

in helping him to adjust normally to his environment. In these days, it is doubtful that any child may reasonably be expected to succeed in life if he is denied the opportunity of an education. Such an opportunity, where the state has undertaken to provide it, is a right which must be made available to all on equal terms. (as quoted in Rist, 1979, p. 3)

It is clear from the above passage that the intent of the justices was to help African American and other disenfranchised and undereducated groups to fit in the present sociopolitical structure. What this "fitting in" meant for schools and in the minds of dominant culture members was not necessarily consistent with what African Americans envisioned for themselves.

In many communities, African Americans, regardless of their educational background, were faced with limited occupational choices. Consequently, although school desegregation might provide equal education, it could not ensure equal opportunity in the workplace or the housing market. Thus the *Brown* decision had to be seen as one with widespread implications for social relations throughout the society.

This broader vision of *Brown* represented the hope of the African American community. The Supreme Court had explicitly affirmed the rights of African Americans to have equal access in the public arena. African Americans interpreted this as an attempt to level the playing field. Not only would African American children have the opportunity to attend better equipped schools, but African American teachers and principals would be able to compete fairly for school positions. The college-educated African American community would be able to break out of the limited occupational options of "teach or preach," African American patronage would be welcomed at stores and restaurants, and housing choice would be a question of affordability, not race.

Unfortunately, the Supreme Court's decision could not be immediately translated into action or acceptance. The shortcoming in *Brown* is that the court proposed an essentially mathematical solution to a sociocultural problem. More specifically, the Supreme Court looked at the sociocultural reality of African American students—that they were consigned to substandard, ill-equipped schools—and proposed that by physically manipulating the students' school placement the problems of inequality would be addressed. They made this decision in the face of scant research evidence concerning the impact of segregation and desegregation (Rist, 1979). The response of many desegregated school districts, immediately after *Brown* was handed down, was to act as if it had never occurred. Rist states that prior to 1964, no systematic data on the implementation of *Brown* were collected, tabulated or analyzed. The general consensus among those who have studied this period is that fewer than one per cent of all black children in the 11 southern states attended desegregated schools. (p. 4)

Little change occurred in public schools immediately following the *Brown* decision. Whites in the South found various ways to resist the decision. This resistance took the form of physical attacks on African American students, legal delaying tactics, and the founding of over 3,000 private academies (Schofield, 1991). It was not until the enactment of the 1964 Civil Rights Act and the Elementary and Secondary Education Act of 1965 that the federal government achieved the legal leverage it needed to ensure that the de jure (state-supported dual systems) segregation of the South was changed. By contrast, the de facto (after the fact, by virtue of housing patterns) segregation of the North was barely affected by this legislation. The mathematical solution proposed by *Brown* meant that the South would close down its African American schools and place the jobs of African American teachers and principals in jeopardy. If the African American schools were eliminated, then all students would be compelled to attend the only available school system. The movement of bodies would mean African American students would attend the previously all-white schools.

In the North, the mathematics was not as simple. There was no separate school system to close. Students attended neighborhood schools, and the neighborhoods were segregated. In addition to not being able to apply a mathematical solution to a sociocultural problem, the courts could not apply a linear mathematical solution to a complex societal organization. The solution to the North's desegregation problems meant moving bodies across neighborhoods. Not only would African American students be asked to attend different schools, white students would also have to leave their neighborhoods.

Other pieces of mathematical data the *Brown* decision failed to factor in were the rising African American birthrates and the increasing immigration rates (Schofield, 1991). The past 20 years have seen a rapid increase in the "browning" of the nation's urban centers. The most elaborate desegregation plans cannot be successfully implemented in cities where white flight and the exercise of private school "choice" have meant that those once labeled minority now constitute the school population's numerical majority.

Schofield's (1991) comprehensive review of the desegregation literature suggests that the failure of studies in this area has been their attention to the "effects of desegregation" while ignoring the more salient questions of "what is going on here" (in desegregated schools) and "what works" (p. 383). More important, Schofield suggests that researchers in this area fail to provide usable insights concerning desegregation's effects because this work tends to be atheoretical. In their eagerness to address social concerns (and to be published), scholars have taken shortcuts to looking at desegregation.

In the subsequent sections, we will discuss further the application of simple mathematical solutions to complex sociocultural problems, take a more in-depth look at the effects of the *Brown* decision, and propose a vision of a desegregated/integrated model of education.

The Mathematical Model Metaphor and *Brown*

The *Brown* case, like most other lawsuits, was formulated in terms of available and authoritative legal doctrine. Yet, this case was different given that equality, a mathematical construct, was reshaped to fit within the legal framework. From *Plessy* to *Brown* to the over 500 pending cases related to these landmark decisions, the ability to transform a mathematical interpretation of equality into a social reality has not been realized.

Crenshaw (1988) provided a possible explanation for the failure of legal remedies to result in equality for blacks. She argued that there are two distinct rhetorical visions in antidiscrimination law. The first is an expansive view that stresses equality as a result. This interpretation of the law looks to eliminate conditions of black subordination and uses the power of the courts to eradicate racial injustice. The second perspective is a restrictive view that coexists with the expansive view. This view emphasizes that equality is a process and minimizes the significance of actual outcomes. Crenshaw (1988) noted the following about the restrictive view:

"Wrongdoing," moreover is seen primarily as isolated actions against individuals rather than as a societal policy against an entire group. Nor does the restrictive view contemplate the courts playing a role in redressing harms from America's racist past, as opposed to merely policing society to eliminate a narrow set of proscribed discriminatory practices. Moreover, even when injustice is found, efforts to redress it must be balanced against, and limited by, competing interests. . . . The innocence of whites weighs more heavily than do past wrongs committed upon blacks and benefits that whites derived from these wrongs. In sum, the restrictive view seeks to proscribe only certain

kinds of subordinating acts, and then only when other interests are
not overly burdened. (p. 1342)

Crenshaw's constructs of expansive and restrictive visions of equality
provide a framework to explore the development of the desegregation
model of equality constructed as a result of *Brown*. Was the *Brown* model
of equality expansive, restrictive, or both?

Von Neumann defined a model as a "mathematical construct which,
with the addition of certain verbal interpretations, describes observed
phenomena. The justification of such a mathematical construct is solely
and precisely that it is expected to work" (Gleick, 1987, p. 273). In science,
given an approximate knowledge of a system's initial condition and an
understanding of natural law, the scientist can construct a model that will
approximate the behavior of the system (Gleick, 1987). Over the last 142
years, civil rights litigators have been constructing a model of equality in
education that equates quality schools for African Americans with the
process of desegregation (Bell, 1987). The evolution of the desegregation
model mandated by *Brown*, metaphorically speaking, meets the Von Neumann criteria of a mathematical model.[2]

The cases preceding *Brown* (e.g., *Roberts v. City of Boston*, 1850; *Plessy
v. Ferguson*, 1896; *Sweatt v. Painter*, 1950) were iterations of the evolving
construct of social equality that led to the desegregation model. Thus these
precedents serve as the approximate knowledge of the education system's
initial conditions of equality. The actual *Brown* decision represents the
verbal interpretation of the desegregation model of equality. The success of
the desegregation model of equality was, and continues to be, contingent
upon its ability to adapt to a cultural ethos of white self-interest. The impact
of white self-interest on the public education system is analogous to the
view that natural laws govern the universe, in that both follow predictable
patterns. Using this mathematical framework, we will examine the restrictive and/or expansive nature of the *Brown* decision.

The Initial Conditions

If the desegregation model of equality is to be understood and classified
as restrictive, expansive, or both, science suggests that the scientist, or in
this case, educators, must have an approximate knowledge of the system's
initial condition. In one of the earliest cases, *Roberts v. City of Boston* (1850),
the plaintiff sought to desegregate Boston's public schools to achieve equal-

ity in education. Lawyers representing the black parents in *Roberts* argued that separate schools tended to create a feeling of degradation in blacks and prejudice in whites (Bell, 1980b). Thus, 104 years before *Brown*, the transitive property of social equality equating desegregation with quality schools and increased opportunities in the marketplace was formulated.[3] The *Roberts* suit was eventually rejected by the Supreme Court of Massachusetts, but black leaders lobbied the legislature for a law against segregated schools and succeeded in acquiring a law prohibiting segregation.

The passage and implementation of this law in Massachusetts should be viewed as a pilot study of the effectiveness of the mathematical model of desegregation. In the case of Boston's education system, the model resulted in a loss of black leaders and teachers, a loss of self-control, and a loss of identity; worst of all, the model impeded the intellectual development of black children (Hall & Henderson, 1984). Even financial support for textbooks, which had been provided to black children during segregation, was ended.

The major gains blacks thought were obtainable with the desegregation model were the very ones lost as a result of not accounting for an important law of the system, white self-interest. School officials argued that white parents would not send their children to all-black schools, nor would they allow blacks to attend their schools. The social law of white self-interest resulted in Boston schools being clearly identifiable by race.

The next major case related to school equality was *Plessy v. Ferguson* (1896). In *Plessy*, the opinion of the court was written in a manner similar to a mathematical property of equality. The court argued,

> If the civil and political rights of both races be equal, one cannot be inferior to the other, civilly or politically. If one race be inferior to the other socially, the constitution of the United States cannot put them upon the same plane. (*Plessy v. Ferguson,* 1896)

Because equality is a mathematical construct, it must conform to the logic of the discipline. From a mathematical perspective, the court's argument has two errors. First, their argument implied that blacks and whites were equally protected under the 14th Amendment. Earlier in this chapter, we argued that Jefferson's view of blacks helped lay the foundation of segregation and was widely accepted as a social norm in America. Assuming benevolence from a nation of people whose cultural ethos conformed to a racial ideology of white self-interest weakens the assumption that a black citizen was equally protected under the law.

The court's argument of equal civil and political rights was completely negated by the fact that blacks were denied political equality by restrictive voting laws. Mathematically speaking, if two groups are considered politically equal, then each group must have exactly the same rights under the law.

A second error in the court's mathematical argument was its failure to define, in measurable terms, the meaning of equal in "separate but equal." Instead, the court used the following reasonableness test:

> [We] cannot say that a law which authorizes or even requires the separation of the two races in public conveyances is unreasonable or more obnoxious to the 14th Amendment than the acts of Congress requiring separate schools for colored children in the District of Columbia. (*Plessy v. Ferguson*, 1896)

In strictly mathematical terms, equality was not addressed in *Plessy*. This important iteration of the desegregation model was principled on false mathematical assumptions. Equal was defined as *reasonable* and its definition was subject to the interpretation of the dominant group. Like the *Roberts* case, white self-interest restricted the transformation of mathematical equality into a social reality. As a mathematical construct, the *Plessy* model is best characterized as an empty set. *Plessy* did not provide a restrictive or expansive view of school equality, because the court's arguments were premised on false mathematical assumptions that rendered the decision meaningless with respect to social equality.

In later cases, the courts began to construct social meaning to the empty conditions of equality referred to in *Plessy* (e.g., *Missouri ex rel. Gaines v. Canada*, 1938; *McLaurin v. Oklahoma State Regents for Higher Education*, 1950; *Sweatt v. Painter*, 1950). In terms of the desegregation model, all of these cases were iterations of the social construction of equal protection in education that led to *Brown*. The construction of equality in education via these cases was analogous to an indirect proof in mathematics.[4]

The legal construction of equality in education always began with the assumption that school inequality did not exist and that it was the plaintiff's responsibility to produce contradictory evidence. Using this method, the court constructed a model of equality by validating educational inequality. There was, and still is, a limitation to using an indirect mathematical proof to achieve equality in a social context. It is a very static process, making it nearly impossible to capture and change dynamic social realities. For instance, in *Sweatt v. Painter,* the court noted numerous inequalities, such as reputation of faculty, experience of administrators, the influence of alumni, and community standing. By defining significant differences between black and white schools, the court constructed the meaning of educational equality. Each new construction by the courts represented the current model of equality in education. Yet, each newly constructed model did not guarantee equality in education for all students. At any given point in time, a school system could initiate or have an ongoing policy that resulted in what could be perceived by a citizen as an impediment to equality in education for African American students. Under our system, the courts assume that inequality does not exist, and thus the burden of providing contradictory evidence or, in essence, the construction of a new model of equality rests with the citizen who is compelled to challenge the school system's policy. The use of an indirect mathematical proof to both legally and socially construct equality was, and continues to be, a time-consuming and restrictive process. Furthermore, the indirect method is not an expansive process that initiates the construction of equality in education or anticipates policies that promote inequalities and prevents their implementation. Nor has this method framed equality as a result. Rather, equality is viewed as a process.

The *Brown* case was consistent with past litigation in the area of education, in that the litigators for the plaintiff used an indirect mathematics proof to construct the meaning of equality in education for African Americans. At the time of *Brown,* the law assumed separate schools were equal. Contradictory evidence provided by social scientists led the court to conclude that the segregation of races in public schools had a detrimental effect on African American children. Thus, the Supreme Court approved the next version of equality in public education, which equated school desegregation with equal protection under the law. The desegregation model has been used to transform the relations between blacks and whites in a variety of social contexts. With respect to public education, the model established in *Brown* has failed to deliver the desired result of educational equality for African Americans.

The difficulties encountered in the judicial and administrative implementation of *Brown* can be attributed to a mathematical flaw. According to Von Neumann (Gleick, 1987), a mathematical model must have "certain verbal interpretations" that describe the phenomenon to be observed. In the case of *Brown,* the phenomenon to be observed was, in theory, an integrated/desegregated public system of education. Yet, in *Brown v. Board of Education* (1955, hereafter *Brown II*) the court failed to give a verbal interpretation of the phenomena of equality to be observed. Instead, it offered the following:

School authorities have the primary responsibility for elucidating, assessing, and solving these problems; courts will have to consider whether the action of school authorities constitutes good faith implementation of the governing constitutional principles. Because of their proximity to local conditions and the possible need for further hearings, the courts which originally heard these cases can best perform this judicial appraisal. (*Brown II*)

Brown II did not provide a verbal interpretation of equality for the lower courts to use as a guide to transform the segregated system of education to an integrated reality. It only described the magnitude of the task. Failure to describe the phenomenon to be observed has resulted in many school districts constructing models of desegregation that have not met the needs of African American children. For example, the Miami and Houston school districts counted Latinos as whites and bused low-income African American students into low-income Latino schools and vice versa (Orfield, 1988). This type of practice may have been avoided if the Supreme Court had articulated a clearer vision for the model. Furthermore, by delegating the responsibility of creating the vision of equality to the lower courts, the *Brown II* model was more susceptible to the law of white self-interest.

According to Gewirtz (1983), the "with all deliberate speed" formula of *Brown II* was an attempt by the court to accommodate white opposition rather than to facilitate administrative adjustments. The combination of a lack of an implementation strategy, white self-interest, and the deliberate speed formula provided school systems the time and freedom to construct resistance strategies. As previously mentioned, resistance to the *Brown* model has taken on many forms that have hampered its implementation: violence, white flight from public education, boycotts, slow-down tactics by officials obliged by law to desegregate, and new versions of segregation.

Further complicating the implementation of the desegregation model today are the demographic realities of America's urban centers. Of the 20 largest public school systems in America, 12 have over 70% nonwhite enrollments (National Center for Education Statistics, 1990). Among these cities, Detroit, Chicago, New York, and Philadelphia have neither a comprehensive nor voluntary desegregation program within their largely nonwhite school systems for the exchange of students with neighboring suburban school districts (Orfield, 1988). The lack of a city-suburban exchange mechanism makes it impossible to desegregate city school systems with majority African American and Latino American student populations. The

Brown II judicial and implementation strategy did not factor the changing demographic conditions into the desegregation model. We can only speculate, based on previous patterns, that white self-interest would be a barrier to city-suburban student exchanges.

The Need for an Expansive Model

Give me that which I want, and ye shall have this that you want . . . it is in this manner that we obtain from one another the far greater part of those good offices which we stand in need of. It is not from the benevolence of the butcher, the brewer, or the baker that we expect our dinner, but from regard to their own self-interest. (Smith, 1937, p. 14)

From Smith's writings on free-market economics to more recent theories of supply-side economics, the unbridled expression of individual self-interest has been characterized as the central ingredient required to maximize the welfare of society (Raboy, 1982). Bell (1980a) suggested that remedies to promote racial equality in education will be considered only when these remedies converge with the interests of whites: "The fourteenth amendment, standing alone, will not authorize a judicial remedy providing effective racial equality for blacks where the remedy sought threatens the superior social status of middle- and upper-class whites" (p. 95).

The law of white self-interest has affected the way the desegregation model of educational equality has been defined and socially constructed via the legal system. From *Roberts* to *Plessy* to *Brown*, this social law has served as an agent to restrict the implementation of the desegregation model of equality. Further accelerating the restrictive power of white self-interest is the lack of a vision for implementing the *Brown* model in a world of ever-changing demographics and other social conditions. The vision for the model must include, yet move beyond, the restrictive process of physical desegregation and focus on an expansive view that incorporates other strategies to achieve equal educational outcomes for all groups.

An Expansive Vision of a Desegregated/Integrated School

With the passage of *Brown*, many African Americans and other people of color equated a "good" education with their children attending well-equipped, well-financed schools with white children. This good education, they believed, would be the result of equal educational opportunity for their children and all other children. Equal educational opportunity would mean that black boys and girls would be treated with the same dignity and respect as white boys and girls. This equal treatment would come about because they would share the same educational space, take the same educational classes, and use the same educational materials. However, this model lacked vision, and African American people soon realized that the educational goals for their children were not being achieved by just experiencing schooling in the same room with white students, often after a long and frightening bus ride. What was needed was a vision of education that challenged the fundamental structure of schools that reproduced the same inequitable social hierarchies that existed in society.

A decade later, with a growing social consciousness that was further enhanced by the passage of the Civil Rights Act of 1965, African American people also wanted to see their boys and girls and other students of color, as well as white children, experience a curriculum that celebrated their culture, accurately told of their ethnic group's deeds and contributions to society, challenged the status quo, and promoted their personal and ethnic group's membership by accepting and affirming them as full members in American society. This good education for many African Americans and other people of color thus far has not become a reality. A recent report, prepared by the directors of the 10 federally funded Desegregation Assistance Centers (DACs), explains how the idea of a good education held by African Americans and other people of color has been shattered, in what the report describes as three failed generations of desegregation efforts since the *Brown* decision (Bates, 1990; Simon-McWilliams, 1989).

The first generation, the effort to stop and eliminate physical desegregation, has seen some progress in urban and suburban areas. It is not unusual to see students of color and white students in school together. This is especially true in magnet schools, or in school areas where the whites are too poor to escape from the city. However, many urban communities are increasingly becoming predominantly black, Latino, and Southeast Asian, with an economic base at or below the poverty level and an infrastructure that is crumbling. Furthermore, with the recent shift in demographics that includes changing immigration patterns and differential fertility rates among various racial groups, school desegregation with students of color and white students is becoming increasingly difficult (Hodgkinson, 1986).

The second generation, the attempt to eliminate inequities within schools rather than between schools, also has experienced slow progress. In mixed-race schools, students of color are often placed on lower academic tracks than are white students (see, e.g., Oakes, 1985), receive more suspensions from school, and are placed in special (remedial or compensatory) classrooms (Irvine, 1990). Also, the school's curriculum and practices are often designed to meet the needs, interests, and lifestyle of the white students. This is especially so in suburban schools, where students of color are bused out each day to attend classes.

The third generation, the achievement of equal learning opportunities and outcomes for all students, is producing mixed results. Whereas more students of color are completing high school and going on to college, the number of students of color not completing their education and/or being pushed out of school is alarmingly high (Hahn, 1987).

Given the work that still remains to be done in order to complete the desegregation of schools, have major improvement in the integration of schools, and deal with the educational challenges brought on with the changing racial demographics, is there a realistic vision of school success and good education that African American and other people of color should hold?

We argue that there is such a vision, and this vision is grounded in the country's rhetoric of democratic principles of equality, equity, and respect and affirmation of ethnic and cultural differences. These principles have not been completely realized by people of color. But, before we discuss the vision, it is important that we acknowledge, at least briefly, that an educational reform effort is under way. And this reform effort is claiming educational excellence and equity for all students.

The Recent Promise of Equal Education

The publication of *A Nation at Risk* (National Commission on Excellence in Education) in 1983 renewed cries in the nation, and especially within the field of education, to provide an equal education for all students. The publication claimed it was founded on twin goals of excellence and equity. The report said, "The twin goals of equity and high-quality (excellence) schooling have profound and practical meaning for our economy and society, and we cannot permit one to yield to the other in principle or in practice" (p. 13).

However, the educational literature and educational efforts since that publication have most often focused on increasing academic excellence in school by: (a) adding the new "basics," which has come to mean more reading, science, math, computer instruction, and technology in the curriculum; (b) increasing the knowledge and competence of those who teach by raising the requirements and standards for who can enter teaching, and providing teachers with greater direction about how to teach; and, important to this article, (c) merely declaring, but not making the effort to see to it, that educational equity exists for all students.

To this day, our review of the educational literature, including the educational reform reports and proposals for educational reform, does not reveal any substantive discussion of a vision of what desegregated/integrated schools would be like. The curriculum, instruction, and other school practices and how the school would meet the needs and interests of its multiethnic, multiracial, language-diverse population have not been articulated.

Can true educational reform, that includes educational equity and excellence for all students, occur without such a vision? We believe not, because without it, educators will not have a plan to prepare all America's children for the present and the future.

An Expansive Vision

As we posited above, the notion of equality can be thought of as restrictive or expansive. The restrictive view concerns itself with process, but not equal educational outcomes. We endorse the expansive view that requires attention to student outcomes as well as numerical equality. Furthermore, we interpret *expansive* to include changes in curriculum, instruction, student interaction, school climate, and parent involvement.

Our vision of schools is that of integrated, multicultural, multilinguistic environments, where those with disabilities have full school citizenship, and students from a variety of homes and living arrangements are welcomed by an understanding and sensitive student body and faculty. They are schools in which students are academically diverse, and achievement is not a function of race, class, or gender. The vital elements of the vision reside within the school's guiding philosophy and manifest in its curriculum, instructional practices, parent/community involvement, and other aspects of the school environment.

Guiding Philosophy

Earlier, we noted that *Plessy* was rendered at a time (1896) when the nation's philosophical disposition and behavior toward African Americans was less than humane. For many whites, the three-fifths clause in the U.S. Constitution was alive and well and only being articulated in other forms.

For example, Justice Brown argued, in approving this separate but equal doctrine,

> The object of the [Fourteenth] Amendment was undoubtedly to enforce the absolute equality of the two races before the law, but in the nature of things it could not have been intended to abolish distinction based upon color, or to enforce social, as distinguished from political equality, or a commingling of the two races upon terms unsatisfactory to either. (*Plessy v. Ferguson,* 1896)

Earlier, we also pointed out that *Brown* was handed down at a time when many in this country believed it was appropriate to move blacks and whites from being separate and unequal to being physically together, with black acceptance of white norms and values. Integration and desegregation were both used as the rallying call, but desegregation was the true password to be acted upon with all deliberate speed. The philosophy of assimilation competed with the philosophy of desegregation to give direction to school policy and procedures.

Presently, we are proceeding at the same deliberate speed. Thus it would be naive and inaccurate to argue that the nation has adopted and acts upon a philosophy of pluralism, equality, and equity for all its citizens. Much reeducation of the citizenry remains necessary to eliminate the behaviors and attitudes that brought forth the killing of Yusef Hawkins, the brutal beating of Rodney King, the belief that most welfare recipients are black women, and the belief that the black family is bankrupt. Nevertheless, we believe it is the role of the school in society to provide an education that promotes cultural pluralism and social and structural equality within all American institutions, especially the houses of government and the judiciary. Schools must advocate a "no-model American philosophy," and they must correct the color-blind attitude when it serves as an excuse for not meeting the needs and interests of students of color.

Student Diversity

Schools must be racially, economically, culturally, and linguistically integrated as opposed to being desegregated. Physical integration of the student population across all areas of school practices is important to a real, quality, multicultural education. For example, in some so-called desegregated high schools, students are tracked in both curriculum and extracurricular classes and activities. The French club, swimming team, chess club, cheering squad, and tennis team are often the province of the white students, whereas basketball and football are the province of students of color, particularly African Americans. Separation, voluntary or forced, can teach racial stereotypes, promote one school activity as being more culturally elite than another, and create racial and class barriers and tensions between students.

Also, along with the curriculum (e.g., textbooks, artifacts, field trips) from which students learn, they must see themselves and their classmates as vital and valuable parts of the curriculum. Learning from each other is important in helping students to critically understand and analyze race, class, and gender issues. It further assists them as they critique each other's ideas and beliefs about the school's curriculum, as well as each other's ideas and beliefs about societal issues.

The importance and value of interactive student diversity is supported by Grant and Sleeter (1986) in an ethnographic study of an integrated, mainstream junior high school. In this study, they reported that the student population truly valued being friends in and out of school. The students used such phrases as "multicultural friendships are fun," and "I don't see Jim as handicapped just because he is in a wheelchair. He goes to parties and dances with his wheelchair. He's not handicapped; he just can't walk." Statements such as these suggest that students are capable of understanding and transcending differences when they participate in education that is multicultural (see Sleeter & Grant, 1987).

Curriculum

Several multicultural education scholars (see, e.g., Gay, 1988; Ladson-Billings, 1991) have written extensively about the nature of curriculum in integrated schools. Space limitations prevent a full discussion here. However, it is important to highlight that the history and contributions of all Americans must be accurately written and infused throughout the entire K to 12 curriculum. More of the curriculum should be organized around social issues that include race, class, gender, and disability as perspectives for analysis. Students' life histories and ethnic communities will often serve as the starting point to teach critical thinking about issues critical to their life circumstances.

Instruction

Instruction must acknowledge that all students have no one best way of learning. It must be designed to enhance all students' self-concept and respect for peers. Instruction must be varied and involve students actively in determining how best to learn about an issue or resolve a problem. It must provide experiences, both for cooperative groups and for individual learning in order for students to learn how to create positive social change.

Parent-Community Involvement

Brown, as well as many of the desegregation cases before and after it, was heard by the judicial system because African American parents and community members were fed up with the quality of education their children were receiving in public schools. Consequently, African American parents were active participants in demanding that the judicial system use its constitutional powers to see to it that their children have an equal opportunity to receive a quality education. The development and continuous fostering of positive parent-community-school relations must be fundamental to the philosophy and practice of the expansive model of education. Parent-school interactions must be (a) interactive at the personal level of teacher-parent-student involvement, (b) interactive at the school building or administrative level, and (c) interactive at the school system or structural level.

Epilogue

We would be among the first to admit the significance and value of *Brown* to all of society, especially people of color. However, *Brown* and all deliberate speed have not provided the quality education for students of color that was expected and hoped for. This model of educational equality, coupled with white self-interest, has not produced (and cannot produce) the expansive vision of equality that will lead to equal educational outcomes regardless of physical placement of students. This expansive vision helps education to fulfill the promise of developing an active citizenry, capable of fully functioning in a democratic and multicultural society.

Notes

1. According to Putnam, Lampert, and Peterson (1990) mathematizing is an activity that

assumes a certain view of the social and physical world, which asserts that the important elements of situations can be represented by numbers and relationships among numbers. In Western society, this view is somewhat of a given, certainly among particular segments of the population who use mathematics to formulate and solve problems and others who consume their work. (p. 98)

For example, in *Johnson v. Chicago Board of Education* (1979), the court sanctioned a school lottery system principled on racial classification. That is, when the percentage of nonwhite children reached 60% in integrated neighborhood schools, the number of children chosen by race exceeding that percentage were selected by lottery for assignment to other schools. The figure 60% represented the important element of this situation. The school board argued that minority enrollments beyond this figure would catalyze white flight. This case illustrates one way mathematizing can be used in the legal system.

2. Williams (1991) contends that theoretical legal understanding is characterized, in Anglo-American jurisprudence, by at least three sets of principles or rhetoric: (a) the hypostatization of exclusive categories and definitional polarities, the creation of clear taxonomies that purport to simplify life in the face of social complexities-rights/needs, moral/immoral, public/private, white/black; (b) the existence of transcendent, acontextual, universal legal truths or procedures, and (c) the existence of "objective" voices by which those transcendent, universal truths find entry into legal discourse. These voices include judges, lawyers, logicians, and practitioners of empirical methodologies (see, e.g., *Johnson v. Chicago Board of Education,* 1979). Similarly, mathematics has been viewed as a paradigm of objective, transcendent, universal truths (Ernest, 1991). In this chapter, the authors use mathematics, and more specifically mathematizing, metaphorically to illustrate the limits of rationality (see, e.g., Wheeler, 1988) of the legal truths that led to *Brown.* Simon (1981) provides additional insight into the limits of rationality. "If natural phenomena have an air of 'necessity' about them in their subservience to natural law, artificial phenomena [e.g., legal truths or procedure] have an air of 'contingency' in their malleability by environment" (pp. ix-x). We do not suggest that the legal system is derived or built on mathematical principles. Instead, we contend that mathematics and the legal system share common characteristics of Western philosophy that allow for a metaphorical analysis.

3. The transitive property of equality states that if a = b and b = c, then a = c. In *Roberts,* the plaintiff's logic was principled on the following: If desegregation implies quality schools and quality schools implies increased opportunities, then desegregation implies increased opportunities.

4. According to Downing (1987), "The method of indirect proof begins by assuming that a theorem is false, and then proceeds to show that a contradiction results. In that case, the theorem must be true" (p. 100).

References

Bates, P. (1990). Desegregation: Can we get there from here? *Phi Delta Kappan, 72*(1), 8-17.
Bell, D. A. (1980a). Brown and the interest-convergence dilemma. In D. A. Bell (Ed.), *New perspectives on school desegregation* (pp. 90-107). New York: Teachers College Press.

Bell, D. A. (1980b). *Race, racism, and American law* (2nd ed.). Boston: Little, Brown.

Bell, D. A. (1987). *And we are not saved: The elusive quest for racial justice.* New York: Basic Books.

Brown v. Board of Education, 347 U.S. 483 (1954).

Brown v. Board of Education, 349 U.S. 294 (1955).

Carson, C., Garrow, D., Harding, V., & Hine, D. (Eds.). (1987). *A reader and guide: Eyes on the prize: America's civil rights years.* New York: Penguin.

Crenshaw, K. W. (1988). Race, reform, and retrenchment: Transformation and legitimation in anti-discrimination law. *Harvard Law Review, 101,* 1331-1387.

Downing, D. (1987). *Dictionary of mathematics terms.* Hauppauge, NY: Barron's.

Dred Scott v. Stanford, 60 U.S. 393 (1857).

Ernest, P. (1991). *The philosophy of mathematics education.* Bristol, PA: Falmer.

Franklin, J. H., & Moss, A. (1988). *From slavery to freedom* (6th ed.). New York: Knopf.

Gay, G. (1988). Designing relevant curricula for diverse learners. *Education and Urban Society, 20,* 327-340.

Gewirtz, P. R. (1983). Remedies and resistance. *Yale Law Journal, 2,* 585-681.

Gleick, J. (1987). *Chaos: Making a new science.* New York: Penguin.

Grant, C., & Sleeter, C. (1986). *After the school bell rings.* Philadelphia: Falmer.

Hahn, A. (1987). Reaching out to America's dropouts: What to do? *Phi Delta Kappan, 69*(4), 256-263.

Hall, D., & Henderson, G. (1984). Brown revisited: Charting a new direction. *Black Law Journal* (UCLA Edition), *9,* 6-37.

Henderson v. United States, 339 U.S. 816 (1950).

Hodgkinson, H. (1986, May 14). Old Americans, young Americans. *Education Week,* pp. 19-25.

Irvine, J. (1990). *Black students and school failure.* Westport, CT: Greenwood.

Jefferson, T. (1954). *Notes on the state of Virginia.* New York: Norton. (Original work published 1784)

Johnson v. Chicago Board of Education, 604 F.-504 (7th Circuit, 1979).

Ladson-Billings, G. (1991). Culturally relevant teaching: The key to making multicultural education work. In C. Grant (Ed.), *Research and multicultural education: From the margins to the mainstream* (pp. 106-121). London: Falmer.

McLaurin v. Oklahoma State Regents for Higher Education, 339 U.S. 637 (1950).

Missouri ex rel. Gaines v. Canada, 305 U.S. 337 (1938).

National Center for Education Statistics. (1990). *Conditions of education.* Washington, DC: Government Printing Office.

National Commission on Excellence in Education. (1983). *A nation at risk: The imperative for educational reform.* Washington, DC: Government Printing Office.

Oakes, J. (1985). *Keeping track: How schools structure inequality.* New Haven, CT: Yale University Press.

Orfield, G. (1988, February). School desegregation in the 1980s. *Equity and Choice, 4,* 25.

Peters, E. (1982). Stereotyping: Moving against consciousness. In *Ethnic notions: Black images in the white mind* (exhibition catalog), Berkeley Art Center, Berkeley, CA.

Plessy v. Ferguson, 163 U.S. 537 (1896).

Putnam, R., Lampert, M., & Peterson, P. (1990). Alternative perspectives on knowing mathematics in elementary schools. In C. Cazden (Ed.), *Review of research in education* (Vol. 16, pp. 57-150). Washington, DC: American Educational Research Association.

Raboy, P. G. (Ed.). (1982). *Essays in supply side economics.* Washington, DC: Institute for Research on the Economics of Taxation.

Rist, R. (Ed.). (1979). *Desegregated schools: Appraisals of an American experiment.* New York: Academic Press.

Roberts v. City of Boston, 59 Mass. (5 Cush.) 198 (1850).

Schofield, J. W. (1991). School desegregation and intergroup relations: A review of the literature. In G. Grant (Ed.). *Review of research in education* (Vol. 17, pp. 335-409). Washington, DC: American Educational Research Association.

Simon, H. A. (1981). *The sciences of the artificial* (2nd ed). Cambridge: MIT Press.

Simon-McWilliams, E. (Ed.). (1989). *Resegregation of public schools: The third generation.* Portland, OR: Network of Regional Desegregation Assistance Centers and Northwest Regional Educational Laboratory.

Sipuel v. Board of Regents of the University of Oklahoma, 322 U.S. 631 (1948).

Sleeter, C., & Grant, C. (1987). An analysis of multicultural education in the United States. *Harvard Educational Review, 57*(4), 421-444.

Smith, A. (1937). *An inquiry into the nature and causes of the wealth of nations.* New York: Random House.

Sweatt v. Painter, 339 U.S. 629 (1950).

Wheeler, D. (1988). The limits of rationality. *For the Learning of Mathematics, 8,* 14-17, 24.

Williams, P. J. (1991). *The alchemy of race and rights: Diary of a law professor.* Cambridge, MA: Harvard University Press.

◧ PART II ◧

Politics of Implementation and School Desegregation

INTRODUCTION

Mwalimu J. Shujaa

This section contains three chapters that focus on the ways in which power and politics affected the interpretations given to school desegregation and approaches to its implementation.

The analysis of the political failure of school desegregation in Yonkers, New York, presented by Judith L. Failer, Anna Harvey, and Jennifer Hochschild in Chapter 3, offers vivid insights into the kind of turmoil that occurs when opponents of school desegregation hold sway over local power dynamics and the desegregation effort is not insulated from such local opposition. Failer, Harvey, and Hochschild provide a theory to explain how the joint and interactive effects of political controversy and institutional structure led to the political failure to desegregate Yonkers's public schools.

Local power relations are further analyzed in Chapter 4, as Jennifer Beaumont presents a case study of the Boston public schools' desegregation under 14 years of court monitoring. Beaumont contends that the actions of the school board, aimed at impeding the court's orders, resulted in the deterioration of many schools, including well-recognized, all-black schools. Beaumont describes how Boston public school officials implemented court-ordered desegregation and examines the impact of desegregation on the stability of school leadership.

The section concludes with Janet W. Schofield's argument in Chapter 5 that school desegregation is too often framed as an event rather than a long process. She contends that goals must include the development of positive intergroup relations within desegregated schools and the avoidance of resegregation. Schofield uses Gordon Allport's contact hypothesis as a conceptual framework for making school policy and practice recommendations.

3

◨

Only One Oar in the Water
The Political Failure of School Desegregation in Yonkers, New York

JUDITH L. FAILER

ANNA HARVEY

JENNIFER HOCHSCHILD

Nearly 40 years after *Brown v. Board of Education* (1954), advocates of school desegregation face a disheartening landscape. Although racial isolation in schools declined sharply in the South between 1964 and 1972 and has decreased gradually in the border, midwestern, and western regions between 1964 and 1989, segregation in public schools has since increased in the South and has consistently risen in the Northeast. In fact, the Northeast is now the region of the United States where black and Latino students are the most racially segregated, with 70% of urban black students in schools that enroll between 90% and 100% blacks and Latinos (Boozer, Krueger, & Wolkon, 1992).

AUTHORS' NOTE: This work benefits from the research of Steven J. Routh, Lawrence Thomas, and Monica Herk. They have our deep thanks, as does Mwalimu Shujaa for his heroic editing. This chapter is adapted from an article in *Educational Policy* (September, 1993); © 1993 by Corwin Press.

Desegregation's limited success (and failure in the Northeast) has led many former proponents of integrated education to doubt whether desegregation will ever secure equal educational opportunity for students of all races. Consequently, many educators now seek to enhance the quality of education for black and Latino students by improving, and sometimes fostering, racially isolated schools. Although we share these doubts, we are not yet ready to give up on desegregation. Racially isolated schools cannot provide the advantages of integrated education in the classroom, playground, and eventually workplace. Black students who attend desegregated schools complete more years of schooling and are more likely to work in white-collar and professional jobs, obtain jobs in more integrated firms, and receive higher wages than black students who attend racially isolated schools (Boozer et al., 1992; Crain & Strauss, 1985). Furthermore, the participants themselves endorse school desegregation; since 1983, more than half of first-year college students of both races have supported the use of busing to achieve racial balance in schools (Cooperative Institutional Research Program, 1987, 1992).

These findings make urgent the need to account for the failure of desegregation in the Northeast. In this chapter, we examine the political reasons for the failure to desegregate schools in New York State. Specifically, we analyze why the public officials responsible for education in New York failed to develop and implement a policy to desegregate Yonkers (a failure recently remedied in *United States v. Yonkers Board of Education,* 1985). Particularly now that courts are more willing to relinquish responsibility for desegregation to legislative and executive authorities (Greenhouse, 1992), the need to understand why this policy is so politically vulnerable, and to suggest how it might be made less so, is of pressing importance.

The Political Failure of Desegregation

Analysts of the political failure of desegregation typically point to the policy's two most controversial aspects. First, desegregation apparently imposes a transfer of resources from a majority of people (better-off whites with children in the better public schools) to a minority of people (worse-off blacks, and sometimes Latinos, with children in the worse public schools). Second, the predictable political conflict generated by downward redistribution is often exacerbated by whites' racially based opposition to desegregation. A policy that challenges both economic and social dominance will be so controversial, the argument goes, that the white majority will be able to shut down integrative actions (Wilson, 1974).

However, political controversy alone cannot account for the failure of desegregation in New York State. The socially and economically redistributive effects of other educational policies also generated strong political opposition, yet those policies were successfully developed and implemented. Case studies demonstrate that the state's and local school board's shared responsibility for public education also affects the political viability of a policy proposal. That is, the combination of majority opposition to desegregation *and* shared institutional responsibility made desegregation politically impossible, whereas similar opposition *absent* shared institutional responsibility allowed other controversial policies to enjoy political success.

The Structure of Educational Authority and Desegregation

As in most states, local school districts carry out the day-to-day administration of education in New York. However, state-level actors in New York have historically had an unusually important role in developing and overseeing implementation of educational policy (Milstein & Jennings, 1973; Murphy, 1974; Usdan, 1963). Many scholars believe that the state's prominent and professionalized role in public education has enhanced educational quality and equity in New York. In particular, the state's relatively centralized and politically insulated educational structure has been assumed to facilitate implementation of controversial policies such as desegregation (Hochschild, 1984).

If state educational institutions were insulated from local controversy, that might be the case. In fact, localities share educational authority with state actors in New York more than do localities in other states. That is, state educational actors and local school boards in New York have increasingly functioned as institutional partners in developing and implementing policy for public education. The terms of this state-local institutional partnership, broadly defined in New York's constitution (Article 5, Section 4) and in statutory law (New York Education Laws 9, sections 101, 215, 301, 305, 306, and 320 l[l]) provide that (a) the Board of Regents promulgates educational policy; (b) the State Education Department (SED) and its commissioner translate these policies into operational regulations (New York Code of Rules and Regulations 8); and (c) local school districts, as agents of the SED, implement them under SED's oversight.

The law does not always specify where the state's responsibility for an educational matter ends and the local districts' responsibilities begin, however. And where the law does not clearly delineate specific duties but does require that certain goals be met, the degree of harmony in the state-local partnership varies with the political context. Where the political will exists, both institutional partners may take actions, even beyond those legally required of them, in order to fulfill shared goals. But where political will is lacking, the partners may refuse or be reluctant to take actions not legally required of them, may drag their feet on their mandated duties, and may impede each other's ability to carry out its share of their joint functions. As we will demonstrate, a less than harmonious partnership played an important role in frustrating policies to desegregate schools in New York.

But just as political controversy alone cannot derail a proposed educational policy, so shared institutional responsibility does not suffice to explain the political failure of a proposed policy. Many new policies have been pursued successfully within New York's educational structure. Rather, it was the combination of high levels of controversy and shared institutional responsibility for public education that frustrated New York's policy for desegregation. That frustration occurred in two distinct ways. First, political controversy and institutional structure joined to prevent immediate implementation of desegregation in the early 1960s. Second, the two variables interacted to create a seesaw dynamic of action and inaction by state and local actors that effectively stymied later efforts by localities such as Yonkers to desegregate their schools.

After presenting our theory of the joint and interactive effects of political controversy and institutional structure, we will illustrate how this framework can help explain the political failure of efforts to desegregate Yonkers. We begin our "regression by hand" by describing the history of desegregation in Yonkers. That history shows how both state and local actors' obstruction of desegregation in the 1960s, and their interactive dynamic of action and inaction in the 1970s, combined to frustrate attempts to desegregate Yonkers. We then turn to two case studies of politically successful educational policies in New York. They demonstrate that the presence of either factor—controversy or shared responsibility—was not enough to block the policy process.

The first case, the provision of state aid to nonpublic schools (parochaid) in the early 1970s, resembled desegregation in that it also generated extensive opposition to its economic redistribution to a disfavored minority. Yet it differed from desegregation in that it was developed in a unified political structure that made local opposition ineffectual. Thus parochaid's political success shows that controversy alone need not impede political action by the state.

The second case, the restructuring of Yonkers's program in special education, resembled desegregation in that both policies had to be negotiated within the structure of New York's shared institutional responsibility for public education. Yet, unlike desegregation, special education was not perceived as redistributing resources to a disfavored minority, and therefore it did not generate great political controversy. Thus its eventual political success shows that a shared institutional structure alone does not necessarily thwart the policy process.

We conclude by examining the implications of our argument, both for Yonkers and for the political prospects of desegregation more generally.

The Political Failure of Desegregation in New York

Political controversy can combine with shared institutional responsibility for educational policy to affect a policy's political chances in two ways. First, the two variables can join to impede implementation. In a partnership in which one majority-controlled partner would bear all the direct costs of a new and controversial policy, that actor has strong incentives to fight the change by refusing to develop and implement it. Unless the second partner has very strong incentives to pursue the policy (strong enough to overcome the costs of doing more than its normal share of the work), the policy will fail.

In New York, local school boards (dominated by white parents and business elites) saw themselves as bearing all of the social and economic costs of desegregating, whereas state actors disagreed with one another about the political payoffs that desegregation might bring. Localities thus had stronger incentives to resist implementation than the state had to enforce it. Predictably, many localities thwarted desegregation policy throughout the 1960s.

The joint effects of controversy and shared authority do not, however, explain why desegregation failed in Yonkers. Twice, school officials became willing partners and tried to join with the state to desegregate Yonkers's schools. Why, when a previously unwilling partner became willing to shoulder its share of the responsibility, did the policy still fail? The answer lies in the interaction of political controversy and institutional structure in New York over time.

This interaction was enabled by the fact that the division of educational authority between the state and the localities in New York is only broadly delineated and is thus subject to the influence of the political context. The commissioner's ability to define the terms of the state-local partnership itself depends on how much the rest of the state government supports a given policy. The less unified the state's support, the less the commissioner can claim to speak for the state, and the less political latitude he has to make his assignment of specific responsibilities stick.

The school boards' status as institutional partners in public education enabled them not only to resist immediate implementation of desegregation, but also to fragment the state's political resolve and capacity to pursue this policy over time. Following the commissioner's failed attempts to desegregate schools in the early 1960s, local boards provided an institutional context within which desegregation's opponents could continue to attract media attention to their refusal to cooperate with the state, thereby ensuring their political visibility to state legislators. Responding to the publicity generated by the protesting school boards, the legislature eventually circumscribed the commissioner's authority to set policies for desegregation. In effect, the (in)actions of the resisting school boards transformed the state itself into a reluctant partner, so that when active support for desegregation coalesced in localities for various idiosyncratic reasons, the state passively (and sometimes actively) frustrated desegregation through its inaction. In this rowboat, only one oar was ever in the water at a time, and the rowboat never reached the shore.

The Political Failure of Desegregation in Yonkers

Twice, able local political and educational leaders in Yonkers were poised to desegregate the district. Twice, they failed. Although the persistence of local (mainly white) opposition clearly helped to derail these efforts, the failures remain difficult to explain until examined in the context of statewide battles over desegregation fought primarily in Albany and in other districts. From this broader perspective, the persistence of segregated schools in Yonkers illustrates how political controversy and shared educational authority joined and interacted to set off a chain reaction of moves and countermoves by the districts and the state that derailed desegregation.

This chain reaction occurred in four stages. First, the commissioner of education directed all school districts to formulate plans for desegregating racially imbalanced schools. Second, many districts delayed responding to the state's directive, drew substantial media attention to their delaying tactics, and pressured their state legislators to undermine the SED's efforts. Third, legislators responded to their most politically effective constituents by weakening the state's capacity to implement relevant policies. Fourth, when Yonkers was finally ready to desegregate its schools, the state lacked the capacity to help. Without the state's financial and technical support, Yonkers could not overcome local opposition and desegregate its schools.

At any given moment in this history, New York's structure of shared educational responsibilities enabled opponents of desegregation to impede immediate action. In addition, opponents actually altered the terms of the partnership between the state and localities over time, creating a climate that made reductions of racial imbalance increasingly unlikely, even when supporters of desegregation gained control of one of the institutional partners.

Yonkers's Segregation

In 1985, a federal district court found the Yonkers Board of Education guilty of intentional discrimination in its schools (*United States v. Yonkers,* 1985). Although some Yonkers schools were segregated as early as 1961, racial balance had never been much of an issue until the late 1960s, when whites began to move out of and blacks and Latinos began to move into the city, changing the demographics of the public schools. Because these new minorities settled in racially secluded neighborhoods, these demographic changes reinforced the racial separation already present in Yonkers's schools. By 1980, segregation was manifest in the racial patterns of student enrollment and faculty and staff assignments, as well as in the distinctly inferior physical plants for black and Latino schools.

Yonkers's Failure to Desegregate

State Action

When Commissioner James Allen, Jr., first called for an end to segregation in New York's schools in 1960 (University of the State of New York, 1960), the state's education law specified neither his nor the districts' role in ensuring racial balance. Following the findings in *Brown,* the regents concluded on January 28, 1960, that segregated schools "damage the personality of minority group children" and "decrease their motivation and thus impair their ability to learn" (University of the State of New York, 1960, pp. 27-28, 28-29). But the regents did not allocate specific responsibilities between the SED and the local districts for identifying imbalanced schools or for remedying the imbalances.

Lacking guidance from New York's education law, Commissioner Allen, began, himself, to define the roles of the state and localities. In 1960, he asked each district to begin eliminating segregation in its schools (University of the State of New York, 1960), and in 1961, he announced a plan to begin desegregation by conducting a racial census of every school. In early 1963, Commissioner Allen directed each district with racially imbalanced schools to inform the state by September of how it planned to achieve racial balance. The same day, the commissioner also responded to a 310 petition (an official complaint) filed the previous year by the NAACP in Long Island's Malverne School District (*Matter of Mitchell,* 1963). His ruling required Malverne to desegregate an elementary school enrolling 75% black children. It was the first time any commissioner in New York had required a local district to desegregate a school.

Local Resistance

Citizens (mainly white) and school boards in many districts were appalled, both with the 310 order in Malverne and with the commissioner's directive on racially imbalanced schools. As the direct targets of a proposed downward redistribution of economic resources and equalization of heretofore unequal racial statuses, these local actors had strong incentives to make their concerns heard. By resisting the commissioner's efforts, local school boards sought to ensure that the majority of citizens did not lose (as they saw it) resources and status in the effort to equalize education for poor and racially subordinated children. Their resistance took several forms.

First, citizens formed pressure groups to protest the commissioner's efforts to integrate their schools. Second, many school boards responded to protestors by refusing to implement Commissioner Allen's orders and by legally challenging his authority to force Malverne to desegregate. Other districts began to cite the litigation as a reason to delay compliance with the commissioner's directives in their own districts (*Vetere v. Mitchell,* 1963). Third, the press covered extensively the politics of desegregation, thereby magnifying the impact of the majority's resistance and the boards' inactions.

In these and other ways, local school boards effectively resisted desegregation. As the partners most directly affected by the policy, they had the incentives and the ability to refuse the state the cooperation necessary for the policy's success ("Allen Directive," 1963).

A Weakened State

The school boards' (in)actions went beyond preventing the immediate implementation of desegregation. They also led to the redefinition of the terms of state-local partnership in educational policy. Previously neutral on the issue of integrated schools, legislators began to react to the potent combination of constituents' protests, districts' defiance of the SED, and the subsequent media circus. Their reactions, over time, diminished the SED's capacity to effect desegregation.

The legislative battle against desegregation began soon after Commissioner Allen issued his 1963 directive. Citing constituents' wishes, legislators had, by March 1964, introduced five bills in opposition to busing and any other compulsory measure to effect racial balance. Between 1965 and 1969, legislators introduced 45 more such bills. In 1969, one antibusing bill passed, becoming Chapter 342 of the State Education Law (a federal court later found the law unconstitutional) (*Lee v. Nyquist*, 1970). Legislators from districts with segregated schools also joined forces with long-term advocates of local rule in sponsoring bills to limit the scope of—and in one case, to abolish—the commissioner's powers and to create an office of inspector general to review the commissioner's 310 decisions.

Although few of these bills became law, they fostered a legislative atmosphere that was suspicious of the commissioner and the SED. Consequently, when Commissioner Allen began to pursue a statewide master plan for integrated education in 1967, the legislature refused to provide the SED with enough money to enact the plan's measures. It underfunded the SED's Division of Intercultural Relations (DIR), the office that administered the department's policies regarding integration and provided technical assistance to desegregating districts. It underfunded, and later canceled, the state's Racial Balance Fund, money earmarked for helping school districts to create and implement programs for achieving racial balance. Lacking sufficient funds and the capacity to claim that the state was behind his policies, the new commissioner, Ewald Nyquist, could by 1970 no longer battle effectively for desegregation on a statewide basis. He was reduced to pursuing integration through his 310 power, and that power was limited to occasions when a district or someone in it filed an official complaint.

Still frustrated that the commissioner continued to use his 310 power to pursue a policy opposed by a conspicuous majority of their constituents, legislators began to pressure the Board of Regents. Some legislators sent letters to the regents, begging them to stop the commissioner from intervening in particular districts. Others called on the regents to fire Commissioner Nyquist. Legislators even began to use an antibusing litmus test when interviewing prospective regents (Clark, 1988).

These efforts were ultimately successful. After several years, the legislature had eliminated from the Board of Regents most supporters of active policies to mandate desegregation and had replaced them with strong opponents of busing and other mandatory desegregative techniques. In 1976, a majority of the Board of Regents voted to fire Commissioner Nyquist.

Recognizing that the legislature and the new regents posed a formidable barrier to mandated desegregation, the next commissioner, Gordon Ambach, no longer pursued the goal of integrated schools and issued no 310 rulings ordering schools to desegregate. Now both partners lacked incentives to pursue the policy.

Local Inaction

Although the state was becoming less willing and able to help local districts achieve racial balance, Yonkers was becoming more segregated. Within Yonkers, citizens and municipal officials disagreed on what to do about their segregated schools. Some (mainly black) parents wrote letters to the SED complaining of racial tension and imbalance; others (mainly white) formed protest groups similar to those in Malverne or altered the mission of extant neighborhood groups to oppose any school reorganization plan that involved busing.

Despite widespread white opposition to, and considerable black ambivalence about, integration, there were at least two times when local educational leaders were willing to cooperate with the state to desegregate Yonkers's schools. The first time occurred in the late 1960s and early 1970s, when Superintendent Paul Mitchell took steps toward improving the racial balance in Yonkers. He planned to open two racially integrated schools and to hire black staff. Superintendent Mitchell also designed workshops to help personnel meet the distinctive needs of black students (*United States v. Yonkers,* 1985). He sought technical aid from the DIR and money from the Racial Balance Fund. Before the state could proffer its limited help, however, Superintendent Mitchell died suddenly in 1970.

Lacking both Superintendent Mitchell's commitment to integration and the state's commitment to supplemental funding, the school board's efforts to desegregate Yonkers ceased. Acting Superintendent James Gallagher later justified his reluctance to pursue Superintendent Mitchell's plans for desegregation by citing the community's resistance. In its increasingly weakened position, the SED did not push Superintendent Gallagher to change his mind. Legislators had just eliminated the Racial Balance Fund, and the DIR was stymied by local opponents whom Superintendent Mitchell had known how to appease (*United States v. Yonkers,* 1985). Without state or local leadership, the momentum from Superintendent Mitchell's efforts dissolved.

Almost a decade later, Superintendent Joseph Robitaille made the next major effort to desegregate Yonkers's schools. A severe budget crisis combined with declining enrollments to make school closings seem essential, and school closings required redistricting. To Superintendent Robitaille, a majority of the school board, and a newly energized NAACP, this was an excellent opportunity to improve racial balance as well. Despite opposition from the mayor and many white citizens, Superintendent Robitaille issued his Phase II reorganization plan on August 5, 1977.

Yonkers, however, was in the midst of a citywide financial crisis and could not pay for desegregation on its own.[1] DIR officials promised technical assistance and came close to promising state funds to help develop and implement Phase II. But the now deeply weakened SED provided no technical assistance and delayed providing funds, and opponents to desegregation became deeply entrenched. By the time the SED informed Yonkers that it could provide no additional money, Mayor Antonio Martinelli had replaced the most active and liberal school board members with conservatives who refused to support programs that would destroy "the tradition of neighborhood schools."[2] After all, as one neighborhood organization observed, why pursue an unpopular program when "there is very little likelihood that the Commissioner [Ambach] would mandate a forced busing program on the city of Yonkers" (Taxpayers Organization of North East Yonkers, 1978; see also Lincoln Park Taxpayers, 1977).

The loss of the apparently promised state money felt, to supporters of desegregation, like the SED had "literally abandoned us and we found ourselves in the soup."[3] The following spring, the board adopted the only two components of Phase II it ever considered: reorganizing the grade structure and transforming one middle school into a school for vocational education. Neither action affected racial balance, and Superintendent Robitaille realized that the school board would never act on this part of his plan. He resigned 6 months later.

In 1980, the local chapter of the NAACP joined with the U.S. Department of Justice to sue the Board of Education and the City of Yonkers for allowing discriminatory schools to persist. After another 5 years, a federal court found intentional segregation in the schools.

Clearly, shared state and local institutional responsibilities for public education allowed local actors' opposition to desegregation to delay or prevent implementation of a mandated state policy. But the joint effects of (local) controversy and shared (state and local) institutional responsibility tell only part of the story. The interaction of the two factors over time is equally important.

More precisely, the shared responsibilities for public education in New York enabled local opponents of desegregation, through the widely publicized warfare between the protesting boards and the commissioner, to substantially raise the costs to legislators of pursuing the policy. Because the shared responsibilities for desegregation were not precisely defined, the legislature could curtail the commissioner's authority and the DIR's resources to act in the state-local partnership, thus rendering the state an unwilling or ineffectual partner. Once the legislature had weakened the state's role in the institutional partnership, the state could no longer help to desegregate communities such as Yonkers—even when local supporters of desegregation got the upper hand. Thus the mutually reinforcing dynamic of action and inaction in Yonkers—the zigzag movements of a rowboat in which only one oar is in the water at a time—resulted from the interaction of political controversy and a particular governmental structure.

The Political Success of Parochaid: Ineffective Controversy

In the early 1970s, parochaid (state aid to nonpublic schools) generated kinds and levels of political controversy similar to school desegregation. Both policies would have involved downward redistribution of scarce educational resources from a wealthier majority to a poorer minority. Both would also have benefited a socially stigmatized minority (in the case of parochaid, predominantly Catholic parochial students). And in both cases, local school boards led the opposition to the state's policy because they were the institutional actors that would bear the brunt of the financial and social costs of the new policy.

Here the similarities end. In the case of desegregation, local school boards could delay implementing the policy until the legislature diminished the state's willingness and capacity to act. In the case of parochaid, however, local opponents could not prevent the legislature, in cooperation with the governor, regents, and the SED, from pursuing the policy.

Why not? Because parochaid was, by definition, a matter of private rather than public education. The policy was therefore developed within an institutional structure—budgetary politics—that involved only state actors; local school boards had no role in effecting the policy. They were simply out of the loop.

As outsiders, local opponents to parochaid lacked both the direct and the indirect levers of protest they enjoyed as members of the educational partnership that controlled desegregation. Without a direct institutionalized voice, they could not delay implementing parochaid by refusing to cooperate with state actors. Their cooperation was irrelevant to the policy's successful enactment and implementation. In addition, school boards and citizen groups had no arena for the dramatic acts of resistance that garnered so much media attention in the case of desegregation, so they were less able to push the legislature into the role of spoiler. Thus they also had little indirect control over the policy. As a result, local opponents of parochaid, despite constituting a majority of voters, were forced to stand by as the state's educational policymakers handed over precious state funds to a relatively poor and socially disfavored minority.

Parochaid first became a political hot potato during the State Constitutional Convention of 1967. Proponents of parochaid seized the occasion to repeal the Blaine Amendment, the state's constitutional ban on the direct or indirect use of state monies to aid schools controlled, either in whole or in part, by religious organizations. Effective campaigning by Catholic interest groups had ensured the election of many convention delegates who were Catholic or who for other reasons supported repeal (Hacker, 1967). Moreover, the church had successfully lobbied for the support of Commissioner Allen, the Board of Regents, the governor, and prominent legislators (Kihss, 1966). Repeal passed the convention with a bipartisan vote of 132 to 49.

Despite the state's unified stand, parochaid remained politically volatile and unpopular. Realizing that they had been outmaneuvered by Catholic interest groups during the convention, opponents to parochaid mobilized to prevent ratification of the proposed constitution in 1967. Interest groups representing public education and civil liberties, including the powerful New York State Educational Conference Board, the United Federation of Teachers (UFT), the United Parents Association, and Jewish and Protestant organizations (Kihss, 1966), formed an umbrella lobbying group in early 1967 called Public Education and Religious Liberty (PEARL) to oppose ratification (Spiegel, 1967).

During the 1967 ratification campaign, these opponents argued that parochaid would unfairly shift educational resources from the public schools (which enrolled 80% of New York's elementary and secondary students) to the nonpublic schools (which enrolled the other 20%). Because the state had refused to increase aid to public schools, citing increasingly severe budgetary constraints, and because taxpayers in many school districts had recently rejected increases in local property taxes, opponents argued that subsidizing the nonpublic schools would draw money and talented students away from the public schools (Farber, 1967; Ronan, 1967; Schumach, 1967;

"Sutton and Cardino," 1967). Anti-Catholic sentiment further infused the controversy, particularly after Jewish and Protestant organizations joined the parochaid opposition. That sentiment led William J. Vanden Heuvel, fourth vice president of the constitutional convention, to condemn the implicit religious hostilities aroused during the ratification campaign (Schanberg, 1967b).

The impassioned fight over parochaid dominated the campaign for ratification, and heavy turnout defeated the proposed constitution by a margin of 3 to 1 (Schanberg, 1967a). Yet even after this conclusive rejection of the policy, legislators of both parties, supported by Governor Rockefeller and the Board of Regents, pledged to introduce a constitutional amendment to repeal the ban on parochaid in the next legislative session ("Salvaging the Good," 1967). Under pressure from Catholic organizations, the Senate's leadership introduced legislation to repeal the Blaine Amendment in 1968, which passed 35 to 17. However, to amend the constitution, both houses of the legislature would have to pass the bill in 2 successive years. The state's voters would then need to ratify it in a referendum. Leaders of the Assembly were sufficiently concerned about the recent electoral defeat of the proposed constitution that they did not introduce a repeal bill in 1968 or in 1969 (Flast & Greenberg, 1968; Ronan, 1968; Schanberg, 1968). But in 1970, both the Senate and the Assembly passed two repeal bills, either of which could be passed again in the 1971 session in preparation for ratification.

By this time, however, leading proponents of parochaid doubted whether the repeal would survive a statewide referendum. Although advocates had downplayed the importance of opposition to parochaid in the defeat of the 1967 constitution, an increasing number privately acknowledged that they lacked the electorate's support. Catholic church officials therefore decided in 1970 to pursue indirect state aid to parochial schools through state budgetary politics rather than through a constitutional amendment (which would again put parochaid to the voters; Lynn, 1971).

The budgetary push for state aid to nonpublic schools was successful. Between 1970 and 1972, the legislature approved assistance to nonpublic schools for state-mandated services (such as testing, record keeping, and building maintenance) as well as direct tuition grants and tax abatements for the parents of students in parochial schools. Three different bills, all with the support of the state's leading educational policy makers, allocated $117 million to New York's nonpublic schools during this period (Clines, 1970a, 1970b; Dugan, 1972; Farrell, 1971; Lubasch, 1972; Lynn, 1970; Narvaez, 1972; Spiegel, 1970a, 1970b).

Opponents of parochaid now faced a grim political situation. Despite the fact that a majority of New York voters opposed parochaid, opponents could not make their opposition effective once the battle was removed to the arena of budget making. They could no longer vote down a proposed constitutional amendment. Furthermore, because state budgetary politics were dominated by organized interest groups such as the Catholic church and other private school organizations, local school boards and private citizens had no significant role in allocating state funds. Lacking means to resist the policy change, opponents could not transfer the costs they were incurring to legislators or other state officials. Without serious electoral costs, and with strong incentives provided by interest groups, state actors continued to fund private schools.

With no political alternatives available, opponents of parochaid turned to the judicial system. In 1971, the U.S. Supreme Court held that state aid to religious schools for the purposes of "secular education services" was unconstitutional. The next year, a federal district court barred New York from disbursing the $33 million it had allocated for such services before the Supreme Court announced its decision (Farrell, 1972; Graham, 1971). Also in 1972, the district court found unconstitutional the annual $28 million of parochaid appropriated in the 1970 Mandated Services Act and the 1972 law that allocated money to nonpublic schools for building maintenance and tuition grants. It barred the SED from disbursing any more of these funds (Graham, 1972; Sibley, 1972).

The state appealed these rulings to the U.S. Supreme Court. In 1973, the court found that all four methods of indirect state aid to parochial schools violated the First Amendment (Peterson, 1973). But the state persisted. The following year, the new governor, Malcolm Wilson, re-quested and received legislative approval for a bill to reimburse parochial schools for the actual costs of state-mandated services, up to $10 million annually (Greenhouse, 1974). A U.S. appeals court found this version of parochaid unconstitutional, as well, in 1976 ("Parochial School Aid," 1976). After 1976, parochaid disappeared as a political issue.

Parochaid was lost in the courts only after it had succeeded in conven-tional electoral politics; desegregation was won in the courts only after it could not be attained through conventional electoral politics. Thus courts are critical to the ultimate success or failure of a policy initiative. But our focus here is less on the ultimate outcome of a policy initiative than on elements of the policy process that lead to political success or failure of proposed policy changes.

Parochaid succeeded politically and desegregation failed politically not because the latter generated more opposition than the former. Both policies were deeply controversial. What distinguished the two cases was how political institutions structured the battles. In the case of desegregation, the institutional structure of shared educational responsibility required that local school boards—the actors that perceived themselves to be paying large costs and gaining few benefits—cooperate in developing and implementing the policy. It was easy for boards to resist and to use that resistance to pressure already ambivalent legislators. In the case of parochaid, the institutional structure of unitary responsibility for the state budget required—and permitted—nothing of local school boards or citizens. The strongest opponents of the policy therefore possessed few institutional means to affect it, and their resistance was politically ineffective.

The Political Success of Special Education

The lesson of desegregation is that shared institutional responsibilities allow either partner to derail a controversial policy. But the case of special education shows that policies can be successfully developed and implemented within a divided political structure. Indeed, joint efforts by the SED and officials in Yonkers improved and sustained programs for children with handicapping conditions beyond what either partner could do alone. What distinguished this partnership from that of desegregation was agreement on goals for special education. Absent political controversy, New York's shared state-local institutional responsibilities for public education pose no barriers to the political success of educational policies.

Both New York State and local districts are responsible for ensuring that eligible children with handicapping conditions receive appropriate special education. To fulfill these responsibilities, commissioners of the SED have promulgated extensive and detailed regulations (New York Code of Rules and Regulations). Districts must provide children with an education that conforms to these standards; the state must set the standards and ensure districts' conformity.

Districts submit extensive plans to the state to ensure that they meet the standards. Although the plans allow districts to set goals, create programs, and devise budgets, they must do so within parameters set by the state. The SED evaluates the districts' policies and plans and sends representatives to conduct on-site reviews. If reviewers find a district out of compliance, the state may withhold all state educational monies until the district can show that its programs meet the state's requirements. Although this rarely happens, the threat of losing funds gives districts, including Yonkers, a strong incentive, to consult regularly with their educational partners in the SED to ensure compliance with the state's regulations.

From the 1960s through the mid-1980s, Yonkers's program in special education was plagued by an overidentification of black and Latino children and the stigmatization of its participants (*United States v. Yonkers*, 1985). Beginning in 1972, Yonkers's Director of Special Education, Gary Carmen, sought to improve the quality of Yonkers's programs for children with handicapping conditions. Carmen installed himself as chair of the selection committee, instituted policies designed to mainstream the students into as many regular programs as possible, and assigned students to schools in their own quadrant of the district.

Working without assistance from the state, however, and facing principals and parents who resisted special education classrooms in their buildings, Carmen's initiatives had mixed results. Moreover, after he retired in 1975, his successor's less vigilant attention to race led to the reappearance of racial bias in assignments (*United States v. Yonkers*, 1985). Acting alone, educators in Yonkers could not effect enduring change in the policy.

In January 1979, the SED's Office for Education of Children with Handicapping Conditions (OECHC) conducted an on-site review of Yonkers's programs in special education. The reviewing team found the district woefully out of compliance with the state's educational regulations (New York State Education Department, 1979). Reviewers were also concerned that Yonkers had failed an inspection by the federal Office for Civil Rights (New York State Education Department, 1982). The latter failure was especially serious because the state could not receive its extensive federal funding for special education unless all districts satisfied federal requirements.

In contrast to its inaction regarding Yonkers's failure to desegregate, the state did not merely remind the district of its responsibilities. Instead, it informed the school board that the OECHC would carefully monitor Yonkers's implementation of corrective actions suggested by the SED (New York State Education Department, 1979). And monitor they did. The SED required the district to document its compliance with federal as well as state regulations (Dodson, 1979). It worked with Yonkers's educators as they planned to reorganize their program and bring it into compliance. Indeed, in a follow-up audit in 1982, the review team credited the "supportive monitoring relationship between the district and the regional representative of the OECHC" as "the basis upon which the district dealt with the compliance issues cited in the 1979 OECHC report" (New York State Education Department, 1982, pp. 8-9).

Once the state stopped monitoring, however, the quality of the program lapsed. In 1987, the OECHC found the program out of compliance on over 100 state mandates (New York State Education Department, 1987). This time when the SED stepped in to help, the OECHC and Susan LaDue, Yonkers's director of special education, not only worked to bring the program into compliance; they also forged a more permanent alliance to enable them to prevent problems from developing.[4] This combined effort of state and local educators has led to careful attention when classifying black or Latino children for special education and to an end to segregation and stigmatization of the program's participants. Yonkers is now in full compliance with state and federal regulations.

Facilitating the state and Yonkers's successful partnership was the fact that special education was not controversial. It did benefit a stigmatized group of students. But prejudice against the handicapped never rose to the level of the racism that intensified political opposition to desegregation or the anti-Catholic sentiment that fueled opposition to parochaid. Furthermore, the state's involvement in special education was not redistributive. The state did spend some of its own monies on these programs, but the programs also brought in large amounts of federal funds. Consequently, both the state and the district were free enough of the pressures created by political controversy that they could act as cooperative educational partners.

Conclusion

As these cases illustrate, the fact that a policy is controversial is not enough to explain its political failure. The fact that a policy requires cooperation from two institutional partners also does not suffice to explain political success or failure. But the combination of a high level of political controversy and the need for a high level of institutional cooperation *is* enough to predict the outcome of a policy initiative—it will fail in the arena of electoral politics (absent some extraordinary intervention).

What does this analysis imply for the political future of desegregation? Initially, our findings may deepen the pessimism of those who have heretofore seen political opposition as a sufficiently daunting barrier to desegregation. Now they must worry about institutional structure, too. But the real lesson to draw from this analysis is that the outlook for desegregation may be more favorable than most assume. Even given citizen opposition, state governments can succeed in desegregating schools if they can be insulated from local influence. After all, the case of parochaid showed that political controversy does not necessarily inhibit state policymakers from taking strong action if they can act without fear of effective local resistance. Thus the political failure of desegregation in New York was not inevitable. It occurred because localities were able to manipulate the state-local partnership in public education so as to render the state a silent partner. But if the school boards had lacked that option, if they had been forced to observe the policy process from the sidelines, as was the case in parochaid, they arguably would not have translated opposition into a veto.

This conclusion implies that praise for New York's unusual structure for making educational policy is sometimes misplaced. The increasing involvement of the state in public education over the course of this century has rendered the state and local school boards mutually dependent partners. But mutual dependence can impede as well as promote action; Yonkers, at least, would have had more desegregation had either the SED or Yonkers's school board had complete control of all the resources necessary to achieve it. Given the degree of local opposition and the strong commitment to desegregate on the part of two commissioners, giving control to the state rather than to the locality would have been a better bet.

Arguing that educational authority over desegregation should reside solely with the state bureaucracy flies in the face of the currently fashionable advocacy of school decentralization (Clune & Witte, 1990). In the current educational and political climate, centralizing educational authority may seem unfeasible. But recent proposals for national educational standards and teacher testing, among others, already support some such centralization. If educators are serious about pursuing school desegregation in their states, and if local resistance in racially imbalanced communities is to be expected, then the first step toward successful desegregation may well be governmental reform. After all, a powerboat will get you to the shore faster than a rowboat with only one oar in the water.

Notes

1. As stated in an interview of J. P. Robitaille on October 29, 1990, conducted by Jennifer Hochschild, Beth Lorenz, and Monica Herk.
2. As quoted by J. Guerney in a November 1, 1990, interview conducted by Beth Lorenz, Steven Routh, and Monica Herk.
3. Stated by R. Jacobson, a former school board member, in a November 26, 1990, interview conducted by Jennifer Hochschild, Steven Routh, and Monica Herk.
4. As discussed in a July 2, 1991, interview with Susan LaDue, conducted by Judith L. Failer and Monica Herk.

References

Allen directive hit by Malverne; Regents policy on rights lacking, attorney says. (1963, August 7). *New York Times*, p. 21.

Boozer, M. A., Krueger, A. B., & Wolkon, S. (1992). Race and school quality since *Brown v. Board of Education*. *Brookings Papers on Economic Activity* (Annual 1992, n. SPISS). Washington, DC: Brookings Institution.

Brown v. Board of Education, 347 U.S. Reports 483 (1954).

Clark, K. (1988). [Deposition given in] Yonkers v. The State of New York, 60 Civ. 6761 (LBS), S.D.N.Y., 14.

Clines, F. X. (1970a, April 18) Church-pupil aid voted in Albany: $28 million is appropriated—Governor favors bill. *New York Times*, p. 16.

Clines, F. X. (1970b, February 28). Regents support repeal of Blaine: Board, in 11-2 vote, backs aid for parochial schools. *New York Times*, p. 3.

Clune, W. H., & Witte, J. F. (Eds.). (1990). *Choice and control in American education* (Vols. 1-2). London: Falmer.

Cooperative Institutional Research Program. (1987). *The American freshman: Twenty year trends, 1966-1985*. Los Angeles: University of California, Los Angeles, Higher Education Research Institute.

Cooperative Institutional Research Program. (1992). *The American freshman: National norms for fall 1992*. Los Angeles: University of California, Los Angeles, Higher Education Research Institute.

Crain, R. L., & Strauss, J. (1985). *School desegregation and occupation attainments: Results from a long-term experiment*. Baltimore, MD: Johns Hopkins University, Center for Social Organization of Schools.

Dodson, R. C. (1979, June 28). Letter from director of Special Services for Yonkers Public Schools to Hannah Flegenheimer. Unpublished document.

Dugan, G. (1972, April 29). Parochial pupils in demonstration: Court ruling barring aid is protested here. *New York Times*, p. 36.

Dunn, G. (1972, April 29). Parochial pupils in demonstration: Court ruling barring aid is protested here. *New York Times*, p. 36.

Farber, M. A. (1967, July 20). School board asks charter parley to keep ban on aid to parochial schools. *New York Times*, p. 19.

Farrell, W. E. (1971, June 6). Albany approves $33-million to aid parochial pupils. *New York Times*, p. 1.

Farrell, W. E. (1972, January 12). Legislators firm on parochial school aid; G.O.P. leaders will press for plan to grant funds to nonpublic schools. *New York Times*, p. 48.

Flast, F., & Greenberg, L. (1968, February 27). Voters' rejection of church-school aid [Letter to the editor]. *New York Times*, p. 42.

Graham, F. P. (1971, June 29). High court, 8 to 1, forbids states to reimburse parochial schools, backs college-level help, 5 to 4. *New York Times*, p. 1.

Graham, F. P. (1972, October 11). Court, 8 to 1, bars Ohio tuition plan: Justices affirm invalidation of grants to parents of private school students. *New York Times*, p. 20.

Greenhouse, L. (1974, April 12). Judge-race shift is voted for city. *New York Times*, p. 29.

Greenhouse, L. (1992, April 1). Justices ease controls in school desegregation case. *New York Times*, p. 1.

Hacker, A. (1967, October 1). The "Blaine Amendment"—Yes or no? *New York Times*, VI, p. 27.

Hochschild, J. L. (1984). *The new American dilemma: Liberal democracy and school desegregation.* New Haven, CT: Yale University Press.

Kihss, P. (1966, October 4). Lindsay seeking more home rule: Says mayors in state will unite for charter change. *New York Times,* p. 1.

Lee v. Nyquist, 318 P.Supp. 710 (1970).

Lincoln Park Taxpayers Association Education Committee. (1977). Report. Unpublished manuscript.

Lubasch, A. H. (1972, April 28). 3 judge panel bars aid by state for parochial school services. *New York Times,* p. 15.

Lynn, F. (1970, December 31). Tactics changed in drive for parochial school aid. *New York Times,* p. 1.

Lynn, F. (1971, January 26). Cooke relaxes stand on Blaine issue. *New York Times,* p. 31.

Matter of Mitchell, Decision No. 7240, 2 Ed. Dept. Rep. 501 (1963, June 17).

Milstein, M. M., & Jennings, R. F. (1973). *Educational policymaking and the state legislature: The New York experience.* New York: Praeger.

Murphy, J. T. (1974). *State education agencies and discretionary funds: Grease the squeaky wheel.* Lexington, MA: D. C. Heath.

Narvaez, A. A. (1972, May 26). Governor signs school-aid bill: Nonpublic institutions could get $56-million a year. *New York Times,* p. 39.

New York Education Laws 9, 101, 215, 301, 305, 306, and 320.

New York State Education Department, Office for the Education of Children with Handicapping Conditions & the Bureau of Bilingual Education. (1979, March 5). *Site visit report of Yonkers public schools.* New York: Author.

New York State Education Department, Office for the Education of Children with Handicapping Conditions. (1982, July 28). *Site visit report of Yonkers public schools.* New York: Author.

New York State Education Department, Office for the Education of Children with Handicapping Conditions. (1987). *Site visit report of Yonkers public schools* (review conducted between January and May, 1987). New York: Author.

Parochial school aid law in New York State stricken. (1976, June 22). *New York Times,* p. 23.

Peterson, I. (1973, June 26). Church schools will stay open. *New York Times,* p. 29.

Ronan, T. P. (1967, August 12). Two groups support school-aid ban: Parents and teachers join against Church-run units. *New York Times,* p. 23.

Ronan, T. P. (1968, January 31). State senate votes to end ban on Church-school aid; Repeal backed 35 to 17. *New York Times,* p. 1.

Salvaging the good proposals [Editorial]. (1967, November 13). *New York Times,* p. 46.

Schanberg, S. H. (1967a, November 8). Constitution beaten, transit bonds win; Jersey G.O.P. captures the legislature. *New York Times,* p. 1.

Schanberg, S. H. (1967b, November 9). Partisan fight shaping up on salvaging of charter. *New York Times,* p. 1.

Schanberg, S. H. (1968, January 3). Travia says he will not support governor on tax increases. *New York Times,* p. 1.

Schumach, M. (1967, April 29). Teachers giving pupils leaflets attacking parochial school aid. *New York Times,* p. 24.

Sibley, J. (1972, October 3). U.S. court bans state aid to private-school parents. *New York Times,* p. 1.

Spiegel, I. (1967, March 7). School-aid foes form state unit: Opponents to battle private use of Albany's funds. *New York Times,* p. 49.

Spiegel, I. (1970a, June 22). Governor, 2 rivals help dedicate Hasidic center. *New York Times,* p. 40.

Spiegel, I. (1970b, January 29). Orthodox rabbis back aid to religious schools. *New York Times,* p. 27.

Sutton and Cardino clash on school aid. (1967, June 30). *New York Times,* p. 33.

Taxpayers Organization of North East Yonkers Education Committee. (1978, March). *TONEY report on "school reorganization phase #2."* Unpublished manuscript.

United States v. Yonkers Board of Education, 624 F. Supp. 1276 (1985).

University of the State of New York. (1960, January 27-28). Regents' statement on intercultural relations in education. *Journal of Regents Meeting.* New York: Author.

Usdan, M. D. (1963). *The political power of education in New York State.* New York: Institute of Administrative Research, Teachers College, Columbia University.

Vetere v. Mitchell, 41 Misc.-200 (1963), *accord,* Vetere vs. Mitchell, 21 AD- 561(1964), aff'd 15 N.Y.- 259 (1965), *cert. denied,* 382 U.S. 825 (1965).

Wilson, J. Q. (1974). The politics of regulation. In J. W. McKie (Ed.), *Social responsibility and the business predicament* (pp. 135-168). Washington, DC: Brookings Institution.

4

Implementation of Court-Ordered Desegregation by District-Level School Administrators

JENNIFER J. BEAUMONT

Forty years after the *Brown v. Board of Education* decision, the debate on desegregation still rages. What were its purposes? What were the most appropriate, effective, and efficient vehicles for meeting those purposes? How would its impact be measured? Expectations ranged widely: from remedying inequities in educational resources (Kaufman, 1991) to increasing academic performances of African American students; from engineered interracial socialization (Braddock, 1985) to ensuring parity between African Americans and European Americans in levels of educational attainment (Willie, 1984, p. 5). Whatever the initial expectations and perceptions of its purposes, districts desegregating their schools had varied results. These variations were usually attributed to voluntary or court-mandated plans, timing of the decision, and the methods used for desegregation. An important element, often missing from the debate, is the significant impact of the commitment district-level school officials had to the implementation phase and the degree of cooperation they exhibited. Leadership plays much more than a catalytic role in school desegregation. Positive, supportive leadership is the most important ingredient in successful school desegregation (Beck, 1980, p. 116).

This chapter is an examination of the implementation of court-ordered desegregation by district-level administrators of the Boston public schools. Within the conceptual framework of institutional and policy history, this study uses document analysis and semistructured interviews to describe how Boston school officials implemented court-ordered desegregation and to examine the impact of desegregation on the stability of school leadership. The chapter begins with a brief review of the literature on the courts as education policy-makers and on the implementation of court-ordered desegregation.

Judicial Role in Education

Although courts cannot initiate the policy-making process, they become policymakers once a matter is brought for litigation. A jurist cannot sidestep making a decision on a matter in litigation. The decision made immediately becomes policy for those specific litigants, and, if accepted by other local and/or regional jurists, becomes policy for all future litigators of that issue (Birkby, 1983, p.1). Once a decision is handed down from the Supreme Court, however, it is national policy and becomes the precedent for all future litigation. According to Justice White, judicial policy making cannot be avoided and is valid because federal courts should be free to devise workable remedies when the state, as representative party, fails to act (Gordon, 1989, p. 205).

Hogan (1985, p. 3) ascribes the concept of equality of education to the Court's application of the Fourteenth Amendment to the schools, with the first cases involving racial discrimination. Although the courts have never considered access to education a constitutional right, they have played a distinctive role in the educational arena since 1789. Federal court involvement in education began in a laissez-faire manner with school matters being left to the states. It was not until the 1950s that judicial reform by the federal courts began to bring state laws in alignment with the U.S. Constitution. Judicial supervision is concurrent with judicial reform, as both federal and state courts expanded their roles into the administration and organization of schools, maintaining oversight and determining the duration of all mandates. In 1973, judicial reform gave way to judicial restraint with the Supreme Court's renewed insistence that education is not a constitutional right (Hogan, 1985, pp. 9-10).

Although courts have to make a decision, they are limited, as regulators, by statutory or constitutional language, precedent, and the presented specifics of the litigation. The enforcement of public policy made by the courts differs from that made by the legislative or executive branches. The courts are unable to directly enforce their constraints (Birkby, 1983, pp. 2-6). They must always rely on other agencies, plaintiffs, or supportive interest groups for the implementation of decrees. Although they face the threat of being held in contempt of court, public officials have ignored directives from the courts or selectively implemented portions of their policy with a frequency that indicates this is not enough of a deterrent to noncompliance. Enactment of judicial policy making as the process of defining rights bears heavily on the process of implementing them (Horowitz, 1977, p. 107).

Thus the efficacy of any judicial regulation can be evaluated by asking: Is the court moving ahead of, in concert with, or contrary to other education policymakers? What is the opposition? What are the political bases for any opposition?

Studying the Implementation
of Court-Ordered Desegregation

According to Nakamura and Smallwood (1980), the implementation of judicial decisions is determined by identifying the actors and arenas relevant to the achievement of policy goals, defining relationships between the actors, and organizing and coordinating the parties to achieve policy goals. Optimal implementation of judicial policy formulation is therefore facilitated or hindered by the quality of communication, the channels of communication, and the commitment of the parties involved. In most cases, the intervening time between the actual decision and its implementation spans many years;[1] this is because the courts have to rely on intermediaries to communicate the decision to those parties affected by the decision but not directly involved in the legalities; the relationships between implementation actors are not constant, and the actors may change while the implementation is in progress; and conflicts between the implementers' personal values and policy requirements may occur.

Variations in the compliance rates of court-formulated policies are often contingent upon the implementation approach selected by the particular judge. There are three broad categories of approaches:

1. Political: The general requirements are set, but the judge does not become involved in the formulation of the details for implementation.

2. Receivership: The court becomes so involved in the implementation of the policy that the normal political process is subjugated to judicial impositions.

3. Technical: The implementation details are sought through impartial but rigid technological systems (Flicker, 1990).

Of course, the approach employed in any situation is determined by the judge's personality and values, the particular environment, and the actors involved. The operant variables for the implementation of any policy include: the costs and benefits, the primary beneficiaries, procedures for monitoring, administrative coordination, the specific standard, the attitudes and commitment of the implementers toward the policy and, most important, how clearly the policy is stated (Bullock & Lamb, 1984). It is necessary to delineate the policy goals, the actors or arenas to be regulated, and the procedures for monitoring to determine the significance of each of these variables.

Conceptual Framework

Neustadt and May's (1986) minimethods were used to look at the institutional histories of the public school system, the governing school board, and the city government. This approach requires delving into the significant events and details of an institution's history. Identifying changes in its internal organization, resource allocation, operating procedures, and incentive systems should reveal an institution's patterns of information processing and decision making, as well as its patterns of interaction with other institutions. An institution's political culture, therefore, becomes the crucible for the implementation factors. Factors such as source of the policy, clarity of the policy, support for the policy, complexity of the administration, incentives for implementers, and resource allocation affect how a policy is implemented (Brewer & deLeon, 1983). Specifically, the political culture of the Boston public schools and its governing School Committee, as well as the factors affecting implementation of court-ordered desegregation by district-level officials, will be analyzed.

Methods

Document analysis was used to get factual information and to understand the institutional history. Document review, in tandem with semistructured interviews, provided the data on the interactions between the school system, the courts, and the community. Secondary data were analyzed in order to describe the impact of desegregation on the student population, total school enrollment, and on the tenure of the superintendents.

History of the Boston Public School System

The Boston public schools served a largely homogeneous Yankee[2] population from 1789 until the early 1900s. There was a strong emphasis on
centralization and professionalization. Commitment to and achievement of
these goals were incorporated into the superintendency, with the first superintendent being appointed in 1851 (Lukas, 1986, p. 120). The first wave of Irish
immigrants arrived in the 1840s (Sheehan, 1984, p. 15). As their numbers
increased, the Irish immigrants wrested control of the school system from the
Yankees between the early and middle years of the 20th century.

Metcalf (1983), like Higgins (1984) and (Clay, 1991), marks the next
pivotal era of the Boston public schools as the period between 1940 and
1960, when the African American population increased from 5% of the total
population to 9.1% (Gelfand, 1990, p. 50), primarily because of newcomers
from the southern states. Metcalf attributes a large part of the school
segregation issues to heightened conflict between the Irish American and
African American groups. It should be noted, however, that in 1849 the
relatively small African American population went to the courts seeking an
end to segregation in the schools. Although the plaintiffs in *Roberts v. City
of Boston* (1850) lost the case, continued public agitation resulted in the
1855 Massachusetts statute abolishing mandated segregated schools (Lukas,
1986, p. 55).[3] It was more than a century later before any concrete steps
were taken to desegregate the Boston public schools.

Desegregation

Official school desegregation orders were handed down to the Boston
School Committee on June 21, 1974 (*Morgan v. Hennigan,* 1974). This
decision came after several years of intransigence by the School Committee,
ushering in an era of violence and hostility unprecedented in the school
system's history. The Massachusetts State Board of Education reviewed
enrollment by race in 1965 and found several school systems operating
racially imbalanced schools. A school was determined to be racially imbalanced if its student body was less than 50% European American. The 1965
Racial Imbalance Act[4] passed by the state legislature required systems
having racially imbalanced schools to submit desegregation plans. Noncompliance with the statute could result in the withholding of federal and
state education funds. Conversely, if new facilities had to be enlarged or
built in order to create racial balance, the state would increase its usual share
of the construction cost from 40% to 65% (*Morgan* at 418).

The State Board of Education charged the Boston School Committee with operating 45 imbalanced schools in 1965; by 1969, there were 62 (*Morgan* at 440). Rather than develop and submit desegregation plans, the School Committee first denied problems were incurred by racial imbalance and then challenged the constitutionality of the legislation. Concurrently, the U.S. Department of Health, Education, and Welfare (HEW) independently investigated the Boston public schools (Metcalf, 1983, p. 198). Its findings supported those of the Massachusetts State Board of Education; thus HEW withheld $25,753,819 in federal funds from the school system (*Morgan* at 420-421).[5]

Limited implementation of the Racial Imbalance Act was achieved because of the activism of African American parents in two organizations: Operation Exodus and the Metropolitan Council for Educational Opportunities (METCO). Both groups received financial and technical resource assistance from the state. In 1965, Operation Exodus began using the open enrollment plan to bus students from the African American community of Roxbury into schools having predominantly European American enrollments. One year later, METCO started busing African American students from the city of Boston into contiguous suburban school districts (Metcalf, 1983, pp. 198-199). Both groups strongly advocated desegregation of the Boston public schools and participated in filing a suit against the School Committee in 1972.

In determining that the School Committee operated a segregated school system,[6] Judge Garrity examined six areas: facilities use; districting and redistricting; feeder patterns; open enrollment and controlled transfers; faculty and staff; and vocational and examination schools (*Morgan* at 425). Although intent was determined in all areas, the evidence was especially strong in the areas of faculty and staff and feeder patterns.

To maintain segregated schools, the School Department created a complex system of grade organizations. Elementary schools served students from K to 5, K to 6, or K to 8. There were middle schools with Grades 6, 7, and 8. There were junior high schools with Grades 7, 8, 9. High schools had two types of grade organizations—Grades 10, 11, and 12 or Grades 9, 10, 11, and 12. The high school a student attended was determined by the grade organization of the elementary and middle or junior high school from which it drew students. Of the 18 high schools the system operated, 9 theoretically accepted students from any school in the city, whereas the other half were "fed" by designated middle and junior high schools. Most of the K to 8 elementary schools and the middle schools had predominantly European American enrollments. Three of the citywide Grades 9 to 12 high schools—Boys Latin, Girls Latin, and Boston Technical—admitted students by examination only. The European American enrollments at these schools were 93%, 89%, and 84%, respectively. The K to 6 elementary schools and the Grades 7 to 9 junior high schools were attended primarily by African American students. Any African American student who wanted to attend a citywide or Grades 9 to 12 high school had to transfer at the 10th grade—an action not highly encouraged (*Morgan* at 426).

Protocols for the hiring of faculty and administrative staff were as complicated as the student feeder patterns. Teachers were hired in three categories: permanent, provisional, and temporary. The distinguishing factors between permanent and provisional status were certification by the State Board of Education, transfer and promotional rights under state law and union contracts, and a $1,500-$2,100 pay differential. A teacher hired in the provisional category could become permanent by gaining tenure after 3 consecutive years of service. About 15% of all teachers in the system during the 1972-1973 school year held 1-year provisional contracts (*Morgan* at 457). African Americans represented less than 6% of the permanent teachers during the 1972-1973 school year (*Morgan* at 459). Temporarily hired teachers worked as substitutes on a daily, as-needed basis. Nearly all administrative positions required 4 to 6 years of teaching experience in the Boston public schools, after earning permanent teaching status. Transfers from faculty to administrative positions were based on seniority. Therefore, African Americans were principals at only 5 of 187 schools, and assistant principals at only 14 (*Morgan* at 459).

Looking at these factors, Judge Garrity requested desegregation plans from the School Committee. Again the School Committee's intransigence prompted the direct and sustained involvement of external actors. Its refusal to submit desegregation plans prepared by the School Department staff resulted in a plan being developed by the State Board of Education's task force (Lukas, 1986, p. 240; Metcalf, 1983, p. 204). The task force's plan was Phase 1 of the remedy. Involving only 40% of the Boston public schools, it was mandated by the state for implementation in September 1974. The School Committee was required to expand the plan into Phase 2 of the remedy. The School Committee refused to endorse any plan that required busing and refused to develop a Phase 2 plan. Implementation of the Phase 1 plan wrought such violence and hostilities that the National Guard had to be brought into Boston.

Finally, on May 10, 1975, Judge Garrity created the Phase 2 plan from the blueprint developed by his appointed team of masters and experts. Judge Garrity administered the implementation of the Phase 2 plan from

September 1975 until 1990, when the court vacated the order. Garrity used the receivership approach. He divided the school system into eight school districts, each reflecting Boston's racial composition; required the busing of one third of the total student population; called for the pairing of public schools with area colleges, universities, and cultural institutions; and created a magnet school district that could serve approximately 25% of the student population.[7]

In addition to racially balanced student populations in the schools, Judge Garrity required that at least 20% of all administrative and faculty positions be filled by African Americans (Ross & Berg, 1981, p. 712). In 1984, Dr. Spillane (1984) said, "We have taken full ownership of what was originally a court-ordered process of affirmative action, and now about 25 percent of our employees in teaching and administrative positions are members of minorities" (p. 11).

The African American representation in administrative positions increased from 12.31% in 1976 to 31.07% in 1992. There were also increases in the representation of other non-European American groups, from 1.37% to 9.51%, during the same period. Similar changes are seen in faculty positions: African American teachers securing permanent positions increased from 8.96% in 1975 to 22.20% in 1992. Within the same category, other non-European American groups increased from 0.51% to 9.01% (Boston Municipal Research Bureau, 1975, 1985, 1992). These changes were not achieved in a context of compliance and progressive growth.

In 1985, and again in 1990, Judge Garrity withdrew from the case and had to reopen it because of the school system's failure to appreciably increase the percentage of African American teachers and administrators ("Desegregation Redux," 1992). Compliance with this aspect of the court order required a radical change for the School Committee, as the city and school system were strongly dominated by the Irish (Clay, 1991; Gelfand, 1990; Higgins, 1984; Wood, 1982). All principals and senior staff were former teachers in the Boston public schools, and before the mid-1960s, there was no active recruitment of teachers outside of Boston-area colleges (Sheehan, 1984, p. 60).

School Committee

Professional employment in the Yankee-controlled private sector was closed to Irish immigrants. Thus the School Committee, controlled by the Irish since the early 1900s, used the school system as the avenue toward professional status (Wood, 1982, p. 455). Administrators and faculty were

Table 4.1 Historical Profile of the School Committee

Year	Changes in Size and Selection	First Appointments
1789	Inception of the school committee as an elected body with 21 members.	
1874	116 members	
1875	24 members	
1902	5 members	
1976	5 members	First African American, John O'Bryant, elected to the school committee
1983	13 members	
1984	13 members	First Hispanic American, Jean Romero, elected to the school committee.
1989	13 members	First Native American, Stephen Holt, elected to the school committee.
1992	7 members. School committee members selected by mayoral appointments.	First Asian American, George Joe, appointed.

SOURCE: Terris (1987).

overwhelmingly Irish (Lukas, 1986, p. 122). This highly politicized committee represented an Irish-dominated, patronage-ridden system. Faculty and other School Department employees maintained their positions primarily through personal contributions and the sale of tickets to events benefiting School Committee members (Dentler & Scott, 1981, p. 9). Although its size fluctuated widely (see Table 4.1), the membership was predominantly Irish Catholic until 1976, when John O'Bryant, an African American, won an at-large seat. Controlling the number of seats on the committee and the selection process were conspicuous displays of power: "Between 1905 and 1977, there were 48 Irish Catholic members, 8 Yankees, 5 Jews, and 2 Italians; after 1942, all but four members were Irish" (Lukas, 1986, p. 122).

In addition to patronage, the School Committee, an elected body until 1992, represented a stepping stone for those members with strong political aspirations (Lukas, 1986, p. 123; Metcalf, 1983, p. 204).[8] By then, the 13-member committee was one of the largest, contemporary school governance bodies in the United States, and each member had a personal administrative staff. In 1989, each member had a $54,000 staff allowance

Table 4.2   Boston Public School Superintendents Since 1963

Superintendent	Dates Served	Length of Tenure
William H. Ohrenberger	Oct. '63-Aug. '72	9 years 11 months
William J. Leary	Sept. '72-Aug. '75	3 years
Marion J. Fahey	Sept. '75-Aug. '78	3 years
Robert Wood	Sept. '78-Aug. '80	2 years
Paul Kennedy (Acting)	Sept. '80-March '81	8 months
Joe McDonough (Acting)	March '81-June '81	4 months
Robert Spillane	July '81-June '85	4 years
Joe McDonough (Acting)	July '85-Aug. '85	2 months
Laval S. Wilson	Sept. '85-March '90	4 years 6 months
Joe McDonough (Acting)	March '90-June '91	1 year 3 months
Lois Harrison Jones	July '91-June '95	4 years

(Koch, 1989, p. 26), adding more than $700,000 to the annual School Department budget. Its political independence ended with the 1992 legislative change to a seven-member mayor-appointed board. Patronage was limited, as the legislation prohibited individual board members from hiring personal staff (Aucoin & Ribadeneira, 1991).

The School Committee acted as an administrative body rather than a policy-making body. Historically, the effective and efficient handling of administrative and planning issues was restricted by the absence of any individual or body other than the School Committee having full authority over the system. According to Dentler and Scott (1981), the superintendent had control of curriculum and program matters only, and the business manager reported directly to the School Committee (Dentler & Scott, 1981, p. 21). The superintendency became a very vulnerable position, as there were no demarcations between the authority and the responsibility of the school leader and those of the School Committee.

Impact of Desegregation Order on Leadership Stability

Prompted largely by the events described above, along with widespread racial tensions among teachers and administrators, generally low student achievement, and the institutionalized ethnic rivalry between the Irish and the Yankees, the Boston public schools entered a new and difficult era marked by high superintendency turnover. As Table 4.2 shows, William

Ohrenberger was the last superintendent to serve more than 5 years. In the 20 years between 1972 and 1992, the Boston public schools had 10 super-intendents with an average tenure of 2 years. During this time, the School Committee terminated or refused to renew contracts for any of the super-intendents. The reasons for the decisions all revolved around the imple-mentation of Judge Garrity's orders.

William Leary, the first superintendent to be involved in the court order, was denied authorization to hire a full-time desegregation coordina-tor in 1973 (Bullard, Grant, & Stoia, 1981, p. 36). By 1975, with several senior administrators in the School Department refusing to become in-volved in assignment of students and faculty, Leary's effectiveness was thwarted. In April 1975, the five-member School Committee voted 3 to 2 not to renew Superintendent Leary's contract because of his efforts to cooperate with Judge Garrity's desegregation orders (Dentler & Scott, 1981, pp. 56-59). Leary's successor, then Associate Superintendent Marion Fahey, served only one term. Unlike Leary, Fahey represented the interests of three influential School Committee members and was appointed by a 3 to 2 vote. As an agent of these members, Fahey denied reappointments to experienced School Department administrators involved in the coordination and im-plementation of the early stages of the desegregation plan (Sheehan, 1984, p. 155). In 1978, with her three patrons losing their bid for reelection to the School Committee, and with the new School Committee President, David Finnegan, proposing a major overhaul of the School Department, Fahey's contract was not renewed. Finnegan's plan, strengthening the superinten-dency while simultaneously reducing the central office administration, was the first administrative reorganization of the School Department since 1905 (Sheehan, 1984, p. 125). Robert Wood, one of the architects of the reor-ganization plan, was Finnegan's choice for the superintendency.

Wood, a court-appointed monitor for the school desegregation case from 1974 to 1976, served as superintendent from 1978 to 1980. Wood was the first outsider to hold the position since 1921 (Sheehan, 1984, p. 125). Before being appointed to the superintendency, Wood was Chancellor of the University of Massachusetts, as well as Undersecretary and then Secre-tary of the U.S. Department of Housing and Urban Development (HUD). His tenure was characterized by constant conflict with the school commit-tee and the school department. Wood's previous public service experiences "did not prepare me to work with an intransigent bureaucracy" (Wood, personal communication, September 10, 1992). The officially stated rea-sons for his termination included improper administration of the 1979-1980 School Department budget, which resulted in an $18-20 million deficit and general dissatisfaction with his performance (Ross & Berg, 1981, pp. 696-697). However, his attempts to bring the School Department in compliance with the order for desegregation, his resistance to patronage as the order of the day, and his cooperation in bringing about the indictment of a School Committee member for extortion seemed to be significant factors also (Ross & Berg, 1981, pp. 701-703; Wood, personal communication, September 10, 1992).[9]

Robert Spillane, on the other hand, ended his tenure voluntarily after 4 years, and with 14 months left in the contract. After superintendencies in Glassboro, New Jersey, and Roosevelt and New Rochelle, New York, Spillane was Deputy Commissioner at the New York State Education Department. He sought leadership of the Boston public schools because he "wanted to be the superintendent of an urban school district" (Spillane, personal communication, August 25, 1992). However, Judge Garrity's manner of oversight in the school desegregation case stymied and frustrated him (Spillane, personal communication, August 25, 1992).[10] Spillane's public opposition to Judge Garrity led to tensions with the African American community. To that community, the courts, hence Judge Garrity, protected its interests (Edwards, 1989, p. 83). Just before leaving in 1985, Spillane changed Judge Garrity's organization of the school system by consolidating the eight school districts into five zones.

Spillane was hired in 1981 by a 5-member School Committee, but in 1984, the number of seats was increased to 13. The 5 members were all selected from at-large elections. The new structure of 9 ward and 4 at-large seats allowed for greater representation. The addition of 8 new members, their personal staffs, and constituent problems from nine districts made working with the new School Committee unwieldy (Spillane, personal communication, August 25, 1992). It was this new School Committee that hired Laval Wilson to be the school system's ninth superintendent in 15 years.

In 1985, John Nucci, the first Italian American to chair the Boston School Committee, initiated a national search to fill the now-vacant chief executive office. Boston was suffering from a negative image problem. It had lost its reputation for being the seat of liberalism in America. The general feeling on the search committee was that a concerted move away from business as usual was needed (Nucci, personal communication, September, 11, 1992). All indicators pointed to the selection of a non-European American, non-Bostonian candidate as a statement of change and healing. The 9 to 4 vote for Wilson represented an unlikely, and definitely uncoordinated, alliance of two groups on the School Committee: European Americans with conservative educational philosophies and three of the four African Americans who voted along racial lines (Edwards, 1989). Wilson's involvement with the long-standing school desegregation order seemed to revolve primarily around staffing and student assignments, as Judge Garrity reopened the case in 1992 because appropriate increases in African American faculty had not been made, especially in the three examination schools (Nueffer, 1990). Although his initial contract was renewed, Wilson served only 2 years of the second contract before it was bought out. The stated reasons were not related to his handling of the implementation of the school desegregation orders.

Conclusion

The 18 years of judicial supervision of the mandated court order to desegregate the Boston public schools did not result in the achievement of a unitary status. Instead, the most visible result was the creation of a new governance structure and an attempt to open up the school system to previously excluded groups. Tension and conflict undergirds the entire process. *Morgan v. Hennigan* was the result of tension and conflict between the African American and European American communities. Clearly, tension and conflict defined the relationships between several groups of actors, and at several levels: between the School Committee and the courts; the School Committee and its superintendents; the School Committee and the larger community, particularly the segments of the African American community.

Neustadt and May (1986) suggest using the historical perspective as a predictor of implementation. The Boston School Committee's pattern of focusing on maintaining itself and being intricately involved in the day-to-day management of the School Department clearly indicated resistance to any policy threatening its power base and reducing its span of influence. Although Judge Garrity chose the receivership approach, implementation of the court order depended entirely upon the School Committee, the superintendent of schools, and the School Department. The actors and arenas necessary for the achievement of the policy goals were known. Missing, however, was the willingness to organize and coordinate the activities. Therefore, as Nakamura and Smallwood (1980) determined, the commitment of the parties is an integral component in the implementation of court orders. School desegregation of the Boston public schools failed, not because of curriculum factors, teaching styles, learning styles, or student abilities. School desegregation of the Boston public schools failed because the policy was reduced to an issue of busing and of student assignments, and because the district-level school administrators actively thwarted the process.

Notes

1. Several cases have had long periods of judicial oversight, for example, Boston, Buffalo (NY), Oklahoma City, Norfolk (VA).

2. The term *Yankee* generally refers to that subset of European Americans who are residents of New England, and particularly to the descendants of the 17th-century Puritan settlers. In this study, the term specifically refers to those descendants of Puritan settlers living in Boston (Thernstrom, 1980).

3. The case was lost of the grounds that the schools, although racially segregated, were equal. This argument set the precedent for *Plessy v. Ferguson* (1896).

4. Unlike the 1974 desegregation order, the Racial Imbalance Act did not address the issue of segregation among faculty or administration.

5. These monies came from grant categories such as the Elementary and Secondary Education Act, Federal Assistance for the Education of Handicapped Children, School Library Resources, Vocational Education Act, and the Education Professions Act.

6. In the 1972-1973 school year, 84% of the European American students attended schools where they made up more than 80% of the population. About 62% of the African American students were in schools where they were more than 70% of the enrollment. Approximately 80% of the 187 schools were considered segregated because they did not reflect the racial composition of the Boston public schools (*Morgan* at 424).

7. At the time, Boston's racial breakdown was 51% European American, 36% African American, and 12% other ethnicities and races. The magnet school district consisted of 12 high schools, 4 middle schools, 9 elementary schools, and a bilingual unit. The magnet school district focused on mathematics, science, and languages and was open to all students regardless of residence (Metcalf, 1983, p. 209).

8. After serving on the School Committee of the 1930s, Maurice Tobin moved on to become mayor of Boston, governor of Massachusetts, and secretary of labor in the Truman cabinet. Similarly, Louise Day Hicks served on the School Committee, on the Boston City Council, and in Congress; she twice ran unsuccessfully for mayor of Boston (Lukas, 1986, pp. 37, 124).

9. On March 10, 1981, School Committee member Gerald O'Leary was convicted on charges of attempting to extort $650,000 from a transportation vendor in order to secure the contract to bus Boston public school students (Ross & Berg, 1981, pp. 702-703).

10. As deputy commissioner of the New York State Department of Education, Spillane was actively involved in the plans to desegregate the New Rochelle public schools. That process represented a collaborative relationship with the presiding judge. Spillane (personal communication, August 25, 1992) found the relationship with Judge Garrity to be constrained.

References

Aucoin, D., & Ribadeneira, D. (1991, December 17). School Board aide's role is in question. *Boston Globe,* p. 33.

Beck, W. B. (1980). Identifying school desegregation leadership styles. *Journal of Negro Education, 49*(2), 115-133.

Birkby, R. H. (1983). *The court and public policy.* Washington, DC: CQ Press.
Boston Municipal Research Bureau. (1975, 1985, 1992). *Boston facts and figures.* Boston: Author.
Braddock, J. H. (1985). School desegregation and black assimilation. *Journal of Social Issues, 41*(3), 9-22.
Brewer, G. D., & deLeon, P. (1983). *The foundations of policy analysis.* Homewood, IL: Dorsey.
Bullard, P., Grant, J., & Stoia, J. (1981). The northeast: Boston, Massachusetts: Ethnic resistance to a comprehensive plan. In C. V. Willie & S. L. Greenblatt (Eds.), *Community politics and educational change: Ten school systems under court order* (pp. 31-63). New York: Longman.
Bullock, C. S., & Lamb, C. M. (1984). *Implementation of civil rights policy.* Monterey, CA: Brooks/Cole.
Clay, P. L. (1991). Boston: The incomplete transformation. In H. V. Savitch & J. C. Thomas (Eds.), *Big city politics in transition* (pp. 14-28). Newbury Park, CA: Sage.
Dentler, R., & Scott, M. (1981). *Schools on trial: An inside account of the Boston school desegregation case.* Cambridge, MA: Abt.
Desegregation redux [Editorial]. (1992, May 17). *Christian Science Monitor,* p. 20.
Edwards, R. (1989). *How Boston selected its first black superintendent.* Unpublished doctoral dissertation, Harvard Graduate School of Education.
Flicker, B. (1990). *Justice and school systems: The role of the courts in education litigation.* Philadelphia: Temple University Press.
Gelfand, M. I. (1990). Boston: Back to the politics of the future. In R. M. Bernard (Ed.), *Snowbelt cities: Metropolitan politics in the Northeast and Midwest since World War II* (pp. 40-62). Bloomington: Indiana University Press.
Gordon, W. M. (1989). School desegregation: A look at the '70s and '80s. *Journal of Law and Education, 18*(2), 189-214.
Higgins, G. V. (1984). *Style versus substance: Boston, Kevin White, and the politics of illusion.* New York: Macmillan.
Hogan, J. C. (1985). *The schools, the courts, and the public interest* (2nd ed.). Lexington, MA: Lexington Books.
Horowitz, D. L. (1977). *The courts and social policy.* Washington, DC: Brookings Institution.
Kaufman, P. W. (1991). Building a constituency for school desegregation: African American women in Boston, 1962-1972. *Teachers College Record, 92*(4), 619-931.
Koch, S. (1989, February 14). School daze: Committee under spotlight for quality of schools. *The Tab,* pp. 1, 26, 50.
Lukas, J. A. (1986). *Common ground.* New York: Vintage.
Metcalf, G. R. (1983). *From Little Rock to Boston.* Westport, CT: Greenwood.
Morgan v. Henningan, 379 F. Supp. 410 (1974).
Nakamura, R. T., & Smallwood, F. (1980). *The politics of policy implementation.* New York: St. Martin's.
Neustadt, R. E., & May, E. R. (1986). *Thinking in time: The uses of history for decision makers.* New York: Free Press.
Nueffer, E. (1990, April 24). Garrity proposes end to desegregation case. *Boston Globe,* pp. 23-25.
Ross, M. J., & Berg, W. M. (1981). *I respectfully disagree with the judge's order.* Washington, DC: University Press of America.
Sheehan, J. B. (1984). *The Boston school integration dispute: Social change and legal maneuvers.* New York: Columbia University Press.

Spillane, R. (1984). Turning around the Boston schools. *American Education, 20*(10), 8-11.

Terris, D. (1987, November 1). A test of democracy. *Boston Globe Magazine,* p. 17+.

Thernstrom, S. (Ed.). (1980). *Harvard encyclopedia of American ethnic groups.* Cambridge, MA: Harvard University Press.

Willie, C. V. (1984). *School desegregation plans that work.* Westport, CT: Greenwood.

Willie, C. V., & Greenblatt, S. L. (1981). *Community politics and educational change: Ten school systems under court order.* New York: Longman.

Wood, R. (1982). Professionals at bay: Managing Boston's public schools. *Journal of Policy Analysis and Management, 1*(4), 454-468.

5

Promoting Positive Peer
Relations in Desegregated Schools

JANET W. SCHOFIELD

American schools have had to deal with a great many difficult challenges in the last several decades. One that many school systems have faced is the desegregation of previously segregated schools. Whether due to a court order, political pressure, or demographic change, many schools now have more heterogeneous student populations than they did in the past. This kind of change is almost always accompanied by considerable controversy and sharp political debate. But concern over whether, when, and which schools will be desegregated, and the major mobilization of political resources often needed to make desegregation happen, have sometimes led those involved to see the establishment of a desegregated school or school system as an event that happened at a specific point in time. The initial desegregation of the schools is undoubtedly an event, generally a very significant event, in the history of a school system. However, it is important to view this event as the beginning of a long process because what occurs in the long run in this ongoing process determines how these desegregated schools affect the students who attend them. Concern about the potentially

This chapter is adapted from an article in *Educational Policy* (September, 1993); © 1993 by Corwin Press.

deleterious social and academic effects of racial isolation has been one of the factors motivating those who have struggled to desegregate school systems, often in the face of protracted resistance. Given the prodigious effort it often takes to desegregate, it is all too easy to assume that, as long as one has achieved reasonable racial and ethnic balance while avoiding actual or threatened violence, all is well. The purpose of this chapter is to argue that this is much too limited a view. Specifically, I wish to highlight the importance of looking at desegregation as a process that goes beyond merely creating racially mixed schools to creating environments that produce both academic and social gains for the students involved.

The importance of creating desegregated schools that foster students' academic achievement is self-evident. This goal of providing students with a strong academic background has often, even generally, been the primary motivation of African Americans and other nonwhites advocating desegregation (Bell, 1980; Blakey, 1989; Sizemore, 1978). Much has been written about strategies that hold promise for increasing the academic achievement of African Americans and other nonwhites in desegregated schools (Cohen, 1984; Hawley et al., 1983; Haynes & Comer, 1990; Miller, 1980; Slavin, 1983a, 1983b). Although acknowledging the crucial importance of this goal, I have chosen to focus this chapter on a second goal, that is, the achievement of positive intergroup relations within desegregated schools. Specifically, I first lay out some of the arguments in favor of focusing a substantial amount of effort and attention on creating and maintaining positive intergroup relations in racially and ethnically mixed schools. Then I discuss how this goal can be achieved. This latter section of the chapter has two parts, one that focuses on an important barrier to the attainment of this goal, resegregation, and the other that uses Allport's (1954) contact hypothesis as a framework for discussing the kinds of school policies and practices that are conducive to the attainment of this goal.

The Importance of Promoting Positive Intergroup Relations in Schools

The goal of improving intergroup relations is both crucially important and often forgotten, or at least relegated to a relatively low position on the list of school system priorities, as long as there is no immediate crisis or obvious danger of serious conflict. Yet I would argue that the social relations that exist in racially and ethnically mixed schools are extremely important for several reasons.

First, because of the pervasive residential segregation in our society, students frequently have their first relatively close and extended contact with those from different backgrounds in school. Hence whether hostility and stereotyping grow or diminish may be critically influenced by the particular experiences students have there. Although there are clearly differing opinions about whether the development of close interracial ties should be a high priority in this country, there is a growing awareness of the very real costs of intergroup hostility and stereotyping.

Second, there is increasing evidence that interracial social networks have positive consequences for African Americans and other nonwhites, ultimate job outcomes. Specifically, recent studies show that African Americans who use racially mixed social networks in job hunting after completion of their school work end up with higher salaries and in a more integrated environment than those who do not (Braddock, 1980, 1985; Braddock & McPartland, 1982, 1987; Crain & Weisman, 1972). There is also evidence of a similar phenomenon with regard to the occupational attainment of Hispanics. Specifically, Mercer and Phillips (1987) report a significant link between having interethnic friends in grade school and high school and occupational attainment in adulthood. If these studies are correct, the state of relations between African Americans and other nonwhites and whites in schools may have important consequences for African Americans and other nonwhites and their economic well-being in later life.

Third, the ability to work effectively with out-group members is an increasingly important skill in our society. Research by Pettigrew and Martin (1987), as well as everyday observation, suggests that many people lack this ability, but demographic trends showing that a growing proportion of the population is made up of African Americans and other nonwhites make this an increasingly important aspect of all children's education. Fourth, of course, is the very real possibility that an inhospitable or conflict-filled environment can interfere with students' academic progress. This kind of environment can lead to a high rate of suspensions, to increased dropping out, or to the diverting of energy from the academic mission of the school to contain social conflict. Thus there is more than ample reason to pay serious attention to intergroup relations in any desegregated school.

Skeptics may argue that a school has no business influencing intergroup relations or that this is just not possible. The fact of the matter is that social learning occurs whether or not it is planned (Schofield, 1989; Schofield & Sagar, 1979). Even a laissez-faire policy conveys a message that there are no serious problems as matters stand or that the nature of intergroup relations is not important enough to be a legitimate concern. Hence a racially and ethnically mixed school cannot choose to have no impact on intergroup relations. It can only choose whether the effect is planned or unplanned.

Resegregation: A Common Barrier
to Improved Intergroup Relations

The first question to ask about intergroup relations in any desegregated school is the extent to which desegregation has truly reduced intergroup isolation rather than just appearing to do so on paper. This is a particular challenge in schools with students whose native language is not English, although there are ways to deal constructively with this complex situation (California State Department of Education, 1983; Carter, 1979; Carter & Chatfield, 1986; Fernandez, 1978; Fernandez & Guskin, 1978; Garcia, 1976; Gonzalez, 1979; Haro, 1977; Heleen, 1987; Milan, 1978; National Institute of Education, 1977; Roos, 1978). It is perfectly possible for a school that has a rather diverse ethnic and racial makeup to be simultaneously an institution in which individuals from the various groups have little or no contact with each other. Such resegregation can be extreme. In one school, researchers who wanted to talk to black and white students at lunch found it literally impossible. Whites would talk to researchers at their tables. Blacks would talk to researchers at their tables. But both were unwilling to sit at the same table at one time (Cusick & Ayling, 1973). In yet another racially mixed school, a student remarked to another researcher, "all the segregation in this city was put in this school," reflecting the fact that, although students from different backgrounds all attended that school, they had little contact with each other (Collins & Noblit, 1978, p. 195). Schools need to be aware of the possibility of resegregation and to plan actively to avoid or minimize it.

How does this resegregation occur? A number of common educational practices lead, often inadvertently, to partial or complete resegregation within desegregated schools. The most obvious and widespread of these are practices designed to reduce academic heterogeneity within classrooms. A whole host of social and economic factors contribute to the fact that minority group students in desegregated schools tend to perform less well academically than their white peers. Thus schools that categorize students on the basis of standardized tests, grades, or related criteria tend to have resegregated classrooms (Epstein, 1985).

Although much resegregation stems from policies such as streaming or ability grouping, it is undeniable that students do often voluntarily resegregate themselves in a variety of situations, from eating lunch to participating in extracurricular activities. The extent of such voluntary resegregation is sometimes remarkable. For example, in one set of studies, the seating patterns in the cafeteria of a school in which the student body was almost precisely half black and half white were recorded for a 2-year period (Schofield, 1979; Schofield & Sagar, 1979). On a typical day, fewer than 15 of the 250 students in the cafeteria during any particular lunch period sat next to someone of the other race. This was so in spite of the fact that there was little overt racial friction. Other studies have reported similarly marked cleavage by race (Cusick & Ayling, 1973; Gerard, Jackson, & Conolley, 1975; Rogers, Hennigan, Bowman, & Miller, 1984).

On the one hand, there is nothing inherently deleterious to intergroup relations about students who share particular interests, values, or backgrounds associating with each other to achieve valued ends. However, to the extent that grouping by race or ethnic groups stems from fear, hostility, and discomfort, it is incompatible with the goal of breaking down barriers between groups and improving intergroup relations. Stephan and Stephan's (1985) work suggests that anxiety about dealing with out-group members is prevalent and can direct behavior in unconstructive ways. Other studies (Scherer & Slawski, 1979; Schofield, 1989) suggest numerous ways in which such anxiety can cause problems, including resegregation, in desegregated schools.

The importance of avoiding a pattern of resegregation within desegregated schools, whether it stems from formal school policies or informal behavior patterns, is made clear by the theoretical and empirical work of many social psychologists (Pettigrew, 1969; Schofield, 1983, 1989). To take just one example, a whole body of work by Tajfel and others (Doise, 1978; Tajfel, 1978; Tajfel & Turner, 1979) suggests that when individuals are divided into groups, they tend to favor the in-group and discriminate against the out-group, even though these groups have no previous history of antipathy. Thus if one creates racially or ethnically homogeneous groups through school policies that resegregate students, already existing tendencies toward stereotyping and discrimination are likely to be magnified.

This suggests that great care should be taken to avoid school policies that lead to resegregation and to adopt policies that may undercut the students' tendency to cluster in racially homogeneous groups because of fear or uncertainty. The particular policies employed to discourage such resegregation would have to depend on the particular situation with which one is dealing. However, policies and practices that undercut resegregation can be easily implemented. For example, teachers can assign seats in a way that creates substantial potential for interracial contact, rather than letting students resegregate themselves. Specifically, teachers can assign students' seats on the basis of the alphabetical order of students' names rather than letting students select their own seats and then institutionalizing this often-segregated pattern with a seating chart (Schofield, 1989). Furthermore, research shows that something as simple as occasionally changing assigned seats increases the number of friends students are likely to make during the school year (Byrne, 1961).

Another policy that can help to avoid resegregation is conscious planning to encourage both African Americans and other nonwhites and whites to participate in extracurricular activities. Sometimes after-school activities become the province of either African Americans and other nonwhites or whites so that one group of students participates in all or most activities and the other hardly participates at all. Another perhaps more common pattern is for particular activities to become associated with students from a particular background so that, although all groups of students participate in some activities, there are few activities in which students from different backgrounds participate jointly (Collins, 1979; Gottlieb & TenHouten, 1965; Scherer & Slawski, 1979; Sullivan, 1979).

Again, the way to prevent these outcomes clearly depends on the specific situation. But often policies can be adopted that do help. For example, if one group of students does not participate because the students live far away and transportation poses a problem, arrangements for transportation can be considered. Similarly, if the faculty advisers of clubs or activities take clear steps to encourage both African Americans and other nonwhites and whites to participate before these activities get a definite reputation as "belonging" to any group, they are much more likely to succeed than if they wait until the resegregation is complete and well-known among the students.

A certain amount of resegregation may be an inevitable consequence of policies designed to advance important goals. For example, it is often hard to serve children for whom English is not a first language without a certain amount of resegregation. Similarly, although there has recently been some movement away from the traditional ready acceptance of tracking policies on the part of policymakers and educators (Carnegie Council on Adolescent Development, 1989; National Governors' Association, 1990), many difficult and complex pedagogical and political issues remain to be resolved about how best to serve students in classrooms in which skill levels vary widely (Oakes, 1992). Furthermore, some kinds of grouping will most likely be necessary for certain defensible purposes (e.g., the teaching of certain specialized courses such as calculus in school systems in which not all students need or wish to take such subjects). In addition, there may be certain extracurricular activities, such as gospel choirs or golf teams, that are likely to be both highly valued by some parts of the community and more attractive to students from certain ethnic backgrounds than others. In spite of such difficulties, any examination of the functioning of a desegregated school needs to address the issue of resegregation, whether it be the consequence of formal policies or student choices, and to devote serious attention to seeing how resegregation, if found, can be eliminated or at least reduced.

Conditions Conducive to
Improving Intergroup Relations

It is important to recognize that the mere absence of resegregation is not enough to create a set of experiences that foster constructive rather than neutral or destructive relations between children from different backgrounds. The quality of those relations is the crucial factor, as Pettigrew (1969) pointed out in making his classic distinction between mere desegregation, which refers to the existence of a racially mixed student body, and true integration, which refers to the creation of an environment conducive to positive relations between members of the various groups present in the school.

If there is one thing that social psychological theory and research have taught us about racially and ethnically diverse schools during the last 40 years, it is that simply putting students from different backgrounds together is not enough to ensure positive social outcomes (Allport, 1954; Cohen, 1972; Eddy, 1975; Orfield, 1975; Rist, 1979; Schofield, 1983). Schools can do a great many things to promote positive intergroup relations (Chesler, Bryant, & Crowfoot, 1981; Cohen, 1980; Crowfoot & Chesler, 1981; Epstein, 1985; Forehand & Ragosta, 1976; Forehand, Ragosta, & Rock, 1976; Hallinan, 1982; Hallinan & Smith, 1985; Hallinan & Teixeira, 1987; Hawley et al., 1983; McConahay, 1981; Mercer, Iadicola, & Moore, 1980; Miller, 1980; Patchen, 1982; Sagar & Schofield, 1984; Slavin & Madden, 1979; Wellisch, Carriere, MacQueen, & Duck, 1977; Wellisch, Marcus, MacQueen, & Duck, 1976). Precisely which specific practices are suitable depends on factors such as the students' ages, the school's racial and ethnic mix, the degree to which minority and majority status are related to socioeconomic background, and the like. Thus, although space limitations make it impractical to discuss each of the myriad possibilities separately, I

would like to discuss what theory and research suggest about the general
underlying conditions that are conducive to building and maintaining
positive intergroup relations, which many of these specific suggestions
embody in one way or another. The most influential social psychological
perspective on the conditions that are necessary to lead to positive outcomes is often called the *contact hypothesis*. Since 1954 when Allport first
proposed it, this approach has stimulated a great deal of research, which,
generally speaking, supports its basic elements. (A volume reviewing, ex-
tending, and revising this theory is Hewstone & Brown, 1986.) Basically,
Allport argued that three aspects of the contact situation are particularly
important in determining whether positive intergroup relations develop.
These are the existence of equal status within the situation for members of
all groups, an emphasis on cooperative rather than competitive activities,
and the explicit support of relevant authority figures for positive relations.
I will discuss these three factors one at a time and illustrate briefly the types
of policies and procedures that schools can adopt to try to create a positive
atmosphere.

Equal Status

First, Allport (1954) argues that the contact situation must be structured in a way that gives equal status to all groups. He argues that if one
does not do this the former stereotypes and beliefs about the superiority or
inferiority of the groups involved and the hostility engendered by these
stereotypes will be likely to persist. Although other theorists have argued
that equal status is not absolutely essential for improving intergroup relations, they generally see it as quite helpful (Amir, 1969; Riordan, 1978). In
a school, as in most organizations, the various positions that need to be
filled are ordered in a status hierarchy. Those on top—the superintendent
at the system level or the principal at the school level—have more power
and prestige than those who serve under them. Allport's argument suggests
then that when one fills the various positions in the organization it is
important that individuals from all groups be distributed throughout the
status hierarchy rather than being concentrated at a particular level. For
example, one could hardly claim that whites and African Americans and
other nonwhites have equal status in a school if the administrators and the
faculty are almost all whites and the teachers' aides are all African Americans and other nonwhites.

Even if a school system does its best to see that the formal status of
African Americans and other nonwhites and whites is equal, it is undeniably

true that desegregation often involves mixing white students from relatively educated and affluent backgrounds with African American and other non-white students from less privileged backgrounds. Thus members of the two groups are likely to have different statuses outside of the school situation. This can create real difficulties for achieving equal status within the school. For example, given the sizable and stubborn link between social class and academic achievement, it is likely that unequal statuses outside of the school will translate into the unequal distribution of students into the more and less advanced tracks. Even if the school recognizes this and decides to avoid formalizing such group differences by eschewing tracking, student performance levels may well still differ in ways that affect their informal status within the school and their peer groups.

Finding effective ways to keep the unequal status of whites and African Americans and other nonwhites in the larger society from creating unequal status within the school is not easy. However, concerted efforts to achieve equal status within the contact situation do appear to make a difference. For example, much has been written about the way in which textbooks and other curriculum components have either ignored or demeaned the experiences and contributions of African Americans and other nonwhites (McAdoo & McAdoo, 1985; National Alliance of Black School Educators, 1984; Oakes, 1985). This hardly creates an equal status environment. Although there are many barriers to remedying this situation (Boateng, 1990), change is possible, and it can have constructive effects (Banks, 1993). For example, Stephan and Stephan's (1984) review of the research conducted on multiethnic curriculum components concludes that a substantial, if methodologically flawed, set of studies generally suggests that multiethnic curricula have a positive impact on intergroup relations, at least when the program elements are of some reasonable complexity and duration.

A controversial issue relating to both equal status and resegregation is the issue of the grouping of students based on their academic performance. As mentioned previously, when desegregated schools group students on the basis of test scores, they often end up with heavily white, high-status accelerated groups and heavily African American and other nonwhite, lower-status regular groups. This means that students are not only resegregated, but that they are resegregated in a way that reinforces traditional stereotypes. Tracking is often instituted or emphasized in schools with heterogeneous student bodies as a mechanism for coping with the diversity. Specifically, it is often seen as a way of ensuring that the academic achievement of the more advanced students is not compromised. It is also sometimes seen as a way of ensuring that less advanced students are presented with materials suited to their current level of performance. However, studies comparing tracked versus untracked schools have not yielded any consistent support for the idea that tracking generally benefits students academically (Oakes, 1992). Furthermore, there is reason to believe that it may sometimes undermine the achievement and motivation of students in the lower tracks and have a negative effect on intergroup relations (Collins & Noblit, 1978; Epstein, 1985; National Opinion Research Center, 1973; Oakes, 1992; Schofield, 1979; Schofield & Sagar, 1977). Epstein's (1985) study of grouping practices in desegregated elementary schools concludes that there is a clear positive link between equal status programs (e.g., programs that emphasize the equality and importance of both black and white students and that avoid inflexible academically based grouping) and higher achievement for African American students. Furthermore, equal status programs positively influenced both white and black students' attitudes toward desegregated schooling.

Although tracking is one of the most visible ways in which status differentials from outside the school get reinforced and formalized inside the school, there are also a myriad of other ways in which this happens. Sensitivity to this issue can suggest seemingly minor, but nonetheless worthwhile, changes in practice that minimize this. For example, schools can add to the traditional practice of honoring students whose absolute level of achievement is outstanding by placing their names on honor rolls or taking special notice of them at school functions honoring students who have shown unusually large amounts of improvement in their academic performance. This reinforces academic values by being more inclusive than traditional practice is.

Such practices are trivial in some respects. Yet, students are often very sensitive to such matters. For example, Schofield (1989) reports an incident in which a racially mixed classroom of sixth graders was shown a televised quiz show in which a team of students from their school competed against a team from another school. A usually well-behaved African American child refused to watch. Later, she explained that she did not want to see the program because the team from her school, which had a student body that was just over half black, consisted entirely of white children. She said with bitterness that the school should not have been called Wexler [a pseudonym]; "Might as well call it White School," she complained (p. 220).

Cooperative Independence

Allport (1954) argues that, in addition to creating a situation that gives members of all groups equal status, it is also extremely important that the activities required in the situation be cooperative rather than competitive. This is important for two reasons. First, given that discrimination is both a historical fact and a present reality in many spheres of life, it is probable that the results of competition will frequently support traditional stereotypes. In addition, considerable research suggests that competition between groups can lead to stereotyping, to unwarranted devaluation of the other group's accomplishments, and to marked hostility, even when the groups initially have no history that might predispose them to negative reactions to each other (Sherif, Harvey, White, Hood, & Sherif, 1961; Worchel, 1979). It is reasonable to expect that this tendency for intergroup competition would lead to hostility and negative beliefs would be reinforced when the groups involved have a history that makes initial hostility or at least suspicion likely.

Both theory and research suggest that the type of cooperation most likely to lead to the reduction of intergroup tensions or hostility is cooperation toward achieving a shared goal that cannot be accomplished without the contribution of members of both groups (Bossert, 1988/1989; Johnson & Johnson, 1992; Sherif et al., 1961). In the nonacademic sphere, examples of this type of cooperation would be the production of a school play, team sports, and the like. In such cases, each individual contributes to a whole that he or she could not possibly achieve alone. Even though different people may contribute different skills, each one is necessary to, and interested in, the final product.

Historically, American schools have stressed competition. However, this is not inevitable or completely unchangeable. First, with the advent of self-paced instructional approaches and the increasing awareness of work on mastery learning, there has been an increasing acceptance of the idea that children may benefit from working at their own pace. Second, in recent years, more and more voices have spoken in favor of an increasing emphasis on the importance of teaching children how to work cooperatively with others to achieve a joint end product. Certainly this trend is sensible given the increasing bureaucratization and complexity of our society, which means that, as adults, individuals are increasingly likely to work with others as part of an organization rather than as individual craftspeople or entrepreneurs.

The use of class committees and teams to create joint projects comes close to being the type of cooperation toward shared goals that appears to be so important for improving intergroup relations. A large number of experiments using a variety of cooperative structures suggest that this does indeed have a positive impact. For example, DeVries and Edwards (1974) found that students who participated in racially mixed work groups that were rewarded for their performance as groups were more likely to help and to be helped by members of the other race than students who received rewards for their individual efforts. They were also somewhat more likely to name a person of the other race as a friend after a month of teamwork, even though the teams met for less than an hour a day. A whole host of other researchers have found similar results in experiments on the impact of cooperative work in the classroom (Aronson, Blaney, Sikes, Stephan, & Snapp, 1978; Aronson & Gonzales, 1988; Bossert, 1988/1989; Cook, 1985; Johnson & Johnson, 1982; Johnson, Johnson, & Maruyama, 1984; Sharan, 1980; Slavin, 1983a, 1983b, 1985). One important feature of such cooperative groups is not only that they appear to foster improved intergroup relations, but they also have positive academic consequences (Johnson, Maruyama, Johnson, Nelson, & Skon, 1981).

Although the use of racially and ethnically mixed teams is one way of fostering student cooperation, such cooperation must be carefully structured (Hertz-Lazarowitz, Kirkus, & Miller, 1992; Miller & Harrington, 1992; Slavin, 1992). Teachers have to take care to see that students contribute to the team efforts in effective ways that do not reinforce traditional modes of interaction between whites and African Americans and other nonwhites. For example, Cohen (1972) has found that when white and black children who are equally capable interact with each other in certain kinds of situations, the white students tend to be more active and influential, even though there is no rational basis for their dominance. Only after a carefully planned program of activities that includes having the black children teach their white peers new skills does this tendency diminish or disappear (Cohen, Lockheed, & Lohman, 1976). Hence a teacher who organizes students into groups must try to find ways to ensure that all children contribute to the groups' final products rather than assuming that the existence of groups, in and of itself, will motivate all children to contribute and to allow others to contribute to the team's work.

Support of Authorities for Positive Relations

Finally, Allport (1954) suggests that the support of authority, law, and custom for positive, equal status relationships between members of all groups is vital to producing constructive change in intergroup attitudes and behavior as a result of intergroup contact. Certainly, a court ruling that requires desegregation (or a decision on the part of a school system to desegregate) is an important sign of government authorities' support for this policy. However, in and of themselves, such events are not nearly enough. For schoolchildren, the most relevant authorities are probably their school principal, their teachers, and their parents. Religious leaders can also be important authorities for some children.

The importance of the principal in a desegregated school can hardly be overemphasized. A large number of studies show that the principal can play a crucial role, both in helping teachers adjust to the new requirements of a desegregated situation and in fostering a social climate that is conducive to the development of positive relations between minority and majority students (Orfield, 1975). Principals can influence the course desegregation takes through their actions toward teachers, students, and parents. For example, one study of a newly desegregated middle school reported that the principal convinced a local foundation to fund in-service training for teachers to help them effectively face the challenge of teaching in classrooms with diverse student populations, as well as a short, integrated summer camp experience for the students who would be experiencing racially mixed classes for the first time. In addition, this principal set up an information center, staffed by volunteers, to help answer any questions that parents or community members had and to distribute accurate information about the school in order to dispel any rumors that might arise (Schofield, 1989).

The principal's support for efforts to achieve positive intergroup relations is important because principals play at least four important roles in influencing desegregation's outcomes. First, they play an enabling function; that is, they make choices that facilitate or impede practices, on the part of others, that promote positive intergroup relations. For example, the principal can play an important role in encouraging teachers to promote cooperation among students on academic projects. Second, the principal can serve a modeling function. It is clear that many people tend to emulate authority. The principal sets a model of behavior for teachers and students. There is no guarantee that others will follow the principal's example, but it is certainly helpful. Third, the principal can play a sensitizing function. The principal is in a good position to argue for the importance of paying attention to the quality of intergroup relations and to put doing so in an important place on the school's list of priorities. Finally, of course, the principal can serve a sanctioning function by actively rewarding positive practices and behaviors and discouraging negative ones.

Teachers are also vital authority figures in the school. They too can facilitate or impede the development of positive relations at the classroom level through the processes of enabling, modeling, sensitizing, and sanctioning. For example, with regard to enabling, teachers often have it within their power to create conditions that are likely to improve intergroup relations between students. Epstein's (1985) research demonstrates that teachers with positive attitudes toward desegregation tend to use equal status instructional programs more than others and that students in such classrooms have more positive attitudes toward desegregation than peers in classrooms not using such approaches. Similarly, teachers with negative attitudes are more likely to use within-class ability grouping.

One way in which authorities such as principals, teachers, or even parents foster the development of positive relations through sensitizing is for them to be aware that students in a desegregated school may misunderstand each other's motives or intentions, either because of cultural differences or because of fears and uncertainties about out-group members. Using this awareness constructively can help students to deal with problems that arise. In an earlier work (Schofield, 1989), I reported a clear example of this kind of behavior. The incident occurred in a school cafeteria after an African American sixth grader reached out and gently put her hand on the long blonde hair of a white girl who was seated near her. The white girl was obviously startled and frightened. She looked around, saw the black girl standing over her, and burst into tears. A teacher who was standing nearby saw the white girl crying and told the black child to stop bothering the white one. Another staff member, a social worker, saw the incident and later talked with both girls about it. The black girl said that she was curious about the way the other girl's hair would feel, so she touched it to find out. The white girl said she thought the other girl was going to hurt her, although she freely admitted that the other girl had not pulled her hair or actually hurt her. The social worker then discussed with both girls the fact that, although there are group differences in hair texture and color, there are also big variations within each group. Both students asked a lot of questions and were obviously interested in discussing their feelings and observations with each other, as well as the social worker.

The problem described above arose because one child misinterpreted the intention of another. No doubt the misinterpretation was aided by the white girl's rather high anxiety level about being in a desegregated school. The first teacher did not recognize the situation for what it really was and chided one student for bothering the other. However, this was really of little help. The white girl still felt she had been threatened for no reason, and the black girl was reprimanded for a relatively harmless action that sprang from a natural curiosity. It took a staff member who served a sensitizing function to bring the incident to a constructive resolution.

With regard to sanctioning, teachers can make an important contribution to the success of desegregated schools by clearly articulating their expectation that students will respect each other's rights and by backing up their stated expectations with disciplinary measures. Most important, the school's expectation that students will get along with each other must be made clear from the beginning, so that students do not think they can violate each other's rights with impunity. If the expectation of harmony and respect is not initially made clear, students are more likely to try to test the limits of the system.

It is common for principals, teachers, and other authority figures involved with desegregated schools to feel that the best and fairest thing they can do is to adopt a point of view sometimes called the color-blind perspective (Rist, 1974). This perspective sees racial and ethnic group membership as irrelevant to the way individuals are treated. Taking cognizance of such group membership in decision making is perceived as illegitimate and likely to lead to discrimination against African Americans and other nonwhites or to reverse discrimination. Two factors make serious consideration of the color-blind perspective worthwhile. First, it is widespread in schools, as well as being a frequently espoused goal in employment, in judicial decisions, and the like. Second, although in many ways color blindness is appealing—and consistent with a long-standing American emphasis on importance of the individual—it easily leads to a misrepresentation of reality in ways that encourage discrimination against African Americans and other nonwhites. Thus I will now turn to discussing some of the consequences of this perspective.

It must be acknowledged that the color-blind perspective may have some positive effects. It can reduce, at least in the short term, the potential for overt racial or ethnic conflict by generally deemphasizing the salience of race and encouraging the even-handed application of rules to all students (Miller & Harrington, 1992). It may also reduce the potential for discomfort or embarrassment in racially or ethnically mixed schools by vigorously asserting that race does not matter.

However, this perspective also has a number of potentially negative effects. Most important, the decision to try to ignore racial considerations—to act as if no one notices, or should notice, race—means that policies that are disadvantageous to African Americans and other nonwhites are often accepted without much examination or thought (Schofield, 1986). For example, disproportionate suspension rates for African American and other nonwhite students may not be seen as a sign of the need to examine discipline policies if school faculty and staff think of students only as individuals rather than facing the difficult issue of whether the school may be treating certain categories of students differently than others. Similarly, a color-blind perspective can easily lead to ready adoption or tolerance of policies that lead to resegregation. Furthermore, this perspective makes it easy for a school to use textbooks and curricular materials that inadequately reflect the perspectives and contributions of African Americans and other nonwhites.

One simple incident (see Schofield, 1989) illustrates the potential dangers inherent in creating an environment in which conscious consideration of an individual's race is deemed illegitimate. Specifically, a white teacher admitted to a researcher that she had purposely miscounted votes in a student council election so that a "responsible child" (a white boy) was declared the winner rather than an "unstable child" (a black girl), who actually had more votes. The teacher seemed uncomfortable with her action, but the focus of her concern was on her subversion of the democratic process. She did not even consider the fact that her action changed the racial composition of the student council, although the proportion of black members was quite low compared to the proportion of the student body that was black. The school's clear color-blind policy made it easy for this teacher to avoid examining the full implications of her behavior.

It is important to emphasize that, in raising questions about the color-blind perspective, I am not arguing that principals or teachers should constantly remind students of their group membership and continually emphasize group differences. This may well reinforce out-group discrimination and hostility (Miller, Brewer, & Edwards, 1985). However, at a policy and decision-making level, school systems, principals, and teachers need to recognize that racially and ethnically mixed schools are intergroup, not just interpersonal, environments and that attention to how various groups are faring is not only appropriate, but likely to be constructive.

Summary

To summarize, desegregation should be viewed as a long-term ongoing process that must be carefully planned and monitored to ensure not only that schools are racially balanced, but that they function in a way that serves the needs and best interests of all students. Serving students' and society's best interests means not only equipping the students with factual knowledge and problem-solving skills but also preparing them to function effectively and constructively in an increasingly diverse society. Thus creating an environment that is welcoming to all students and that promotes positive relations among them is a challenge to which desegregated schools must rise.

Theory and research in social psychology suggest some ways in which this can be accomplished. First, it is important to avoid resegregation, which can occur either as a result of common school policies or as a result of students' negative attitudes toward members of other groups. However, avoiding resegregation is not enough. School policies and practices need to be closely examined to ensure that, insofar as possible, they promote equal status and cooperative interdependence between African Americans and other nonwhites and whites. Those in positions of authority can support the development of positive intergroup relations by enabling others, as well as by modeling, sensitizing, and sanctioning. Recognizing that the school is an area in which intergroup as well as interpersonal relations develop should help those in authority to perform these functions in an effective manner.

References

Allport, G. W. (1954). *The nature of prejudice.* Cambridge, MA: Addison-Wesley.

Amir, Y. (1969). Contact hypothesis in ethnic relations. *Psychological Bulletin, 71*(5), 319-342.

Aronson, E., Blaney, N., Sikes, J., Stephan, G., & Snapp, M. (1978). *The jigsaw classroom.* Beverly Hills, CA: Sage.

Aronson, E., & Gonzalez, A. (1988). Desegregation, jigsaw, and the Mexican American experience. In P. A Katz & D. A. Taylor (Eds.), *Eliminating racism: Profiles in controversy* (pp. 301-314). New York: Plenum.

Banks, J. A. (1993). Multicultural education: Historical development, dimensions, and practice. In L. Darling-Hammond (Ed.), *Review of research in education* (Vol. 19, pp. 3-49). Washington, DC: American Educational Research Association.

Bell, D. (1980). *Brown* and the interest-convergence dilemma. In D. Bell (Ed.), *Shades of Brown: New perspectives on school desegregation* (pp. 91-106). New York: Teachers College Press.

Blakey, W. A. (1989). *Public school desegregation: Education, equal protection, and equality of opportunity.* Unpublished manuscript, Center for Research on Minority Education, University of Oklahoma, Norman.

Boateng, F. (1990). Combatting deculturalization of the African-American child in the public school system: A multicultural approach. In K. Lomotey (Ed.), *Going to school: The African-American experience* (pp. 73-84). New York: State University of New York Press.

Bossert, S. T. (1988/1989). Cooperative activities in the classroom. In E. Z. Rothkopf (Ed.), *Review of research in education* (Vol. 15, pp. 225-250). Washington, DC: American Educational Research Association.

Braddock, J. H., II. (1980). The perpetuation of segregation across levels of education: A behavioral assessment of the contact hypothesis. *Sociology of Education, 53,* 178-186.

Braddock, J. H., II. (1985). School desegregation and black assimilation. *Journal of Social Issues, 41*(3), 9-22.

Braddock, J. H., II, & McPartland, J. (1982). Assessing school desegregation effects: New directions in research. In R. Corwin (Ed.), *Research in sociology of education and socialization* (Vol. 3, pp. 209-282). Greenwich, CT: JAI.

Braddock, J. H., II, & McPartland, J. (1987). How minorities continue to be excluded from equal employment opportunities: Research on labor market and institutional barriers. *Journal of Social Issues, 43*(1), 5-39.

Byrne, D. (1961). The influences of propinquity and opportunities for interaction on classroom relationships. *Human Relations, 14,* 63-69.

California State Department of Education. (1983). *Desegregation and bilingual education—partners in quality education.* Sacramento: California State Department of Education.

Carnegie Council on Adolescent Development. (1989). *Turning points: Preparing American youth for the 21st century.* Washington, DC: Carnegie Corporation of New York.

Carter, T., & Chatfield, M. L. (1986). Effective bilingual schools: Implications for policy and practice. *American Journal of Education, 95,* 200-232.

Carter, T. P. (1979). *Interface between bilingual education and desegregation: A study of Arizona and California.* Washington, DC: National Institute of Education. (ERIC Document Reproduction Service No. ED 184 743)

Chesler, M., Bryant, B., & Crowfoot, J. (1981). *Making desegregation work: A professional guide to effecting change.* Beverly Hills, CA: Sage.

Cohen, E. (1972). Interracial interaction disability. *Human Relations, 25,* 9-24

Cohen, E. (1980). Design and redesign of the desegregated school: Problems of status, power, and conflict. In W. G. Stephan & J. R. Feagin (Eds.), *School desegregation: Past, present, and future* (pp. 251-278). New York: Plenum.

Cohen, E. (1984). The desegregated school: Problems in status power and interethnic climate. In N. Miller & M. B. Brewer (Eds.), *Groups in contact: The psychology of desegregation* (pp. 77-96). Orlando, FL: Academic Press.

Cohen, E., Lockheed, M., & Lohman, M. (1976). The center for interracial cooperation: A field experiment. *Sociology of Education, 49,* 47-58.

Collins, T. W. (1979). From courtrooms to classrooms: Managing school desegregation in a deep south high school. In R. C. Rist (Ed.), *Desegregated schools: Appraisals of an American Experiment* (pp. 89-114). New York: Academic Press.

Collins, T. W., & Noblit, G. W. (1978). *Stratification and resegregation: The case of Crossover High School, Memphis, Tennessee* (Final Report). Washington, DC: National Institute of Education.

Cook, S. W. (1985). Experimenting on social issues: The case of school desegregation. *American Psychologist, 40,* 452-460.

Crain, R. L., & Weisman, C. S. (1972). *Discrimination, personality, and achievement: A survey of northern blacks.* New York: Seminar Press.

Crowfoot, J. E., & Chesler, M. A. (1981). Implementing "attractive ideas": Problems and prospects. In W. D. Hawley (Ed.), *Effective school desegregation* (pp. 265-295). Beverly Hills, CA: Sage.

Cusick, P., & Ayling, R. (1973, February). *Racial interaction in an urban secondary school.* Paper presented at the meeting of the American Educational Research Association, New Orleans, LA.

DeVries, D. L., & Edwards, K. (1974). Student teams and learning games: Their effects on cross-race and cross-sex interaction. *Journal of Educational Psychology, 66,* 741-749.

Doise, W. (1978). *Groups and individuals: Explanations in social psychology.* Cambridge: Cambridge University Press.

Eddy, E. (1975). Educational innovation and desegregation: A case study of symbolic realignment. *Human Organization, 34*(2), 163-172.

Epstein, J. L. (1985). After the bus arrives: Resegregation in desegregated schools. *Journal of Social Issues, 41*(3), 23-43.

Fernandez, R. R. (1978). *The political dimensions of bilingual education in the context of school desegregation in Milwaukee: A case study.* Unpublished manuscript.

Fernandez, R. R., & Guskin, J. T. (1978). Bilingual education and desegregation: A new dimension in legal and educational decision-making. In H. LaFontaine, B. Persky, & L. H. Glubshick (Eds.), *Bilingual education* (pp. 58-66). New Jersey: Avery.

Forehand, G. A., & Ragosta, M. (1976). *A handbook for integrated schooling.* Washington, DC: U.S. Department of Health, Education, and Welfare.

Forehand, G. A., Ragosta, M., & Rock, D. (1976). *Conditions and processes of effective school desegregation* (Final report). Princeton, NJ: Educational Testing Service.

Garcia, G. F. (1976). The Latino and desegregation. *Integrated Education, 14,* 21-22.

Gerard, H., Jackson, D., & Conolley, E. (1975). Social context in the desegregated classroom. In H. Gerard & N. Miller (Eds.), *School desegregation: A long-range study* (pp. 211-241). New York: Plenum.

Gonzalez, J. M. (1979). *Bilingual education in the integrated school.* Arlington, VA: National Clearinghouse for Bilingual Education.

Gottlieb, D., & TenHouten, W. D. (1965). Racial composition and the social systems of three high schools. *Journal of Marriage and the Family, 27,* 204-212.

Hallinan, M. T. (1982). Classroom racial composition and children's friendships. *Social Forces, 61*(1), 56-72.

Hallinan, M. T., & Smith, S. S. (1985). The effects of classroom racial composition on students' interracial friendliness. *Social Psychology Quarterly, 48*(1), 3-16.

Hallinan, M. T., & Teixeira, R. A. (1987). Students' interracial friendships: Individual characteristics, structural effects and racial differences. *American Journal of Education, 95,* 563-583.

Haro, C. M. (1977). *Mexican/Chicano concerns and school desegregation in Los Angeles.* Los Angeles: Chicano Studies Center Publications, University of California.

Hawley, W., Crain, R. L., Rossell, C. H., Schofield, J. W., Fernandez, R., & Trent, W. P. (1983). *Strategies for effective school desegregation: Lessons from research.* Lexington, MA: Lexington Books.

Haynes, N. M., & Comer, J. (1990). Helping black children succeed: The significance of some social factors. In K. Lomotey (Ed.), *Going to school: The African-American experience* (pp. 103-112). New York: State University of New York Press.

Heleen, O. (Ed.). (1987, Spring). Two-way bilingual education: A strategy for equity [Special issue]. *Equity and choice, 3,* 1-64.

Hertz-Lazarowitz, R., Kirkus, V. B., & Miller, N. (1992). Implications of current research on cooperative interaction for classroom application. In R. Hertz-Lazarowitz & N. Miller (Eds.), *Interaction in cooperative groups* (pp. 253-280). Cambridge: Cambridge University Press.

Hewstone, M., & Brown, R. (Eds.). (1986). *Contact and conflict in encounters.* Oxford: Basil Blackwell.

Johnson, D. W., & Johnson, R. T. (1982). The study of cooperative, competitive, and individualistic situations: State of the area and two recent contributions. *Contemporary Education, 1*(1), 7-13.

Johnson, D. W., & Johnson, R. T. (1992). Positive interdependence: Key to effective cooperation. In R. Hertz-Lazarowitz & N. Miller (Eds.), *Interaction in cooperative groups* (pp. 174-199). Cambridge: Cambridge University Press.

Johnson, D. W., Johnson, R. T., & Maruyama, G. (1984). Goal interdependence and interpersonal attraction in heterogeneous classrooms: A meta-analysis. In N.

Miller & M. B. Brewer (Eds.), *Groups in contact: The psychology of desegregation* (pp. 187-212). Orlando, FL: Academic Press.

Johnson, D. W., Maruyama, G., Johnson, R., Nelson, D., & Skon, L. (1981). Effects of cooperative, competitive, and individualistic goal structures on achievement: A meta-analysis. *Psychological Bulletin, 89,* 47-62.

McAdoo, H. P., & McAdoo, J. W. (Eds.). (1985). *Black children: Social, educational and parental environments.* Beverly Hills, CA: Sage.

McConahay, J. (1981). Reducing racial prejudice in desegregated schools. In W. D. Hawley (Ed.), *Effective school desegregation* (pp. 35-53). Beverly Hills, CA: Sage.

Mercer, J. R., Iadicola, P., & Moore, H. (1980). Building effective multiethnic schools: Evolving models and paradigms. In W. G. Stephan & J. R. Feagin (Eds.), *School desegregation: Past, present, and future* (pp. 281-307). New York: Plenum.

Mercer, J. R., & Phillips, D. (1987). *Factors predicting adult status attainment of Chicano students: 20 year follow-up.* Unpublished manuscript, University of California, Riverside.

Milan, W. G. (1978). *Toward a comprehensive language policy for a desegregated school system: Reassessing the future of bilingual education.* New York: Arawak Consulting Company.

Miller, N. (1980). Making school desegregation work. In W. G. Stephan & J. R. Feagin (Eds.), *School desegregation: Past, present, and future* (pp. 309-348). New York: Plenum.

Miller, N., Brewer, M. B., & Edwards, K. (1985). Cooperative interaction in desegregated settings: A laboratory analogue. *Journal of Social Issues, 41*(3), 63-79.

Miller, N., & Harrington, H. J. (1992). Social categorization and intergroup acceptance: Principles for the design and development of cooperative learning teams. In R. Hertz-Lazarowitz & N. Miller (Eds.), *Interaction in cooperative groups* (pp. 203-227). Cambridge: Cambridge University Press.

National Alliance of Black School Educators. (1984). *Saving the African American child.* Washington, DC: Author.

National Governors' Association. (1990). *Educating America: State strategies for achieving the national educational goals.* Washington, DC: Author.

National Institute of Education. (1977). *Desegregation and education concerns of the Hispanic community.* Washington, DC: Government Printing Office.

National Opinion Research Center. (1973). *Southern schools: An evaluation of the effects of Emergency School Assistance Program and of school desegregation* (Vols. 1 & 2). Chicago: Author.

Oakes, J. (1985). *Keeping track: How schools structure inequality.* New Haven, CT: Yale University Press.

Oakes, J. (1992). Can tracking research inform practice? Technical, normative, and political considerations. *Educational Researcher, 21*(4), 12-21.

Orfield, G. (1975). How to make desegregation work: The adaptation of schools to their newly-integrated student bodies. *Law and Contemporary Problems, 39,* 314-340.

Patchen, M. (1982). *Black-white contact in schools: Its social and academic effects.* West Lafayette, IN: Purdue University Press.

Pettigrew, T. (1969). The Negro and education: Problems and proposals. In I. Katz & P. Gurin (Eds.), *Race and the social sciences* (pp. 49-112). New York: Basic Books.

Pettigrew, T. F., & Martin, J. (1987). Shaping the organizational context for black American inclusion. *Journal of Social Issues, 43*(1), 41-78.

Riordan, C. (1978). Equal-status interracial contact: A review and revision of the concept. *International Journal of Intercultural Relations, 2*(2), 161-185.

Rist, R. C. (1974). Race, policy, and schooling. *Society, 12*(1), 59-63.

Rist, R. C. (Ed.). (1979). *Desegregated schools: Appraisals of an American experiment.* New York: Academic Press.

Rogers, M., Hennigan, K., Bowman, C., & Miller, N. (1984). Intergroup acceptance in classrooms and playground settings. In N. Miller & M. B. Brewer (Eds.), *Groups in contact: The psychology of desegregation* (pp. 213-227). New York: Academic Press.

Roos, P. D. (1978). Bilingual education: The Hispanic response to unequal educational opportunity. *Law and Contemporary Problems, 42,* 111-140.

Sagar, H. A., & Schofield, J. W. (1984). Integrating the desegregated school: Problems and possibilities. In M. Maehr & D. Bartz (Eds.), *Advances in motivation and achievement: A research manual* (pp. 203-242). Greenwich, CT: JAI.

Scherer, J., & Slawski, E. (1979). Color, class, and social control in an urban school. In R. C. Rist (Ed.), *Desegregated schools: Appraisals of an American experiment* (pp. 117-153). New York: Academic Press.

Schofield, J.W. (1979). The impact of positively structured contact on intergroup behavior: Does it last under adverse conditions? *Social Psychology Quarterly, 42,* 280-284.

Schofield, J. W. (1983). Black-white conflict in the schools: Its social and academic effects. *American Journal of Education, 92,* 104-107.

Schofield, J. W. (1986). Causes and consequences of the colorblind perspective. In S. Gaertner & J. Dovidio (Eds.), *Prejudice, discrimination and racism: Theory and practice* (pp. 231-253). New York: Academic Press.

Schofield, J. W. (1989). *Black and white in school: Trust, tension, or tolerance?* New York: Teachers College Press.

Schofield, J. W., & Sagar, H. A. (1977). Peer interaction patterns in an integrated middle school. *Sociometry, 40,* 130-138.

Schofield, J. W., & Sagar, H. A. (1979). The social context of learning in an interracial school. In R. C. Rist (Ed.), *Desegregated schools: Appraisals of an American experiment* (pp. 155-199). New York: Academic Press.

Sharan, S. (1980). Cooperative learning in teams: Recent methods and effects on achievement, attitudes, and ethnic relations. *Review of Educational Research, 50,* 241-272.

Sherif, M., Harvey, O. J., White, B. J., Hood, W. R., & Sherif, C. (1961). *Intergroup cooperation and competition: The Robbers Cave experiment.* Norman, OK: University Book Exchange.

Sizemore, B. A. (1978). Educational research and desegregation: Significance for the black community. *Journal of Negro Education, 47,* 58-68.

Slavin, R. E. (1983a). *Cooperative learning.* New York: Longman.

Slavin, R. E. (1983b). When does cooperative learning increase student achievement? *Psychological Bulletin, 94,* 429-445.

Slavin, R. E. (1985). Cooperative learning: Applying contact theory in desegregated schools. *Journal of Social Issues, 41*(3), 45-62.

Slavin, R. E. (1992). When and why does cooperative learning increase achievement? Theoretical and empirical perspectives. In R. Hertz-Lazarowitz & N. Miller (Eds.), *Interaction in cooperative groups* (pp. 145-173). Cambridge: Cambridge University Press.

Slavin, R. E., & Madden, N. A. (1979). School practices that improve race relations. *American Educational Research Journal, 16,* 169-180.

Stephan, W. G., & Stephan, C. W. (1984). The role of ignorance in intergroup relations. In N. Miller & M. B. Brewer (Eds.), *Groups in contact: The psychology of desegregation* (pp. 229-255). Orlando, FL: Academic Press.

Stephan, W. G., & Stephan, C. W. (1985). Intergroup anxiety. *Journal of Social Issues,* *41*(3), 155-175.

Sullivan, M. L. (1979). Contacts among cultures: School desegregation in a polyethnic New York city high school. In R. C. Rist (Ed.), *Desegregated schools: Appraisals of an American experiment* (pp. 201-240). New York: Academic Press.

Tajfel, H. (Ed.). (1978). *Differentiation between social groups.* London: Academic Press.

Tajfel, H., & Turner, J. C. (1979). An integrative theory of intergroup conflict. In W. Austin & S. Worchel (Eds.), *The social psychology of intergroup relations* (pp. 33-47). Monterey, CA: Brooks/Cole.

Wellisch, J. B., Carriere, R. A., MacQueen, A. H., & Duck, G. A. (1977). *An in-depth study of Emergency School Aid Act (ESAA) schools: 1975-1976.* Santa Monica, CA: System Development Corporation.

Wellisch, J. B., Marcus, A. C., MacQueen, A. H., & Duck, G. A. (1976). *An in-depth study of Emergency School Aid Act (ESAA) schools: 1974-1975.* Santa Monica, CA: System Development Corporation.

Worchel, S. (1979). Cooperation and the reduction of intergroup conflict: Some determining factors. In W. G. Austin & S. Worchel (Eds.), *The social psychology of intergroup relations* (pp. 262-273). Monterey, CA: Brooks/Cole.

◙ PART III ◙

School Desegregation's Impact on African American Community Life and Life in Schools

INTRODUCTION

Mwalimu J. Shujaa

There are four chapters in this section. The two opening chapters focus on African American community life. Van Dempsey and George Noblit reconstruct the cultural narrative of a historically African American school silenced by desegregation in Chapter 6. They found that this school (pseudonym Rougemont), which was closed in 1975, had been the center of a close-knit African American community and a source of pride. Most of Rougemont's students were redistricted to the desegregated Liberty Hill school (also a pseudonym). In contrast to the sense of family experienced at Rougemont, African American students found that the environment at Liberty Hill was characterized by notions of "we" and "other." Dempsey and Noblit conclude that decisions about school desegregation were essentially reflections of cultural ignorance about the roles that many historically African American schools played in their communities.

In Chapter 7, Patricia A. Edwards focuses on the nature of parental involvement in historically African American schools and desegregated schools. Returning to her childhood community, Edwards recounts her own experiences in a historically African American school and shares recollections from her mother and elementary school principal. We are presented with first-person accounts of how the people who studied, worked, and sent their children to one African American school in Georgia viewed the changed nature of parental involvement in desegregated schools controlled by the local white elites. Edwards challenges researchers and policymakers to look beyond desegregation to consider the importance of broader sociopolitical contexts.

The two concluding chapters address African American life in schools, both K-12 and postsecondary. It is argued in Chapter 8 that, by focusing too narrowly on equality of educational access and opportunities, advocates for quality schooling in K-12 schools undervalue the significance of the learning environment. In this chapter, Ronald D. Henderson, Nancy M. Greenberg, Jeffrey M. Schneider, Oscar Uribe, Jr., and Richard R. Verdugo present findings from studies about how the organizational features of schools and active monitoring of quality indicators have an impact on the conditions of teaching and learning.

In Chapter 9, Carolyn J. Thompson writes about an area that has received limited treatment by scholars. She draws our attention to the success of African American student leaders in negotiating college and university environments. Thompson's aim is to contribute to the future success of African American students in predominantly white colleges and universities by developing a better understanding of their successes rather than their failures.

6

Cultural Ignorance and School Desegregation
A Community Narrative

VAN DEMPSEY
GEORGE NOBLIT

School desegregation was a classic case of educational policy accompanied by ignorance. Burlingame (1979) has argued that this is often the case with policy decisions. To act at all, we must act "as if" we do not know things that could divert us from our intended agenda. The issue here is not being unknowing, but rather acting as if we were ignorant to pursue some policy. Certainly this was true in school desegregation. We acted as if we were ignorant of the fact that desegregation was disproportionately burdening African Americans with the bulk of busing, with the closure of African American schools, and with the demotions and firing of African American educators (Irvine & Irvine, 1983; Smith & Smith, 1973).

There were many levels of ignorance at play. We were ignorant of the taken-for-granted assumptions made by whites and the courts. For example, whites and the courts assumed that African Americans would benefit from merely associating with the dominant culture and would assume more desirable status and beliefs (Coleman, Mood, Weinfeld, & York, 1967). We

This chapter is adapted from an article in *Educational Policy* (September, 1993); © 1993 by Corwin Press.

were equally ignorant of the culture of African Americans. In fact, school desegregation in many ways ignored the possibility that there could be desirable elements in African American culture worthy of maintenance and celebration. In practice, we seemed to ignore that there was an African American culture at all. The result was that we could not even consider that school desegregation could have destructive consequences for African Americans, and that school desegregation could actually destroy important elements of African American culture. Irvine and Irvine (1983) refer to such destructive consequences as *iatrogenesis,* a medical label applied when a remedy brings about an unhealthier situation than the one the remedy was meant to cure in the first place. Irvine and Irvine suggest that the term *iatrogenesis* may apply to our efforts at school desegregation.

In each of these cases, ignorance was based in assumptions more than in a lack of knowledge. There were people who disagreed with the *Coleman Report* (Moynihan & Mosteller, 1972), people who understood that we were desegregating schools on white terms (Bell, 1975), and people who were concerned that school desegregation could be cultural genocide for African Americans (Hardy, 1979). Yet we proceeded to ignore these issues in earnest pursuit of school desegregation, acting as if they were not reasonable concerns. To us, this is a special kind of ignorance, a cultural ignorance, driven both by the assumptions of the majority group and the logic of educational policy. Cultural ignorance is presumptive in that it devalues aspects of what is known so that we act as if it was not known. It is an ignorance based in intention—the intention to make something happen, regardless of reasonable concerns raised about the intention. The tragedy is that in this case the intention was about race equity, and it required us to act as if the culture of African Americans was of no concern at all.

Had we been more sensitive to African American culture or even culture itself (Bellah, Madsen, Sullivan, Swidler, & Tipton, 1985; Eisenhart, 1989), we might have reconsidered desegregation and fashioned a remedy that was less destructive of African American beliefs. Possibly we could have prescribed a remedy that enhanced the communicative competence of African Americans to change and maintain their culture (Bowers, 1984), rather than make their culture reflect the dominant one. But we did not. We did not, even though some African American communities resisted school desegregation because they saw the remedy fashioned in the courts and in policy as destructive (Cecelski, 1991). Educational policymakers and whites in general were not only ignorant of African American culture, they chose to ignore efforts by African Americans to enlighten them. As Burlingame argued, educational policy seems to require us to act as if we are ignorant and, moreover, to reject opportunities that would educate us. Now, more than 40 years after *Brown v. Board of Education,* it is time for us to better understand what we chose to be ignorant of and to follow the lead of African Americans who seek a fresh understanding of desegregation and a new approach to educational policy about equity (e.g., Bell, 1980).

Our ignorance about desegregation and its impact on African American culture has persisted partly because we have failed to recollect and celebrate the stories that were lost in the desegregation era. We thus lost important lessons about how we might become more sensitive to diverse cultures in schools today. Across America, thousands of schools, and in some cases communities, were lost in the movement to provide equity in education. Also lost in those communities and schools were the stories of their cultures, of their lives, of how education worked for them. It is one of those stories on which we will focus here. It will reveal a case of culture almost lost by our cultural ignorance.

In the fall of 1987, we were part of a research team of four invited into a small southern elementary school we called Liberty Hill. The principal had asked us to help him build a sense of unity among his faculty. New to the school, he was concerned with the amount of tension that existed within the faculty, both among themselves and between the school and its community. We suggested that the faculty and the research team produce a history of the school as a cohesion-building project. In the process of creating that history, we found that the school, which opened in 1915, was the oldest school in the city still in operation. Liberty Hill School had a long and proud tradition as one of the best schools in the city, referred to consistently in our interviews as being "like a private school."

This, by the way, is not the school we will be describing at length. In the process of researching the history of this school, we found that a nearby school, which we called Rougemont, had played an inextricable role in the history of Liberty Hill. To reconstruct the histories of the two schools and understand what life was like in and around them, we examined various documents, including school board minutes dating back to 1919, PTA minutes, journals, scrapbooks, personal records and artifacts, church histories, and public archives. Our richest data by far, however, came from over 75 interviews we conducted in the Rougemont and Liberty Hill schools and communities. These included current teachers at Liberty Hill, former students, teachers, and principals of both schools, and members of the school communities. (All names and references used here are pseudonyms.)

Our role was to help reconstruct the narrative silenced by school desegregation. We should always remember not to confuse narrative with "factual" history. Narratives are ways for people to be linked to the future; to have the meanings they value become part of a wider human discourse. That is to say, the narrative that follows is part of the Rougemont community's effort to construct and reconstruct its culture. This construction is sentimental because the community's project is constructing sentiment itself. It is likely that everyday life in Rougemont was much more contested than the narrative reveals, but sentiment recalls that which people wish to be perpetuated in their narrative, and it is thus selective. For us, the significance of the story that follows is that people wish this to be their story and as such are no longer silenced.

Because our initial focus was on Liberty Hill School, our entry into the field for research about Rougemont School did not begin in earnest until almost 1½ years later, in January 1989. We were introduced to the Rougemont community in a rather dramatic way: through an interdenominational church service in Rougemont. We were there to introduce ourselves and to have our history project sanctioned by the community. We had already done some interviews with people from Rougemont but in general had received a luke-warm response. We learned a telling lesson: The remaining vestiges of a formerly close-knit community with strong and visible leadership and a powerful sense of identity were its churches. The only way for us to be introduced to the community was to go to the one gathering still reflective of community: the interdenominational service that incorporated all the churches that served Rougemont whenever there was a fifth Sunday in the month.

The fifth-Sunday service rotated through the five Rougemont churches, and this night, it met in a church that was geographically centered in the community. The church seated about 200 people, with half that many in attendance, including those of us representing the school history project. As we waited for the service to begin, an elderly woman inquired as to why we were there, and having learned of our intent, launched into a description of how the community had changed during her lifetime. "We didn't have to shut our doors," she began her portrait of a community people nostal-gically recall. A community without crime in its boundaries. Homes that could be left open without fear of robbery or assault. Neighbors who were lifelong friends, free to go into each other's houses at will and encouraged to supervise and discipline each other's children. She said her feeling of safety ended about 15 years earlier when her husband died just as the community began to change. Fifteen years earlier—when Rougemont School was closed as the city desegregated its schools.

The diminished sense of safety is part and parcel of the changes in the Rougemont community since its school was closed in 1975. There are other related changes. Home ownership has decreased, and the population is more transient. The children of the community no longer see the neighborhood as the idyllic community their parents were raised in, and they move to other neighborhoods to raise their families. There are no longer visible leaders of the community or cooperative efforts to help those in need, the aged, or the infirm, as was the case in the past. Yet the church service was evidence that there was still some sense of community, and it was a testament to Rougemont's struggle to survive.

The service was the most moving introduction to a community any of us had ever witnessed. It came when we were afraid that we would not be able to write a history of Rougemont School. We were having difficulty identifying people who worked at and attended the school, and even when we could identify them, few were willing to talk with us. That evening, one of the church elders took it upon himself to arrange a Saturday meeting at the church where people could come and talk with us. Another woman offered to share a history she had assembled about the community that focused on the churches. Others recounted how central the school had been to the community, and how much they wished it was still in operation. People repeated that its closing marked the beginning of decline in the community. We were well on our way to learning what Rougemont School could teach us about education, had its voice not been silenced. Rougemont was trying to hold fast to its traditions, even as outside forces rent the boundaries and soul of the community.

A Place for Us

As Relph (1976) argues in his *Place and Placelessness,*

> people are their place and a place its people, and however readily these may be separated in conceptual terms, in experience they are not easily differentiated. In this context places are public—they are created and known through common experiences and involvement in common symbols and meanings. (p. 34)

Rougemont had been created as a pocket of opportunity for African Americans. There was employment, largely at a nearby university, and home ownership was its material base. But what made Rougemont a community was its park, its school, its churches, and its political organization. All of these provided for common experiences, symbols, and meanings. And they were all created by the community as essential to their social and cultural lives. With only the churches left, it was becoming harder and harder to find people who identified themselves as "from Rougemont." Even place was dissolving.

Rougemont was settled in the late 19th century, when Randolph College moved from Trinity County to the outskirts of Treyburn, at the time a southern town growing around the tobacco industry. Charles Walters, an African American employee of the college, decided to move with the college and built a home in a nearby woods. He cleared a path between home and work that was destined to become the main thoroughfare of Rougemont. Other African Americans similarly found employment at the college and built small homes. The path became a dirt street, and eventually the farmland became a neighborhood with definite boundaries. In the era of enforced segregation, Rougemont was in part bounded by other neighborhoods, including College Park, built by white employees of the college and by white professionals and businesspeople of Treyburn. It was also bounded by the college itself on the south and a notorious district of gambling and bootleg houses on the north. The boundaries were so rigid that people recalled the special meaning of Mr. Fred Brewer's hayrides for the children. They were billed as a "trip around the world," for Mr. Brewer dared to take his horse-drawn haywagon full of children beyond the reaches of Rougemont, circling the entire city.

Rougemont was not then a community of poor African Americans, but neither was it a neighborhood of higher-status African Americans. The latter community was across the city, surrounding Treyburn State College. Rougemont, rather, was a community of stably employed people, originally at Randolph College and later in the local mills or as maids and servants in the adjacent white neighborhoods. Although the vestiges of this are still evident, residents lament the influx of unemployed people and transients.

Rougemont was a close-knit community. "Everyone was one big family," according to residents. Friends visited and neighbors helped each other out. If someone was sick, neighbors pitched in and took food to the home. As a longtime Rougemont resident described it,

> I used to joke, especially when I started driving, . . . "I wish I had a third hand." Because knowing everyone in Rougemont [meant] when you went down the street, I would have liked to have two hands just to wave as I went by and have my third hand on the wheel. But walking or riding or whatever, you knew everybody.

The elderly were looked in on, and the elderly looked out for the children. Child rearing was also seen as a community venture. If an adult saw a child misbehaving, the adult would generally punish the child and then report the infraction and the punishment to the parent:

> It would not bother your parents at the time if someone took you in their house and gave you a spanking if they saw you doing something wrong. And when you got home you got another one. There was that kind of closeness.

Another resident remembered the epitome of the close-knit discipline network—Ma Franklin:

> All the families were close, close-knit families. There was a lady there all the kids called Ma Franklin. She's still living, she's about 90 years old now. We still call her Ma Franklin. She was everybody's mama. If she caught you doing something wrong or fighting she might spank you and then take you home. . . . She was everybody's mom.

Rougemont was a community of strong, shared values: hard work, religious faith, discipline, and individual and collective responsibility. Residents took care of their own and expected each to look to the other's welfare. It was their place, and they shared responsibility for it.

The neighborhood included all the amenities of a small town: grocery and clothing stores, barbershops and beauty salons, churches, scout troops, and recreation centers. The citizens even reclaimed a garbage dump to create a park for the residents. It became a place for children to play, adults to stroll and visit, and families to picnic. It was also the site of community celebrations. It symbolized just how much Rougemont was a place especially of and for them.

Rougemont was not an incorporated town and was not active in the wider political world of the city or of the African American population of Treyburn. It enjoyed few community services and had no representative in the wider political structure of the city, neither situation unusual for African American neighborhoods in cities, especially in the South. Isolated from the wider political apparatus, Rougemont created its own. The "Bronze Mayor" and his "Board of Directors" took care of everything from voter registration to helping people in trouble. These positions were honorary, going to the men with the most money and know-how in the community.

The Board of Directors organized community projects and lobbied with the local political structure for needed public services.

Rougemont was a community unto itself, with boundaries, churches, stores, and a political system. It was solidly working class, even if such employment was limited to domestic and service employment. Traditional employment patterns continued as Randolph University employed Rougemont residents as custodians, cooks, and dormitory workers. Some were employed in the local mills and tobacco companies; but in general, Rougemont people had little exposure to the wider African American and white communities. Connections with the other African American communities in the city were largely through the teachers at Rougemont School, who came from the middle-class neighborhoods around Treyburn State College, where they also studied. In this respect, Rougemont was one step down from the influential African American community and from the white communities. All of this contributed even more to Rougemont's insularity. Its residents' struggle was defined as being stalwart and hard-working, investing in education, religion, and their community. Rougemont citizens struggled to improve their lives, their churches, and their school, but they engaged little in the wider struggles for civil rights in the community.

This insularity is at no time more evident than in the 1960s, when civil rights was a major issue in all African American communities. Rougemont kept a "very low profile" in civil rights protests, according to a resident. "Our first lady," one person commented, knew how to deal with people, and Rougemont adopted the posture: "Just let Lillie do it." Lillie, the Bronze Mayor's wife, would go to meetings and talk with people. The community saw her as effective in getting the things the community desired, but there came a point when Rougemont recognized the need for collective action. In the early 1960s, African American leaders from other areas of the city came to Rougemont and held a meeting at St. John's Church to plan and elicit support for a boycott of downtown stores. The community voted to boycott. However, it was also recognized that it would be necessary for African Americans to become more active in the electoral process if they wished to have a voice on the local political scene. The Bronze Mayor and the Board of Directors organized voter registration drives in Rougemont and campaigned to get out the vote. Rougemont, however, was a minor actor in the local civil rights movement, inasmuch as the leadership came from other neighborhoods. Equally important was Rougemont's basic insularity. Residents continued to invest in their community, never realizing that the investment would contribute to the community's demise and ultimately to the demise of the most significant project in the history of the community, Rougemont School.

A School of Our Own

Although we were unable to find an exact origin of Rougemont School, it dates back to roughly the turn of the century. The first classes were held in a church in the community, with a schoolhouse constructed eventually with the help of the Rosenwald School movement. Rougemont School became a symbol of the community, achieved through exclusive service to students from Rougemont, through its presence in the neighborhood, through its long-standing faculty, through its reinforcing of community values, and through its identity as "a school of our own." Rougemont School was the community's ultimate cultural symbol and reflected the basic patterns and beliefs of Rougemont. Rougemont community was characterized as a family, and this was also true of the school. Rougemont expected its school to "educate the children and to be involved in the community," even though most of the teachers lived outside of Rougemont. The teachers at Rougemont fulfilled an educational and ideological role in the community. Beyond the usual responsibilities of teaching, they were expected to be present "every time there was something at the school." They had to attend all picnics, celebrations, and community meetings held at the school. The teachers were clearly to be role models for the children. They were to dress well, to be respected and exemplary citizens, and to foster close relationships between the school and community. They were, for example, expected to attend church services in Rougemont periodically. The community reciprocated by treating them with deference and respect equal to that accorded to the ministers of the churches they would attend. In the services, their presence would be publicly announced, and ministers would take time in the service to thank them for attending. According to one resident,

> You have to remember, too, that for many years . . . and this was certainly true when I was a child . . . for many black people, for most black people, the teacher was *the* person in the community. . . . That was because primarily [teaching] was the profession that most blacks went in if they wanted to get ahead and so forth. So, when the teachers came to church, then everybody took a back seat and they were always allowed to speak. . . . It was a really a big thing when they would come [to church].

A former Rougemont school student recalled. "There was prestige. My parents thought preachers were good, but teachers were great!"

Rougemont teachers had expectations of their own, mostly directed at their students. Teachers attempted to instill in children a sense of the importance of success in school. As a former principal explained, "They expected kids to learn. They expected high performance and the kids gave it. Kids responded like that. [Rougemont School] wasn't somewhere to run and hide and be lazy." Another former principal elaborated, "The teachers wanted their kids to be proud of themselves. They wanted their kids to have an understanding of their culture and history, and what they were doing . . . , what they were needing to do."

Teachers expected students to approach school with purpose. Teachers wanted their students to *want* to learn and to do well. Rougemont teachers were of one mind. According to a former student,

> You knew when you went to school that morning that you will be doing whatever you were told to do and you were going to stay there until you finished it. That was another thing . . . you didn't finish your work, you didn't go home when the other kids went home.

She went on to explain what the teachers communicated to the students: "You're going to learn. You're going to do well. You're going to excel and you're going to compete with anyone. They didn't take excuses lightly."

Growing from a faculty of 2 in 1921 to 18 by 1974 had little effect on the stance of the teachers nor how they were regarded by the community. As one mother whose children attended the school across three decades of the 1950s, 1960s, and 1970s, recalled: "They had a good group of teachers, some of the best. They were extra good." One former principal, who worked at the school during the early 1970s, summed it up succinctly, "I found a lot of good teaching going on." Another explained how the teachers got the children to believe that they were able to live up to the high expectations: "There was a lot of praise, there was a lot of boosting. But not illegitimate praise, not a facade, not a false sense of pride trying to be instilled."

Community/School Atmosphere

> I have heard every teacher and principal say who has been at Rougemont that there was really something special about that community, but I think the relationship was because of the parents really taking interest in the children and really working together.

Students, teachers, principals, and community members all expressed feelings similar to this about the relationship between Rougemont School and the community: "It was a community school, and everybody seemed like they loved it." This teacher continued, "It was a wonderful community [where] people [stuck] together, that cared about each other, that loved each other. It was just great. They were fully involved in the school. Whatever went on, they were there."

The close bond between Rougemont School and the community was best expressed in a description of the spring carnival in Rougemont Park across the street from the school. As a former teacher recalled,

> We had, I remember, the parents there. They always planned the social gathering in the spring over at the park. That was beautiful. It reminded you of a family type of situation. This was in the spring. This is where the parents would, like in the olden days, I guess. I'm from the country where people would pack picnic lunches, go to church and spread. Well, they would do these things in the park for the kids. They would grill food and things of that sort. That was a very good relationship. It was other things. You could almost feel how, you know, people care. You could just feel the warmth.

The school and community also came together at school fund raisers such as the school carnival. Grade mothers would work with the teachers in planning events such as movies, hot dog stands, and sock hops. All of the materials were donated to the school by the community, and the profits were used to buy instructional materials. As a former student said, "I remember that well when I was a little girl. It was a closeness, a sense of family because of some of the projects like that."

One student remembered the carnival as the "biggest event at our school." The carnival was something everybody looked forward to. Students would play games such as "go fish" for prizes:

> You might pull up a baby doll on a fishing pole, or some spectacular gift, not a little spider or things like we do now. But the parents in the neighborhood went way out, because that was the main event of the year at our school. Like people have baby dolls and stuff, they clean it up at home, and make new clothes for it. And if you were lucky you'd pull up a baby doll or a yo-yo, which was big thing then, or a bat and ball, you know, little things. And you might pull up a booby prize, but you know, you're lucky to pull a good prize.

The Rougemont parents were integrally involved with Rougemont School on a daily basis, not just at special events. As one teacher described the parents' effect on the school,

> They were special. They would come to the school. You didn't particularly have to go to them. They would come to you. . . . For parents that is good, you know. They'd want to know how they could help. What can they do? If you had a problem at school, or maybe if you needed something and you would say, "Oh I need such and such a thing," they would try to get it for you. If there was a problem with a child, they would do that. If we would say, OK, we're having some particular thing at school, whether it included the total school, whatever was needed, they would get it. Would try to help anyway.

A former principal said: "The parents liked the school. The community enjoyed their school. The community would come in to visit and to eat with the kids. It wasn't like pulling eye teeth to get people in." Another principal said,

> The PTA was there 100%. They always had a large crowd. Any principal or leader would call, and they would help out. The attitude toward the teacher was different. The parents wouldn't say anything negative. It was a family school, like being a member of a family.

As mentioned earlier, the family atmosphere of the community made disciplining children a shared responsibility. Teachers were allowed to make full use of that network. As a principal stated,

> I knew it was a tight-knit community that had always been tight-knit. Folks helped each other. Relatives lived a couple of blocks away, so there was extended family in the area. There was a grandmother or uncle nearby. I was just as free to talk to them as to the parents. Whatever you said would get back to the parents verbatim, and in some instances the relatives would just handle it.

Students were fully aware of the parental support teachers received as disciplinarians: "Well, in those days we got a spanking. Your teachers spanked you and called your mom, and then you went home and knew what you were going to get when you go home—the same thing!" Another student recalled,

If you were disobedient, oh yeah, the call was made that very day and you didn't want your parents to know that you had misbehaved because the rule was if you got it at school, you got it again when you got home.

Many teachers and principals discussed school-community interaction in terms of problems brought into Rougemont School by students from home. Children would at times bring in problems first thing in the morning to which the teacher lent a friendly ear. Although students generally got along well in the school, sometimes problems were brought in from the previous evening or weekend, and teachers would attempt to diffuse the problem early.

Teachers visited the homes and would eat with the families. The relationship was strong enough for teachers to go to homes whenever necessary. One teacher commented,

And I guess the parents, as I said, were right there whenever there was a problem. I had a little thing where I would walk home. At 2:30 if I had a problem with a kid that day, then they knew, "I'll walk home with you today." And I guess this was one thing that kept the children from having so many problems.

As stated in this teacher's comment, having a parent literally at the fingertips of the school cut down on a great many discipline problems. With parents so close to the school, in many cases walking children to school, parents had ample opportunity to converse with teachers. Required home visits by the teacher as well as voluntary ones helped to build a great deal of rapport between parents and teachers, strengthening the connection between home and school.

Primarily if [teachers] would visit in the afternoon after school it was because of a problem that was going on, and they would try to get with the parents before it got out of hand, which again I think is really important. And I think that personal touch really showed the concern, the interest.

One teacher remembered a particularly poignant example of teachers going into the community to deal with a problem:

I remember one year, Sarah [another teacher] and I were involved with a family that was in—I think one of the kids was in her room and one was in mine. This particular child, this is where the teacher would enter to help with the family. We noticed that the child needed assistance and [was] not getting it from Social Services. We went in to help. . . . It was cold this particular day, and very rainy. We went by to see the parents, and this was a little old lady. The little fella, he and his sister were living with their grandmamma. She was too old to care for the children. So after going in there we found that they didn't have any heat, and at that time we came across [the city] to Scott Coal Company, got coal, went home, got blankets and things of this sort.

A Comparison of Two Cultures

Accreditation reports provided one of the sources of information through which we could triangulate data and enhance our description of Rougemont and Liberty Hill schools. During the 1973-1974 school year both schools underwent Southern Association accreditation. The accreditation process involved self-study, whereby committees of teachers and administrators evaluated all aspects of their school, including not only academic programs such as social studies, math, and science, but other areas such as (to use the study's terms): The Children Served by the School, Philosophy, Organization for Learning, and Facilities. All schools that underwent the accreditation process followed the same plan and carried out the evaluation in the same amount of time. The self-studies, a selective data source in themselves, can help in our reconstruction of the silenced narrative of Rougemont School. In many ways, they provide text to the context we have discussed above.

Rougemont and Liberty Hill schools were both required to undergo the accreditation process in the 1973-1974 school year. At the time of accreditation, both schools had nearly achieved a 50-50 African American to white racial balance by altering attendance lines. There were important differences in context to each study. One was prepared at a historically African American elementary school with a predominantly African American faculty, whereas the other was prepared at a historically white elementary school with a predominantly white faculty. Another key difference was that the Rougemont community was more weighted toward middle- and lower-income neighborhoods, whereas Liberty Hill tended toward middle- and upper-middle-class neighborhoods. Because the schools were evaluated at the same time, the self-study reports by each school in April 1974 provide an opportunity to examine the two faculties' responses to the same questions about the same educational issues at the same time. The studies provide an opportunity to compare the two schools from roughly the same vantage point. Given that the two reports were written at the same time, and were written about schools only six city blocks apart, it is easy to assume similarities will appear, but it is the difference in the tone of the two documents that makes the comparison interesting. Following are comparable sections selected from each study that help enhance understandings of the contexts of each school and community.

Rougemont

In the section on The Children Served, Rougemont referred to attendance and absenteeism by stating, "The general health of the students at Rougemont School is good and a high rate of absenteeism is not a problem." The Rougemont document made a general reference to the state of manners and language of the children: "The manners and language usage of the students are fair, but some improvement is needed in this area." To further describe the children, more specifically their aspirations, the authors of the study asked the students what they would like to be when they grew up. Following are some student responses:

Teacher	1	Veterinarian	4	Doctor	4
Secretary	5	Dentist	1	Policeman	6
Nurse	13	Pilot	4	Athlete	8
Oceanographer	2	Artist	8	Janitor	1

The Rougemont study also contained children's answers to what they did after school.

Play	107
Work at home, then play	16
Do homework	33
Watch TV	47
Read	2
Work at a job	4

Rougemont seemingly found the children to be worthy of providing information, and teachers took the time to include them as part of information gathering.

The Rougemont Philosophy, another self-study section, described how the school helped children cope with the world at the present: "We at

Rougemont Elementary School believe that the challenges of speed, complexity, and impersonality of modern day living in today's changing world are frightening experiences for many of our elementary school children." At issue was how children's understanding of the world affected the fulfillment of their needs as students. "Therefore, an atmosphere must be obtained in which a child's social, emotional, intellectual, physical, and moral needs can be met on an individual basis." The Rougemont philosophy viewed the school as part of the community. "We believe that the school is an integral and vital part of the community. Therefore the school should strive to serve the needs of the community." School and community were partners in the education of children: "Only when both the school and the community acknowledge their responsibility to support and develop each other can the needs of children in school be met." The community was viewed as a participant in the educational process, not just a beneficiary of it.

Emergency School Assistance Aid (ESAA), another section of the self-study, described the use of funds provided to school districts in the early 1970s to help alleviate problems brought on by desegregation. (Both Rougemont and Liberty Hill used ESAA funds to attempt to improve math and reading performance among students.) The Rougemont study stated, in the ESAA section, that "racial tension still exists in our community and probably will for a number of years. . . . The fine work of professional groups, student groups, and several community groups has given the community a relatively good base for human relations."

The Rougemont study also gave background to their problems in areas pertaining to ESAA. "Many participants come from homes which are economically, educationally, and socially disadvantaged, and many have (a) poor attendance records, (b) low self-concepts, (c) low aspirations, and (d) lack of motivation in the home environment." The Rougemont study went on to describe the children on whom this project was focused:

> Children are born with intellectual curiosity, as proven by the thousands of questions they ask from the time they start talking until they are turned off by some who ridicule, laugh at, or belittle them. We feel that the project teachers and aides with the help of the central office staff will rekindle this curiosity.

In the Language Arts section, Rougemont teachers recognized variance in ability levels of children and attempted to "accept the child as he is." Oral expression was to be developed according to student needs, with encouragement to "broaden his vocabulary and cultivate a more fluent, correct usage of the English language," thus making the student part of the standard.

In a discussion of the Teaching-Learning Process at Rougemont School, factual knowledge was held to be valuable because of its present utility, not its potential utility.

> A sound approach to the learning process will recognize that learning is the interaction of the learners with a situation which includes, among other things, a problem, material to help solve the problem, and, in the case of the child, an adult to help and guide.

This was "the best preparation for living in the future." The teacher's purpose was to help the child find value in knowledge: "It is the teacher's privilege to help the child establish goals and clarify hazy purposes." By taking advantage of the personality of the student, "the teacher can bring the goals of the children and the objectives of the school into closer harmony."

Liberty Hill

Under the section The Children Served, the Liberty Hill study states: "The children like Liberty Hill as a school and are loyal to it. There are no dropouts here in elementary school." Liberty Hill implied that "dropouts" were nonachievers, uninterested in college, and disloyal, with no association between absenteeism and health. In their description of the children, the Liberty Hill study associated poor language with a particular group, drawing a distinction between those who use proper language and those who do not: "Most of the students are cooperative and polite. A very few, due to poor home environment, use language that is not up to our standards. Constant efforts are exerted to improve this." Liberty Hill used language and manners to group students, one being problematic for the school, whereas Rougemont portrayed its students as one body, albeit in need of improvement. It is also interesting how the future plans of the children at Liberty Hill are discussed: "Most of the children who attend Liberty Hill School are eager to achieve. Quite a number plan to go to college, and some plan to go to technical schools."

There was also quite a difference in the discussion of leisure time between the two schools. Liberty Hill gave one statement that "teachers encourage pupils to have things to do in their leisure time." Liberty Hill made a general statement about the children in the school whereas Rougemont used a more emic approach.

The Liberty Hill Philosophy treated school as a prerequisite to children's lives and their later integration into the community:

> The faculty at Liberty Hill School believes that the elementary school should aid in the development and adjustment of the child for the assumption of his personal role in American society. Our philosophy is that each child is an individual who should be helped toward a self-realization of his potential as a member of his community.

At Liberty Hill, education was preparing to be, as opposed to being. The goal of Language Arts at Liberty Hill was "clear diction, correct grammar, and a good vocabulary." The authors set as the standard the socially accepted way children were supposed to express themselves "in both formal and informal situations," a standard both monolithic and external to the student.

Liberty Hill stated as its ESAA goal "preventing a gradual regression of a pupil's achievement level in the math and/or reading area." Its target is "the slow learning child." Also in this section, and in sharp contrast to a critical statement made in the introduction to the Rougemont self-study, the Liberty Hill study claimed, "Integration was no big problem here." (While it is possible that one school may have experienced tensions and the other not, it is interesting that being as close together as these schools were geographically, with significant overlap in populations, their perception of racial tension would be so different.) It is also ironic that the tone of the Liberty Hill study implied a dichotomized student body, brought about through the identification of a disadvantaged group in the school. The Rougemont study implied at least the perception of a more unified school. Rougemont did not scapegoat the child and had a more ambitious goal for ESAA than "preventing a gradual regression of . . . achievement level."

At Liberty Hill, the teacher dominated the Teaching-Learning process. "The faculty of Liberty Hill School believes that the teacher is the key to the learning process." There was no mention of the student's place in the process, other than "pupil-teacher planning," and "teacher-pupil-parent relationships."

A Comparison of the Two Schools

Both Liberty Hill School and Rougemont School created texts to tell about themselves. Both stories focused on communities that each school considered "home" to the school. Each dealt with a population that was extremely different from that historically dealt with at each school. Here the similarities end. The Rougemont text told "who we are." It was in some instances an interpretative text, but it also offered a description from which the reader could build his own story about the Rougemont community and school. Rougemont told a candid story of who children are.

The Liberty Hill study told a different story, one where the authors dichotomized *us* from *them,* and *we* from *they.* Those who achieved were singled out from those who did not. Successes originated in the school, whereas failures originated elsewhere. The Liberty Hill authors interpreted for the reader. There was little description; the story was built. The Liberty Hill text was a managed one, where the image was created for the audience. When the Liberty Hill text became specific, it was to displace blame. Liberty Hill told who parents are and what children will be.

The Rougemont text was about one community. The Liberty Hill story was about two. Liberty Hill School saw itself serving two "communities," and thus told two stories when the difference between the two warranted recognition. There was at Liberty Hill one group that achieved and had achieved. There was another that did not and had not.

Ultimately, the self-studies are not about factual description of the two schools. They are rather narratives of the two schools. In these representations, the language of the Liberty Hill self-study manifested the kinds of cultural ignorance and nonrepresentation to which we point. Factual or not, the dichotomizing and marginalizing language embodies the ignorance.

Rougemont's Closing

Differences in the cultures of schools, and in the tone of documents reflecting those cultures, such as the self-studies described above, provide valuable insights into the stories that institutions such as schools have to tell about themselves. For schools and school cultures such as Liberty Hill that have survived institutionally, such documents are important. But in situations where schools and their cultures may have been lost to social and political events and needs—or ignored—the ability to reconstruct the stories becomes crucial for the maintenance of those schools' narratives and their cultural identities.

As noted above, the self-study reports were released by Rougemont School and Liberty Hill School in April 1974. In less than a year, Rougemont School became the subject of a much more significant process and report. On October 30, 1974, the U.S. Middle District Court advised the city that new desegregation plans would be developed. Four schools in the city were under consideration to be closed, Rougemont being one of them. At the end of the 1974-1975 school year, Rougemont community's children were redistricted into other schools, one of them being Liberty Hill. The teacher who remembered the story cited earlier of delivering coal to a student's home finished her story by reflecting on the closure decision: "You know these are things I miss from Rougemont because it was really, that was a very good atmosphere to work. I loved it. When that school closed I cried for almost a week."

For Rougemont, the end of its school was at least in part the end of the community. Education in Rougemont had been in and of community, and as one resident of the community said, "The closing of Rougemont was the end of social organization, the end of home visits. Nobody knew what anyone else was doing. You didn't see people the way you did." As one former Rougemont principal put it, "The kids in the heart of Rougemont went to Liberty Hill School."

One Rougemont citizen commented that the closing of the school had a definite impact on Rougemont. "It hurt the community; everybody. We had one of the best schools in [the city]. We had good teachers. Why did they want to change it?" It is ironic that the answer to this man's question might lie in the very community strength that had made the school success- ful for so many years. The Rougemont School and its community had done an effective job of defining themselves as a community—and in the harsh political realities of desegregation—as an African American community (even though, ironically, by 1974 the school was 50% white). In the end, the insularity that had for so long served Rougemont led to its downfall. The insularity meant that Rougemont was excluded by, and excluded itself from, the wider community's politics surrounding desegregation. Its resi- dents were not participants in the politics of desegregation, rather they were the victims. A citizen who helped lead the community fight to save the school said, "The school was good. It was new with new facilities. It was set up as one of the best schools. Being in a black community closed it. We had good teachers. They took interest in children."

It is also ironic, and in a sense tragic, that the best evidence of the power of the relationship between Rougemont School and the community came in both institutions' destruction. A former principal described the closing of the school as the "destruction of [the] community focal point."

The unraveling of Rougemont School and the community reflects the importance of the relationship between place and people described by Relph earlier, and the damage that can occur by severing that relationship. For the children of Rougemont, who had for years known limited boundaries to their world, the abrupt expansion of boundaries that came with desegregation must have been traumatic. For Rougemont community writ large, relationships that had for years defined community unraveled. Relph (1976) asserts that community and place reinforce the identity of each other in a "very powerful" relationship (p. 34). In an extension of his discussion of community, "the identities of places are founded . . . on the interaction of . . . three opposing poles of the I, the Other, and the We" (p. 57). The I and the Other are able to communicate with each other through the signs and symbols of the We. "To wish to separate the I, the Other, and the We is to desire to dissolve or to destroy consciousness itself" (p. 57). In a sense, it was consciousness that was lost in the closing of Rougemont School, for it was the one place where the signs and symbols of a community came together and were shared. It was at Rougemont School that all the threads of the close-knit community were woven; where the Rougemont family could unite and reunite. Rougemont School was synonymous with Rougemont community. Much like Erickson's (1976, p. 215) description of loss of community through a natural disaster, in *Everything in Its Path*, the people of Rougemont were "enmeshed in the fabric" of their school and their community. Each one—community and school—was dependent on the other for completing its character, and completing and holding together the "knit" in the Rougemont fabric. When the school was taken away, the fabric was shredded. The resident who talked about social disintegration above described well the danger of being forced out of the community:

> Being poor was not a stigma [at Rougemont], they understood. [After the closing of Rougemont] people became afraid to come to school because of limited background or lack of education. Many students from the area stopped education after integration came. There wasn't a strong push. Things seemed to have broken down.

The teacher who shared the story of the gathering in the park, and the story of the home visit that ended in delivering coal and blankets to children and their grandmother, said of the school's closing, "It was just like you were losing a friend, which I did."

Conclusion

Featherstone (1976), in a discussion of the desegregation of the Boston Schools, commented on the African American experience with the process:

Blacks inherit more than their share of American faith in schools; but
in the past, this was grounded less in naive idealism than in a shrewd
assessment that schools were the only game in town that would let
them in, albeit on condescending racist terms. Schools kept blacks out
and oppressed them; but separate black schools and colleges served as
havens, turfs, and sources of jobs. (p. 191)

The Rougemont community's elementary school served in many senses as
a haven and a turf, if not a source of jobs. In the period since the school's
closing in 1975, that haven and turf have not only been taken away, they
have been replaced with a school community that is "separate" in ways
seldom envisioned in the desegregation movement. The Rougemont students were reassigned to schools like Liberty Hill, which resegregated them
by scapegoating and stigmatizing the children. In the process of resolving
the inequity between African American and white schools, schooling for
Rougemont children was separated from their community, from their
history, from their traditions, and from their culture. The result of school
desegregation for Rougemont was a cruel irony. The cost of being integrated in schools was the disintegration of community. The children were
separated from their culture. Moreover, the community lost the only social
institution that served all of them and celebrated their lives and beliefs.
Today, it is only on fifth Sundays, when all the churches meet together, that
there is a chance for community and a chance for shared cultural beliefs.

The lesson of Rougemont is a brutal one. It teaches African Americans
to be wary of education policies that are intended to benefit them, for these
policies may well be based in cultural ignorance. Cultural ignorance is more
damaging than simply not knowing another's culture, because it assumes
the superiority of one's own beliefs. Sadly, cultural ignorance legitimates
educational policymakers treating other beliefs as detractors to the implementation of policy. The lesson, then, is that any educational policy that is
not equitable in its development and implementation is unlikely to be
equitable in its results.

It is, of course, impossible to turn back the clock, to act as if desegregation never occurred. Our intent, rather, is simply to try to reclaim a little
of what was lost. Clearly, the story of Rougemont is but a reconstruction of
a narrative of African American life that was silenced by school desegregation. Yet the process of reconstructing such narratives is vital. In these
stories are what remains of a culture that equated education with emancipation, that valued schools as cultural entities, and that built communities
with schools. These are values worth upholding in all our communities. In

better understanding the cultural consequences of school desegregation for African Americans, we may come to understand what we all need in our communities and from our schools.

References

Bell, D. (1975). The burden of *Brown* on blacks. *North Carolina Central Law Journal, 7* (Fall), 27-39.

Bell, D. (1980). *Shades of* Brown: *New perspectives on school desegregation.* New York: Teachers College Press.

Bellah, R., Madsen, R., Sullivan, W., Swidler, A. & Tipton, S. (1985). *Habits of the heart.* Berkeley: University of California Press.

Bowers, C. A. (1984). *The promise of theory: Education in the politics of cultural change.* New York: Teachers College Press.

Brown v. Board of Education, 347 U.S. 483 (1954).

Burlingame, M. (1979). Some neglected dimensions in the student of educational administration. *Educational Administration Quarterly, 15*(1), 1-18.

Cecelski, D. (1991). *The Hyde County school boycott.* Unpublished doctoral dissertation, Harvard University Graduate School of Education.

Coleman, J., Mood, A., Weinfeld, F., & York, R. (1967). *Equality of educational opportunity.* Washington, DC: Government Printing Office.

Eisenhart, M. (1989). Reconsidering cultural differences in schools. *Educational Foundations, 39,* 51-68.

Erickson, K. T. (1976). *Everything in its path.* New York: Simon & Schuster.

Featherstone, J. (1976). *What schools can do.* New York: Liverstone.

Hardy, C. (1979). Motivation: Making the extra effort!!! again. *Southern Exposure, 7*(2), 94-98.

Irvine, R. W., & Irvine, J. J. (1983). The impact of the desegregation process on the education of black students: Key variables. *Journal of Negro Education, 52,* 410-422.

Moynihan, D., & Mosteller, F. (1972). *On equality of educational opportunity.* New York: Random House.

Relph, E. (1976). *Place and placelessness.* London: Pion.

Smith, J., & Smith, B. (1973). For black educators: Integration brings the ace. *Urban Review, 6*(3), 1-11.

7

◨

Before and After School Desegregation
African American Parents' Involvement in Schools

PATRICIA A. EDWARDS

One of the few times a parent's voice was heard and taken seriously by policymakers occurred when the Rev. Oliver Brown objected to his daughter having to attend a distant, all-black school, even though she passed an all-white school in her neighborhood. Since the *Brown v. Board of Education* decision, parent voices have received scant attention by policymakers in their discussions of the strengths and weaknesses of school desegregation. I argue that not only should parents' voices be heard by policymakers, but that the voices of teachers and administrators should be heard as well. In this chapter, I summarize three generations of desegrega-

AUTHOR'S NOTE: I wish to thank my mother, Mrs. Annie Kate Edwards, and my elementary school principal, Mr. Erasmus Dent, for sharing their rich and insightful recollections of how parents, teachers, and the black community supported each other before school desegregation. I especially appreciate their recollections about what happened in segregated schools that allowed African American children to gain access to the education they rightfully deserved.

This chapter is adapted from an article in *Educational Policy* (September, 1993); © 1993 by Corwin Press.

tion efforts since the *Brown* decision with the intent to highlight parent voices. I argue that researchers and policymakers should turn their attention to the importance of broader sociocultural facets of desegregation. I provide recollections from my mother and elementary school principal that African American parents did not have to be formally invited to participate in their children's education before school desegregation. I also give my own recollections of PTA meetings, fund-raising activities, social gatherings, and visits to my classroom by my mother. I describe the efforts since school desegregation to invite African American parents to become involved in school affairs. I suggest that educators must examine whether African American parents feel invited or uninvited.

Parents: The Forgotten Voices
in the Three Generations of Desegregation

The first generation of desegregation, marked by the historic 1954 decision by the U.S. Supreme Court case in *Brown v. Topeka Board of Education,* focused primarily on efforts to end physical segregation and on court-ordered desegregation plans to accomplish this. Bates (1990) admits, "When Rev. Brown brought his suit, there were substantial disparities between schools for blacks and those for whites with regard to buildings, books, and facilities" (p. 10). He also admits that

> most people assumed that these disparities would be eliminated only if black families were given access to schools that had been all-white, schools that in 1954 appeared to be far superior to those grudgingly offered to black families by white legislators and policymakers. (p. 10)

Even though Lightfoot (1980) was only 10 years old when the *Brown* decision was handed down in 1954, she describes the memory of the moment when the news of the *Brown* decision reached her house. She recalls that

> jubilation, optimism, and hope filled my home. Through a child's eyes, I could see the veil of oppression lift from my parents' shoulders. It seemed they were standing taller. And for the first time in my life, I saw tears in my father's eyes. "This is a great and important day," he said reverently to his children. And although we had not lived the pain and struggle of his life, nor did we understand the meaning of his words, the emotion and the drama of that moment still survives in my soul today. (p. 3)

Lightfoot also recalls,

> I truly believed at that moment, that black brothers and sisters in
> southern schools would now have an equal chance, taste the sweetness
> of the American pie, and learn to value their black skin, their history,
> and their children. I forgot momentarily the subtle exclusion and
> microaggressions that I experienced daily in my almost all-white
> northern, middle-class school. (pp. 3-4)

Trent (1992) describes a quite different scene in his house. The scene
takes place a few years after the historic 1954 decision. The scene is a family
conference in which the discussion focuses on whether to attend an all-
white school or not.

> I remember vividly a day during the mid-1960s when my parents
> called my brother and me to the kitchen table for a family conference.
> They had just received a letter from the school board office indicating
> that a free-choice school plan was in effect. This plan would give
> parents the opportunity to send their children to one of several
> segregated, white schools in this rural Virginia district. In this way,
> county school board officials could document that they were moving
> toward gradual school desegregation. The question from our parents
> was, "Which school do you want to attend?" Being the oldest sibling
> still in school, I quickly announced, "I don't want to go to no white
> school." My younger brother concurred. My father signed the form
> indicating that we wished to remain in our same school, and that was
> the end of our family conference. We returned outside and continued
> to shoot some hoops. (pp. 291-292)

After he returned outside to shoot some hoops with his brother, Trent
(1992) recalls he wondered "how [his] parents might have reacted had [he
and his brother] requested to attend one of the White schools" (p. 292).
Trent provides several reasons why his parents allowed him and his brother
to remain in a segregated school setting, but one of the most revealing
reasons he shares is described below.

> Perhaps, though, at the heart of this choice was my parents' fear that
> enrollment in one of the white schools would place us in physical,
> psychological, and emotional danger. They feared that our mere
> presence in one of the newly integrated schools would aggravate and

intensify the hatred that had maintained our segregated communities, our segregated existence, for centuries. (p. 292)

Trent's parents, like many African American parents, wondered what would happen after black and white children were no longer physically separated.

Lightfoot (1980) also wondered what would happen after black and white were no longer physically separated, and the questions she raises reflect her concern:

> How was the message going to be translated into the realities and lives of teachers and children in schools? Black and white bodies could be moved into the same schools. Children could experience greater physical proximity. Did any of this have anything to do with increasing reading scores, quality education, or greater self-esteem for young children? Whose agenda was being met, and for what social, political, and economic reasons? How was desegregation going to be accomplished against the massive resistance of threatened and insecure whites? Why did a large majority of blacks want desegregation? What were their motives, hopes, fears, and anticipated compromises? What would happen to the enduring relationship between communities, families, and schools as populations shifted and strangers invaded once homogeneous and protected enclaves? (p. 4)

Unfortunately, few policymakers raised questions or expressed concerns about the mixing of black and white bodies in the schools. Too few policymakers asked themselves, Is a school desegregated just because children of different descent attend it? Does the technical definition of desegregation result in the implied meaning of desegregation? Can a desegregated school maintain segregation in how it treats its students, their community, and their parents?

As the process of desegregation continued, many of the questions I raised, as well as the questions that Lightfoot raised over a decade ago, have resulted in the second generation of desegregation problems faced by today's school districts. According to Bates (1990),

> These problems stemmed from inequities *within* schools rather than between schools. They included such educational matters as unequal access to classrooms and programs, and the disproportionately high rates of suspension and dropping out among minority students. At the same time, it was becoming very clear that, in addition to segregation

by race, in-school segregation was also occurring by gender and national origin. (p. 10)

It is not surprising that today's school districts are faced with a second generation of desegregation problems. Many of these problems have surfaced because trying to attack racism within the school system was never a part of the desegregation package. Simply put, desegregation put African American children in a racist context, hoping that they would learn anyway because, at least, they then could share in the same material benefits of an integrated school. However, Trent and Artiles (1993) point out that

> when Black children entered integrated schools, they were met generally by white administrators and teachers who were unprepared to deal with their cognitive styles, social values, beliefs, customs, and traditions. Because of the discontinuity that developed overnight between home and school cultures, these personnel began teaching black children with preconceived notions and stereotypical views about how they functioned. (p. 29)

Two well-known cases support Trent and Artiles's (1993) observation. In the 1978 case that has come to be known as the "Black English Case," *Martin Luther King Junior Elementary School v. Ann Arbor School District Board,* the parents of 11 black children charged school officials with denying their children equal educational opportunities by failing to help the children overcome a language barrier. Cobb-Scott (1985) reported, "The court found it appropriate to: require the defendant Board to take steps to help its teachers to recognize the home language of the students and to use that knowledge in their attempts to teach reading skills in standard English" (p. 63). Judge Charles W. Joiner himself said,

> The research evidence supports the theory that the learning of reading can be hurt by teachers who reject students because of the "mistakes" or "errors" made in oral speech by black English-speaking children who are learning standard English. This comes about because "black English" is commonly thought of as an inferior method of speech and those who use this system may be thought of as "dumb" or "inferior." (1978 at 18)

Another notable case where black parents had to fight for their children's rights was that of *Larry P. v. Riles* (1972). The *Larry P. v. Riles* case was filed on behalf of black elementary schoolchildren who allegedly were inappropriately placed in classes for students with mental retardation. In the court settlement, a preliminary injunction regarding future testing with the Wechsler Intelligence Scale for Children and the Stanford-Binet was granted. According to Swanson and Watson (1989), "The repercussions of this case have been far-reaching and have affected minority children both positively and negatively. Most significant has been the effect on services to students" (p. 387).

The two cases cited above are representative examples of second-generation desegregation problems, but the implications of these two cases are concerns of the third-generation of desegregation. Bates (1990) contends that third-generation problems are more challenging because they focus on the achievement of equal learning opportunities and outcomes for all students. To the dismay of many, the achievement gap between blacks and whites is widening (Hale-Benson, 1990). Bates laments that

> While third-generation issues are not as blatant as physical segregation, they are no less painful and debilitating to minority children in our schools. Third-generation issues are closely related to teacher attitudes toward and expectations of minority students. When teachers expect little or nothing of minority students, minority students often respond accordingly. (p. 11)

More than 40 years have passed since the historic *Brown* decision, and some African American parents are still wondering what the decision has accomplished for them and their children. For many African American parents, the emotion faded many years ago and, in its place, there is cynicism, withdrawal, and pessimism. Bell (1983) is one of the few policy-makers who actually admitted that African American parents should have played a larger part in the *Brown* decision. He apologizes by saying,

> Had we civil rights lawyers been more attuned to the primary goal of black parents—the effective schooling of their children—and less committed to the attainment of our ideal—racially integrated schools—we might have recognized sooner that merely integrating schools, in a society still committed to white dominance, would not ensure our clients and their children the equal educational opportunity for which they have sacrificed so much and waited so long. But from the beginning many black parents and their community leaders realized what some civil rights lawyers have not yet acknowledged. There can be no

effective schooling for black children without both parental involvement in the educational process and meaningful participation in
school policy making. (p. 575)

What Policymakers Failed to Address: The Social Ramifications of School Desegregation

Many predicted that it was inevitable that desegregation as it was
conceived was doomed to failure. It was so doomed primarily because the
solutions proposed for the desegregation of schools were simplistic and
unrealistic arrangements (Irvine & Irvine, 1983; Lightfoot, 1980). Lightfoot
reveals that

> the solutions lacked an awareness of the complex, multifaceted pro-
> cesses of education and negated the strong, enduring, resistive quali-
> ties of institutional and cultural inertia. Most important, although the
> *Brown* decision focused on schooling, it disregarded the development
> of children and the perspectives of families and communities. (p. 4)

Lightfoot also says that

> a critically important ingredient of educational success for black and
> white children lies in the power relationship between communities
> and schools, rather than in the nature of the student population.
> Mixing black and white bodies together in the same school and
> preserving the same relationships and perceptions between schools
> and the families they serve is unlikely to substantially change the
> structures, roles, and relationships *within* schools that define the
> quality of the educational process. The nature and distribution of
> power among schools, families, and communities is a crucial piece of
> the complex puzzle leading toward educational success for all chil-
> dren. (p. 17)

A similar, but slightly different, message is offered by Irvine and Irvine
(1983). They contend that early proponents of school desegregation rushed
to measure the so-called educational benefits of desegregation for African
American children's achievement, but failed to examine the broader sociocultural facets of desegregation's dynamics. Irvine and Irvine correctly
point out that "assessing the effects of desegregation independent of the

contextual significance of the broader sociocultural and historic roots of blacks, as a people, misses the central component of how such a system is implicated in the learning process" (p. 412).

Irvine and Irvine (1983) used three units of analysis to show how the primary and secondary effects of desegregation affect African American student achievement within the broader sociocultural context. The units of analysis they used were at the interpersonal, institutional, and community levels. At the interpersonal level, the disappearance of African American teachers and administrators negatively affected the self-esteem and self-awareness of African American children. At the institutional level, the African American school was a "security blanket" for African American children and their families. For the most part, it was a place where African American principals and teachers were in control. Irvine and Irvine argue that "these schools represented and took on uniquely stylized characteristics reflective of their members—patterns of communications, cultural preferences, and normatively diffused modes of behavior" (pp. 415-416).

The African American community was also an institution African American parents and children looked to for strength, hope, and security. More important, the African American community set both a floor and a ceiling on achievement and educational attainment for its members. Billingsley (1968) conceives the black community in this respect. He states,

> In every aspect of the child's life a trusted elder, neighbor, Sunday school teacher, schools, or other community members might instruct, discipline, assist, or otherwise guide the young of a given family. Second, as role models, community members show an example to and interest in the young people. Third, as advocates they actively intercede with major segments of society (a responsibility assumed by professional educators) to help young members of particular families find opportunities which might otherwise be closed to them. Fourth, as supportive figures, they simply inquire about the progress of the young, take a special interest in them. Fifth, in the formal roles of teacher, leader, elder, they serve youth generally as part of the general role or occupation. (p. 99)

The policy (product) called integration eroded much cultural strength among African American communities, the cost of the goal of equity in education. Segregation of the biggest order and inequity have been maintained in integration, at the cost of losing community control and cultural maintenance because the policy of integration never took on the true cause of inequity as measured in our institutions and our history as a nation, that is, racism. Two recent publications, Hacker's (1992) *Two Nations: Black and White, Separate, Hostile, Unequal* and Kozol's (1991) *Savage Inequalities: Children in America's Schools* discuss in detail the racism that still divides blacks and whites today.

Hacker contends that African Americans remain a subordinate class because "being Black in America bears the mark of slavery. Even after emancipation ... blacks continued to be seen as an inferior species, not only unsuited for equality but not even meriting a chance to show their worth" (p. 14). Hacker believes that these convictions persist today and are the basis for the existence of two nations—separate, hostile, and unequal. Kozol describes the effects of poverty and inadequate funding on education. He eloquently argues that the American educational system is still separate and unequal more than 40 years after the historic *Brown* desegregation decision.

The views on racism by Hacker and Kozol come as no surprise. Johnson (1954) predicted nearly 40 years ago that desegregation would alter the unique institutional arrangements of the African American community, particularly African American schools. His prediction became a reality because African American students and their parents saw their schools dismantled. They also saw the African American teachers and administrators whom they had come to love and admire reassigned, demoted, or in some cases dismissed. Since that great day in 1954, few researchers and/or policymakers have paid serious attention to the voices of parents, teachers, and principals who were affected both personally and professionally by this historic decision.

Parent Involvement in a Southwest Georgia Segregated School

Unfortunately, few researchers have highlighted the voices of African American principals (Foster, 1991; Lomotey, 1993). Fewer researchers have highlighted parents' voices and the communities they represent. Irvine and Irvine (1983) point out that "literature is woefully lacking in the treatment of the [African American] community as a structure that had a collective stake in the educational process of [African American] youth in the community" (p. 419). Lightfoot (1978) echoes a similar message. She contends that

Black families and communities have been settings for cultural transmission, survival training, moral and religious instruction, role modeling, myth making, and ideological and political indoctrination. But very little of this "informal" education has been systematically documented by scholars because it has been considered distracting and divergent from the formal schooling of black children; because much of it seems incomprehensible and mysterious to white scholars; because it is thought to bear no direct connection to the successful accommodation of blacks to mainstream life; and because it contradicts our sacred myths about the great American melting pot. (p. 129)

As a woman who grew up in the South, I remember vividly that the family, the school, and the community contributed to the educational achievement of African American children like myself. I was born and raised in a midsize southwest Georgia community. I entered school a few years after the 1954 U.S. Supreme Court's landmark *Brown* decision, which declared segregation in education unconstitutional. I grew up in a stable, close-knit neighborhood where I knew many eyes watched me and would tell my mama when I misbehaved. My elementary school principal and most of my teachers lived in my neighborhood. Consequently, there were many opportunities outside of school for my principal and teachers to talk with my parents about my progress and behavior in school. My principal, teachers, neighbors, as well as my parents, all shared and reinforced similar school and family values.

Before school desegregation, African American parents knew their place in the school. They felt comfortable coming and going in the school at their leisure. The faces of teachers and administrators were familiar to them because, in many instances, the teachers and administrators were their friends, neighbors, and church members. Parents could voice their concerns, opinions, and fears about their children's educational achievement, and teachers and administrators listened and responded.

Parent involvement prior to school desegregation connoted active participation, collaboration, co-generative discussions with teachers and administrators. It meant African American parents had some control of the schools and school systems that molded the minds of their children. For example, teaching personnel were accountable to the community and therefore had to teach if they wanted to maintain their jobs. School performances were relevant to the life experiences and needs of African American children and provided motivation to learn. African American children developed self-worth and dignity through knowledge of their history and culture and through the images provided by community leaders and teachers. African American parents had control through coalition. The schools maintained continuous communication with African American parents and developed with these parents a structure that included them in the governing of the schools. African American parents could exert influence to protect their most precious resources, their children.

My mother was president of the PTA throughout my entire six years of elementary school. When I asked my mother to talk with me about her role as PTA president, I was astonished to find that she had actually saved a copy of her opening address as PTA president. In it, she said,

> Education is the key. Our children have to go farther than we did in school. We don't want our children working hard for nothing. Times are tough and we want our children to have the education to get a good job. We want them to make something out of themselves. We want them to be strong men and women. We want them to not have to put up with what we have to put up with on our jobs. We don't want them to be treated unfairly and feel that they cannot do anything about it.

Mama said her eyes welled with tears, but she continued her speech by saying,

> We all know what happened in Alabama to Rosa Parks. You work all day, and white folks want you to go to the back of the bus or get up and let a white person have your seat. That's not right, and all of us know that they know that's not right. [According to mama, this statement received several emotional outbursts from teachers and parents.] We will no longer accept this type of treatment. Oh no, we will not tolerate it. We will fight to the end, and our children will take up where we left off. The way we can stop this treatment is to work with the teachers to help them educate our children. We need to reinforce at home what the teachers and principal are trying to do at school.

Parents of all different educational and economic levels bonded together to support the principal and teachers. African Americans were not allowed to eat in restaurants or live in hotels, so the school became a social gathering place for parents, teachers, and the principal to discuss social, economic, and political issues. Consequently, PTA meetings and social gatherings were well-attended. Fund-raising activities were also well-supported by parents.

My mother, Mrs. Annie Kate Edwards, is still involved in school activities. She volunteers at the Lincoln Fundamental Magnet School where her two granddaughters are enrolled. I asked her about her role as PTA president at River Road Elementary School, which is now Martin Luther King Drive Elementary School; she listed many areas of parental involvement.

- Parents participated in committees that directly influenced school curricula and policies. Committees consisted of parents, teachers, and the principal.
- Parents worked on sponsorship and implementation of curriculum-related and family-oriented activities, for example, cultural arts contests/displays, Family Fun Night.
- Parents made instructional materials for classroom use, as directed by teachers.
- Parents assisted in the school library, checking out and shelving books.
- Parents participated as room mothers or room fathers.
- Parents supervised on class trips or chaperoned at school functions.
- Parents attended classroom plays, presentations.
- Parents attended school assembly programs.
- Parents attended competitive games and athletic events at school.
- Parents attended promotion ceremonies.
- Parents attended parent/teacher conferences.
- Parents were encouraged to help children with homework at home. You know some of them couldn't help, but they found other people in the community who could help their children.
- Parents were involved in PTA fund-raising activities.
- Parents were asked to join the PTA.

Mr. Erasmus Dent was principal of River Road Elementary School throughout my entire elementary school career. He lived across the street from me, and until this day he maintains the same residence. Even though Mr. Dent is retired, he continues to consult with the school district, and he mentors young principals, especially young African American principals.

Instead of engaging in an interactive dialogue with me around the questions, Mr. Dent chose to make a statement that addressed the questions.

I am Erasmus Dent, who was the principal of River Road Elementary School for more than 30 years. This school, basically black, is located in the southern portion of the city of Albany, Georgia. The school at one time had 1,100 students, but gradually decreased down to 550 students. River Road Elementary School, which is now Martin Luther King Drive Elementary School, is located in a totally impoverished area in south Albany, Georgia, with most of the parents and students being deprived economically and socially. The parents were mostly uneducated, with the majority being low literate. However, because of housing patterns in this city, some educated families and persons with good social and economic lives were part of our school community. Therefore, the leadership in our school and community resulted in a fever pitch desire for value-rich experiences, improved education and better lives. The dream for our children to become successful doctors, dentists, lawyers, politicians, engineers, etc. [was the reason].

The parents felt a very close relationship to the community schools and realized their responsibility in ensuring quality education for the students. Parent organizations, which were 100% PTA at that time, concerned themselves with physical, academic, and moral conditions and the improvement of our students. This led to the attempts at supplementing school finances through drives, a system of broadening experiences through trips and imported cultural groups, and suggestions regarding activities and personnel. Through being encouraged to participate in all efforts to continue and improve education for their children, the parents developed confidence in and respect for the principal and teachers.

They and the downtown administrative personnel allowed the school's principal to staff and to direct its program and activities. This, with community input, led to well-controlled schools with few serious internal problems involving students, teachers or community. Though most parents were unable to assist their children with schoolwork and projects because of their former educational levels, they participated in such things as school programs, school trips, special projects, etc. Working with the school was encouraged and resulted in massive attendance at PTA meetings and other functions and strong support of our activities.

Being located in the low socioeconomic and educationally impoverished area gave impetus to our efforts in the segregated settings. Our school was very successful and proud of many in our community and in our school. The result is evidenced by the success of our students, many of whom have become highly successful in industrial, technological, scientific, legal, social, and educational pursuits.

After the integration of faculty, the role of parents decreased at River Road, and things were never the same. Efforts, however, were less intensified because of less encouragement by disinterested faculty. The influx of a vast majority of white teachers, and the removal of our better black teachers, resulted in changes regarding selection, management, and overall quality of teachers and teaching. Prior to this time, selection, assignment, and control of teachers and staff were primary responsibilities of the building principal. The staffing policy changed to the extent that the principal had little or no control over who became a part of the teaching staff.

The selection and assignment differences resulted in a decline in scope and intensity of efforts to enrich the lives of our students. No longer was effort put forth to employ individuals with skills beyond their specific area of expertise. Also, the school system no longer enforced its policy that attendance at PTA was required. Many, or rather most, of the teachers were ill-prepared and were unwilling to deal with our students—meaning black students—using effective methods and on the pupil's level. Hence, there was a dramatic decline in pupil progress along with more than quadruple the number of discipline problems.

Due to the attitudes of white parents and the downtown administrative personnel toward black teachers, students, and administrators, the situation saw very slow improvement. This resulted in much friction between parents and teachers. The school was subsequently zoned to receive white students from a comparable area just across the Flint River. Because of racial tensions and cultural experiences, the problems were compounded. The cooperation with school policies, activities, and projects ultimately differed greatly after integration.

Initially, white parents attended PTA and other school functions in great numbers out of concern for their children's new environment. However, after some time, everyone became comfortable with the new school and support declined. The loss of support was partially attributed to no longer having compulsion to cooperate with the school's programs and because of the community's having been divided. And this was no longer a one-community school.

United efforts of parents as well as the overall aggressiveness of the students seemed to be less evident after integration of the schools. Perhaps much of the decline can be attributed to such things as weakened pupil-teacher relationships, extension of school attendance area to include white communities, less effective strategies for selecting personnel, racial tensions, discipline differences by black and white teachers, community and personal attitudes toward the school, and the loss of effectively motivating parents to support the school. Integration in my opinion hurt black communities, principals, teachers, and students. We simply lost something. I think it was racial pride in our schools, drive and motivation to take control of the schools. To me, the "I can't" attitude rather than the "I can" attitude surfaced in our teachers, parents, and children after school desegregation.

My mother and my elementary school principal spoke candidly about how the school and home supported each other. They spoke about the importance of the community in assuring the stability of the school. Comer (1990) supports their beliefs by saying,

> When schools were an integral part of stable communities, teachers quite naturally reinforced parental and community values. At school, children easily formed bonds with adults and experienced a sense of continuity and stability, conditions that were highly conducive to learning. (p. 23)

From my mother and my elementary school principal, we learn that before school desegregation in their southwestern Georgia community, parents, teachers, and administrators examined the existing educational structure and revised it to meet the needs of African American children and the communities in which they lived. These individuals made the educational system a functional one for African American children and parents. The schools became tools that shaped and molded African American communities and that helped African American students and parents to fully understand *what* was taught, *why* it was taught, and *for what* roles African American children were preparing themselves. Last, but more important, we learn that parents, teachers, and administrators joined together to protect African American children against educational injustices and systematic genocide.

Parent Involvement After School Desegregation:
An Overview

Published a decade after school desegregation, Moynihan's (1965) report on African American families sparked debates that sometimes extended into the national media. The Moynihan report, as well as reports by other researchers, tended to highlight negative accounts of black urban life and education. For example, Etzkowitz and Schaflander (1969) wrote that "love, warmth, hygiene, education, and family stability [were] absent from Negroes" (p. 14) and that there were "practically no pluses in Negro ghetto culture. . .[only] bitterness and despair, nihilism, hopelessness, rootlessness, and all the symptoms of social integration in the poor speech, poor hygiene, and poor education" (p. 15). Haskins and Adams (1984) point out that the overwhelming evidence seemed to be on the side of a more pathological view of the poor. For example,

> They could not cope with life, their children, their economic status, the schools, nor society in general. Thus, the poor became the focus of large-scale social programs intended primarily to improve their children and themselves. Throughout the 1960s and 1970s, such parent programs gained momentum with support from the social and behavioral sciences. In addition, there was local pressure from disadvantaged groups themselves for greater opportunities, power, and influence. (pp. 347-348)

Only a few writers, such as Riessaman (1962) and Chilman (1966), emphasized the "overlooked positives" of disadvantaged groups and the strengths of poor families. In a more recent discussion, Reginald Clark (1983), in his book *Family Life and School Achievement: Why Poor Black Children Succeed or Fail*, dispels myths about the limitations of family structure or income on children's school achievement. To support his contentions, Clark conducted 10 intimate case studies of African American families in Chicago. All of these families had incomes at the poverty level, and one-parent and two-parent families were equally represented, as were families that had produced both high- and low-achieving children. Clark made detailed observations on the quality of home life, noting how family habits and interactions affected school success and what characteristics of family life provided children with "school survival skills," a complex set of behaviors, attitudes, and knowledge that are the essential elements in academic success.

Despite the fact that African American families have positive attributes and the desire to help their children, many school systems were unsuccessful in attempting to establish home-school partnerships with African American parents. Nevertheless, several school systems continued to reach out to these families. Their efforts were supported by two decades of federal programs and legislation for parent involvement (Head Start, 1965; Head Start Planned Variations, 1967-1971; Follow-Through Programs, 1967;

Follow-Through Planned Variations, 1968-1971; Education of All Handicapped Children Act, 1975; Title I, 1981, and its successor, Chapter I, 1974-1975). A major focus in all of these federal initiatives was recognizing parents as the principal influence on their children's development, thus acknowledging the importance of close cooperation between home and school.

Once the parent education movement was in motion, however, the following questions arose: Where was it going? Whom would it serve? How would it serve them? Ira Gordon (1979) emphasizes "the need to clarify the goals of parent education before plunging into program development, because different goals will pose different problems in implementation" (p. ix).

Several national reports—A Nation at Risk (National Commission on Excellence, 1983) and Becoming a Nation of Readers (Anderson, Hiebert, Scott, & Wilkinson, 1985)—have highlighted the importance of parents to their children's school success. Researchers such as Epstein (1987) have reported that "parent involvement is [still] on everyone's list of practices to make schools more effective, to help families create more positive learning environments, to reduce the risk of student failure, and to increase student success" (p. 1).

A number of researchers have described the kinds of roles that parents could assume (Berger, 1987; Henderson, Ooms, & Marburger, 1986). Berger states that parents could be involved as teachers of their own children, spectators, volunteers, paid employees, and policymakers. Henderson et al. provide a similar but slightly different list of roles parents could assume. They revealed that parents could be partners, collaborators, problem solvers, an audience, supporters, and advisers and/or co-decision makers. Even though these researchers identified the roles parents could assume and the critical need to involve them, several barriers prevented (and still prevent) African American parents from being involved in school.

Barriers to African American Parents' Involvement in Desegregated Schools

An interesting barrier to African American parent involvement is the way they are viewed by the school. Some school personnel believe that African American parents did not support and reinforce their children's school achievement. A statement by White (1975) expresses this view. If the family provided their children with school appropriate behaviors, then the school could do its job better, White said; however, if parents failed to do their job, "there may be little the professional can do to save the child from mediocrity" (p. 4).

Ron Edmonds, a strong advocate in the school effectiveness movement, vehemently disagrees with White's position. Ulric Neisser (1986) summarizes the remarks Edmonds made at a Cornell conference prior to his death on July 15, 1983. Edmonds argues that

> minority children's failure to learn can just as easily be seen as the school's failure to teach them. The fact that many poor and minority children fail to master the school curriculum does not reflect deficiencies in the children, but rather inadequacies in the schools themselves. Variability in the distribution of achievement among school-age children in the United States derives from variability in the nature of the schools to which they go. Achievement is therefore relatively independent of family background, at least if achievement is defined as pupil acquisition of basic schools skills. (p. 6)

Another barrier to African American parents' involvement was the way that schools solicited their assistance. The schools mainly communicated with these parents by sending home notes. Gandara (1989) warns that "a school does not become a part of a community by sending home notes" (p. 39). France and Meeks (1987) note that "functionally illiterate and illiterate parents [many low-income African American parents fit into this category] have been largely ignored by the schools, which go on sending home notices, report cards, homework assignments, information packets, survey forms, and permission slips as though they believe every parent can read and write" (p. 227). They suggest that

> when there are indications that parents are failing to respond to parent involvement programs because of literacy problems, teachers should take the time to call and arrange conferences during which they can describe some of the ways in which academic success can be fostered outside of direct instruction. (p. 226)

Epstein (1986) suggests that teachers can increase the amount of involvement of parents (including African American parents) who have little schooling. Epstein compares teachers who were active in seeking parental support with those who were not. Differences in these parents' reports of their involvement in learning activities at home from those of more educated parents were significant only in classrooms of teachers who failed to show leadership in parental involvement. Epstein concludes that teachers who got parents involved "mitigated the disadvantages typically associated with race, social class, and level of education" (p. 279).

Inviting African American Parents Back to School: Some Examples

More than 17 years ago, Sara Lawrence Lightfoot (1978) argued that

> the educational institution is a threatening monolith, not only in the sense that the power of knowledge makes [poor and racial minority parents] feel inadequate because many of them are illiterate and uneducated but because every bit of communication from the school comes as a negative appraisal of their child, a destructive comment about their lives. (p. 36)

In response to Lightfoot's contention, Purkey and Novak (1984) believe that school should be "the most inviting place in town" (p. 2). The four principles of invitational education outlined by Purkey and Novak (1984, p. 2) include the following:

1. People are able, valuable, and responsible and should be treated accordingly.
2. Teaching should be a cooperative activity.
3. People possess relatively untapped potential in all areas of human development.
4. This potential can best be realized by places, policies, and programs that are specifically designed to invite development and by people who are personally and professionally inviting to themselves and others.

Comer (1980, 1990) and Edwards (1991b), both African American researchers, have designed programs to invite African American parents back to school. The School Development Program designed by Comer and the book reading program, Parents as Partners in Reading Program, developed by Edwards, are presently being used in multiple sites around the country (see Edwards 1990a, 1990b). The Yale Child Study Center School Development Program was designed as a building-level attack on the barriers to appropriately serving at-risk students and their parents. Key to the Comer process is that schools must make adjustments to bring all adults in the school community together in a supportive way—to create an ethos and tone that are supportive of children. Comer and his colleagues created a school governance and management team that was led by the principal but was representative of all of the adults in the building. It included teachers selected by teachers, parents selected by parents, and a member of the mental-health team (made up of the support staff, including the social worker, psychologist, and special-education teacher). This group developed a comprehensive building plan focused on the school social climate and the academic program.

The small rural Louisiana community where Edwards developed the Parents as Partners in Reading Program was 80% black, and almost all of the students were poor. Edwards (1991b) reveals that although teachers requested that parents read to their children, they did not take into account that 40% of the parents were illiterate or semiliterate. The Parents as Partners in Reading Program provided a structure for these parents to participate in book-reading interactions with their children. The book-reading program became a vehicle for changing these low-income African American parents' attitudes toward school, themselves, and how they could contribute to their children's growth as readers and writers (see Edwards, 1995).

Conclusions and Recommendations

School systems in the inner cities and some in rural communities, which may be almost entirely populated with African American children, are in fact often dominated by a majority white and wealthy school board, majority white administrators, and definitely a majority white teaching staff. Teachers of color in the United States have dwindled to fewer than 5% within the last 5 years.

Racism permeates our society. Most teacher preparation programs require little or no work on racism or even multiculturalism and, when such study is included, it is extremely weak. School desegregation never had antiracist training as an agenda, goal, or requirement for staff who work with African American children and their parents. Moreover, most teachers do not live in the communities in which they teach. Could these factors have anything to do with why parent involvement looks so different in integrated schools than segregated schools? My response is, yes, they do. Schools will not become successful unless they stress the unique importance of African American people and their communities. Lightfoot (1978) reiterates this point by saying that "in order for schools to successfully teach black children, they will have to incorporate the cultural wisdom and experiences of black families and meaningfully collaborate with parents and community" (p. 129). Wright (1970) argues that "when schools are too largely removed from a sense of immediate responsibility to their clientele, education is in danger. The institution becomes the master rather the servant of those it teaches" (p. 270). Educators can no longer continue to think of equality in terms of "things" such as buildings, books, and curriculum. According to Hawkins (1970), "In all that is done in the name of equalization of opportunities, it is necessary that educators keep in mind that *what* is done is important, but *how* it is done is more important" (p. 43). The relationship between the home and the school must be one of depth.

The invitation for African American parents to come to school before school desegregation was evident by the personal accounts given by my mother and my elementary school principal. All parents, irrespective of their economic or social status, felt welcome to come to school. This should send a message to schools of today. Today's school personnel must closely examine their school's history to determine if past policies and practices made African American parents feel invited or uninvited. Epstein (1988) noted that "Schools of the same type serve different populations, have different histories of involving parents, have teachers and administrators with different philosophies, training, and skills in involving parents" (p. 58). Epstein's observation should encourage school personnel to ask themselves a number of questions:

- What is our school's history of involving African American parents?
- What is our school's philosophy regarding African American parents' involvement in school activities?
- What training and skills do we need for involving African American parents in school affairs?

In addition, schools must develop creative strategies that are culturally sensitive to African American parents. The programs developed by Comer (1980) and Edwards (1991b) are successful because they are culturally sensitive to African American parents. The key to a successful parent involvement program is to know the parents as individuals, with varying experiences, situations, and backgrounds. They differ in their relationships with their own children and in their feelings about school. Some have a high regard for education. For others, their children's schooling is a relived struggle amid more pressing concerns (see Edwards, 1991a). The goals and values of individual families will vary, and they may differ from those of the teacher and school. This individuality that parents, especially African American parents, bring to school involvement efforts challenges today's educators. When parent involvement strategies ignore these important variations, the efforts can be disappointing. When schools acknowledge the range in dispositions, backgrounds, experiences, and strengths among African American families, efforts to establish sound home-school communications and involvement are more successful.

References

Anderson, R. C., Hiebert, E., Scott, J. A., & Wilkinson, I. A. G. (1985). *Becoming a nation of readers: The report of the commission on reading.* Washington, DC: The National Institute of Education.

Bates, P. (1990). Desegregation: Can we get there from here? *Phi Delta Kappan, 72*(1), 8-17.

Bell, D. (1983). Learning from our losses: Is school desegregation still feasible in the 1980s? *Phi Delta Kappan, 64*(8), 572-575.

Berger, E. H. (1987). *Parents as partners in education: The school and home working together.* Columbus, OH: Merrill.

Billingsley, A. (1968). *Black families in white America.* Englewood Cliffs, NJ: Prentice Hall.

Brown v. Topeka Board of Education, 347 U.S. 483 (1954).

Chilman, C. S. (1966). *Growing up poor.* Washington, DC: U.S. Department of Health, Education, and Welfare.

Clark, R. M. (1983). *Family life and school achievement.* Chicago: University of Chicago Press.

Cobb-Scott, J. (1985). The King case: Implications for educators. In C. K. Brooks (Ed.), *Tapping potential: English and language arts for the black learner* (pp. 63-71). Urbana, IL: National Council of Teachers of English.

Comer, J. P. (1980). *School power: Implications of an intervention project.* New York: Free Press.

Comer, J. P. (1990). Home, school, and academic learning. In J. I. Goodlad & P. Keating (Eds.), *Access to knowledge: An agenda for our nation's schools.* New York: College Entrance Examination Board.

Edwards, P. A. (1990a). *Parents as partners in reading: A family literacy training program.* Chicago: Children's Press.

Edwards, P. A. (1990b). *Talking your way to literacy. A program to help nonreading parents prepare their children for reading.* Chicago: Children's Press.

Edwards, P. A. (1991a). *Differentiated parenting or parentally appropriate: The missing link in efforts to develop a structure for parent involvement in schools.* Paper presented at the third annual roundtable on Home-School-Community Partnerships, Chicago.

Edwards, P. A. (1991b). Fostering early literacy through parent coaching. In E. Hiebert (Ed.), *Literacy for a diverse society: Perspectives, programs, and policies* (pp. 199-213). New York: Teachers College Press.

Edwards, P. A. (1995). Connecting African American families and youth to the school's reading program: Its meaning for school and community literacy. In V. L. Gadsden & D. Wagner (Eds.), *Literacy among African American youth: Issues in learning, teaching, and schooling* (pp. 263-281). Cresskill, NJ: Hampton Press.

Epstein, J. L. (1986). Parents' reactions to teacher practices of parent involvement. *Elementary School Journal, 86*, 27-94.

Epstein, J. L. (1987). Parent involvement: State education agencies should lead the way. *Community Education Journal, 14*(4), 4-10.

Epstein, J. L. (1988). How do we improve programs for parent involvement? *Educational Horizons, 66*(2), 58-59.

Etzkowitz, H., & Schaflander, G. M. (1969). *Ghetto crisis: Riots or reconciliation?* Boston: Little, Brown.

Foster, M. (1991). Just got to find a way: Case studies of the lives and practices of exemplary black high school teachers. In M. Foster (Ed.), *Readings on equal education: Qualitative investigations into schools and schooling* (pp. 273-309). New York: AMS Press.

France, M. G., & Meeks, J. W. (1987). Parents who can't read: What the schools can do. *Journal of Reading, 31*, 222-227.

Gandara, P. (1989). "Those children are ours": Moving toward community. *NEA Today, 7*, 38-43.

Gordon, I. J. (1979). Parent education: A position paper. In W. G. Hill, P. Fox, & C. D. Jones (Eds.), *Families and schools: Implementing parent education* (Report No. 121, pp. 1-5). Denver, CO: Education Commission of the States.

Hacker, A. (1992). *Two nations: Black and white, separate, hostile, unequal.* New York: Scribner's.

Hale-Benson, J. (1990). Achieving equal educational outcomes for black children. In A. Barona & E. E. Garcia (Eds.), *Children at risk: Poverty, minority status, and other issues in educational equity* (pp. 201-215). Washington, DC: National Association of School Psychologists.

Haskins, R., & Adams, D. (1984). Parent education and public policy: Synthesis and recommendations. In R. Haskins & D. Adams (Eds.), *Parent education and public policy* (pp. 346-373). Norwood, NJ: Ablex.

Hawkins, L. (1970). Urban schoolteaching: The personal touch. In N. Wright, Jr. (Ed.), *What black educators are saying* (pp. 43-47). New York: Hawthorn.

Henderson, A. T., Ooms, T., & Marburger, C. L. (1986). *Beyond the bake sale: An educator's guide to working with parents.* Columbia, MD: National Committee for Citizens in Education.

Irvine, R. W., & Irvine, J. J. (1983). The impact of the desegregation process on the education of black students: Key variables. *Journal of Negro Education, 52*(4), 410-422.

Johnson, C. S. (1954). Some significant social and educational implications of the U.S. Supreme Court's decision. *Journal of Negro Education, 23*, 364-371.

Kozol, J. (1991). *Savage inequalities: Children in America's schools.* New York: Crown.

Larry P. v. Riles, 1972.

Lightfoot, S. L. (1978). *Worlds apart: Relationships between families and schools.* New York: Basic Books.

Lightfoot, S. L. (1980). Families as educators: The forgotten people of *Brown.* In D. Bell (Ed.), *Shades of Brown: New perspectives on school desegregation.* New York: Teachers College Press.

Lomotey, K. (1993). African American principals: Bureaucrat/administrators and ethno-humanists. *Urban Education, 27*(4), 395-412.

Martin Luther King Junior Elementary School Children v. Ann Arbor School District Board, 473 F. Supp. 1371 (E.D. Mich. 1979).

Moynihan, D. P. (1965). *The Negro family: The case for national action.* Washington, DC: Office of Policy Planning and Research, U.S. Department of Labor.

National Commission on Excellence in Education. (1983). *A nation at risk: The imperative for educational reform.* Washington, DC: U.S. Department of Education.

Neisser, U. (1986). New answers to an old question. In U. Neisser (Ed.), *The school achievement of minority children: New perspectives* (pp. 1-17). Hillsdale, NJ: Lawrence Erlbaum.

Purkey, W. W., & Novak, J. M. (1984). *Inviting school success: A self-concept approach to teaching and learning.* Belmont, CA: Wadsworth.

Riessaman, F. (1962). *The culturally deprived child.* New York: Harper & Row.

Swanson, H. L., & Watson, B. L. (1989). *Educational and psychological assessment of exceptional children: Theories, strategies, and applications.* Columbus, OH: Merrill.

Trent, S. C. (1992). School choice for African American children who live in poverty: A commitment to equity or more of the same? *Urban Education, 27*(3), 291-307.

Trent, S. C., & Artiles, A. J. (1993). *Serving culturally diverse students with behavior disorders: Broadening current perspectives.* Manuscript submitted for publication.

White, B. L. (1975). *The first three years of life.* Englewood Cliffs, NJ: Prentice Hall.

Wright, N., Jr. (1970). Our schools. In N. Wright, Jr. (Ed.), *What black educators are saying* (pp. 269-271). New York: Hawthorn.

8

⊠

High-Quality Schooling
for African American Students

RONALD D. HENDERSON

NANCY M. GREENBERG

JEFFREY M. SCHNEIDER

OSCAR URIBE, JR.

RICHARD R. VERDUGO

Many school desegregation experts would agree that desegregating the public schools was an effort to equalize the quality of schooling. It was argued that racial imbalance was linked to educational imbalance—that moving African American students from "bad" to "good" schools would equalize educational access and opportunity. But if the resultant educational attainments of African American students are taken to be indices of the success or failure of this effort, then desegregation has failed miserably.

Could it be that the decision makers and advocates for the equality of educational access and opportunities focused their attention and energies

AUTHOR'S NOTE: With the exception of R. D. Henderson, the authors' names are listed alphabetically. The views expressed in this chapters are not necessarily those of the National Education Association.

on only one small part of the problem? The same question applies to those who would focus attention simply on improving the test scores of students in predominantly African American schools. Should not the solution be sought in the learning environment itself—in the conditions of teaching and learning that enable quality outcomes? Nowadays, such a viewpoint makes greater sense than tinkering with the demographics of the student population.

The purpose of this chapter is to present and describe a different approach to improving education quality. Rather than focusing on the demographics of schooling or the singular attributes of programs, our research focuses on improving the conditions of teaching and learning at the school building. We propose looking at a school's organizational features and quality outcomes.

In addressing this issue, we have organized the remainder of this chapter in the following manner. Section 2 is divided into three subsections: (a) a brief recounting of the school quality and desegregation literature, (b) a review of the literature concerned with the educational achievement of African American students, and (c) a brief history of the Conditions of Teaching and Learning study (CTL). Section 3 describes our methods, sample, and measures and also examines the relationship between several kinds of CTL measures and the educational achievement of a sampling of students, almost all of whom are African American. Section 4 summarizes our findings and draws several conclusions from our analyses.

Background

The Problems of Desegregation as a Quality of Schooling Variable

After years of assessing the effects of desegregation on academic performance, there is yet to be a clear, concise answer as to whether the academic accomplishments of African American students have actually improved. Researchers do find statistically significant relationships (both positive and negative) that persist even after controlling for socioeconomic status (SES), gender, and other relevant factors. But inconclusive research findings have led to varying conceptions of the size and impact of the effect.

Research on the effects of school desegregation on the academic achievement of African American students can be classified into two basic approaches. The first approach has been large-scale national studies. An outstanding example of this approach is the work of Coleman (1966), who concluded that other factors (e.g., SES) were more important than desegregation efforts in predicting the achievement of African American students. A variant of this approach was the Bridge, Judd, and Moock (1979) attempt to synthesize desegregation research. They concluded that African American students attending predominantly white, high-SES schools score higher on achievement tests. Although this approach provided much valuable information, it also obscured differences that may have existed within individual districts. In any event, much of the early debate about the desegregation-achievement relationship grew from the review of single studies or variation within a small number of studies (e.g., Armor, 1972, 1978; Pettigrew, 1975).

A second approach to studying desegregation and achievement involved analyses of the literature. An example of this approach was Weinberg's 1975 review of the literature. In both this project and in his later reexamination (1977), Weinberg included an amazingly complete review of the research literature on African American school achievement. However, Weinberg made little or no attempt to control for the methodological competencies of the studies he included. In another example of this approach, St. John (1975) sought to remedy Weinberg's deficiency. St. John included 43 studies classified according to research design, which allowed her to observe the relationship between methodology and the impact of desegregation on student achievement. She concluded that although the quality of the studies was too nebulous and the results too mixed to lead to any definitive statements, the preponderance of work suggested that school desegregation improved the achievement of African American students.

In 1977, Bradley and Bradley also conducted a review of the research literature. They found so many methodological problems that they concluded it was impossible to draw accurate generalizations about the effects of desegregation on the academic achievement of African American students. The authors, however, did not attempt to expand knowledge of research methodology beyond St. John's analysis. In 1980, Krol reviewed 71 studies applying a meta-analysis framework. This ensured that individual studies were screened for minimum adequacy and that results were converted to standardized estimates based on a ratio of test means to their standard deviations, thus allowing researchers to better estimate the magnitude of desegregation effects. Krol concluded that desegregation had a very small positive (but statistically nonsignificant) effect on the academic achievement of African American students of about .16 of a standard deviation. In effect, this amounts to between 1.5 and 3 months of progress during an academic year.

Crain and Mahard (1978) also used meta-analysis to study the effects of desegregation on minority student achievement. They found that desegregation raised the achievement test scores of African American students. Crain and Mahard intentionally included studies with weaker designs in order to test the impact of design on the reported desegregation effects. They concluded that the size of the overall effect mean was a nonsignificant .065 of a standard deviation. However, a significant positive effect of .3 of a standard deviation was found under two conditions—if a plan was implemented before first grade and if it was implemented in metropolitan areas.

Wortman (1982) felt that Crain and Mahard's approach was flawed because it allowed for the inclusion of many methodologically flawed studies and "cross sectional surveys" lacking the necessary statistical information to analyze desegregation effects. Therefore, Wortman undertook a meta-analysis using 31 studies that met his requirements concerning minimum methodological quality. Wortman concluded that desegregation had a definite positive effect on the achievement of African American youths.

Given the social importance of this body of research and the many theoretical and methodological problems plaguing this research, the National Institute of Education (NIE) (1984) commissioned a set of papers and a conference in which these papers were read and discussed. The objectives of the conference were to clarify the desegregation-achievement link, identify areas of consensus, and reconcile differences of interpretation. Principal participants in this project included Robert Crain, Paul Wortman, David Armor, Norman Miller, Walter Stephan, Herbert Walberg, and Thomas Cook. These participants agreed upon a comprehensive set of criteria for selecting studies to be analyzed. Upon applying their criteria, they discovered that only 19 studies could be included. From these 19 studies, the panel concluded that African American students make slight gains in reading when they are taught in desegregated schools, but no gains in mathematics.

Reflecting on these approaches, we have concluded that studying desegregation as a quality of schooling variable is probably a mistake. First, desegregation cannot be treated as if it were a uniform program in all racially mixed schools. Rather, desegregation is a complex process and needs to be studied cautiously. Racial balance does not necessarily change power structures or attitudes within schools (Cohen, 1980), and it takes more than racially based ratios to "restore the victims of discriminatory conduct to the position that they would have occupied in the absence of such conduct" (*Bradley v. Milliken*, 1974). Also, although lower courts in the South frequently required more than moving pupils (sometimes mandating remedial education, the desegregation of teachers, and in-service training), it was not until *Bradley v. Milliken II* (1977) that the Supreme Court ruled that a broad array of components related to educational quality were essential to redress the wrongs of a segregated educational system. District court decisions in Wilmington (*Evans v. Buchanan,* 1978) and Cleveland (*Reed v. Rhodes,* 1978) followed the same pattern.

Perhaps desegregation has important effects on African American student achievement, but the nature of these effects may vary with type of student, type of school, type of community, SES, gender, and other related factors. Perhaps desegregation does not have a single effect, positive or negative, on the academic achievement of African American students, but rather some strategies help, some hurt, and still others make no difference whatsoever. It is clear to us that focusing simply on demographic issues detracts from focusing on improving schools.

School Quality Factors and the Academic Achievement of African American Students

It is only recently that we have understood enough about attaining quality outcomes to carry out the Supreme Court's mandate in *Bradley v. Milliken II* (1977). No strategy can achieve quality unless it begins with an understanding of desired outcomes, and with an understanding about how different schooling practices produce different results. The importance of creating high-quality schools for all types of students is underscored by legal and demographic trends that indicate most African American students will continue to attend schools that are predominantly African American.

The research literature on the academic achievement of African American students is quite extensive and covers several major determinants. These factors fit quite nicely into three areas: family background, student traits and psychology, and school factors. In brief, research findings within the first two of these three areas can be summarized in this fashion (see Verdugo, 1981, for a review). Generally, the greater the socioeconomic resources of students, the better (when all else is constant) their educational achievement (Luster & McAdoo, 1994). Moreover, students who are more motivated, have high educational and occupational expectations, and have certain kinds of coping skills perform better in school (Pollard, 1989). However, the effects that school factors have on African American student achievement are difficult to determine.

Studies of the climate that schools perpetuate offer some evidence of the influences of school factors on the academic achievement of African American students. Such factors as teacher expectations about student potential and a curriculum that emphasizes the basics are found to affect all students, including African Americans. These findings emerge in the recent literature on Catholic schools. For example, Bryk, Lee, and Holland (1993, p. 207) use their analysis of Catholic schools to develop a set of characteristics they feel would enhance student learning, including the learning of African American students. They conclude that effective Catholic high schools function on the basis of four foundation characteristics: a delimited technical core, communal organization, decentralized governance, and an inspirational ideology.

The authors argue that these school characteristics are able to transcend any background traits (e.g., poverty; race, socioeconomic status) that students bring with them to school and transform them into achievers.

Earlier effective school and Total Quality Management (TQM) research has defined a number of characteristics that are found in a quality school. This research has found that a quality school is one where all participants are able and willing to collect and use data in assessing all processes. Furthermore, all participants must be encouraged to base their educational decisions upon those data. In addition, all participants must perceive that they are responsible for accomplishing the school's objectives and that the quality of their activities and decisions is perceived inside and outside the school.

Staffs in quality schools are found to have high expectations, are highly efficacious, practice broad cooperation, and possess a clear sense of purpose about student achievement (Brookover & Schneider, 1975). African American students, as well as other students, perform well (Brookover & Schneider, 1975; Brookover et al., 1978; Eubanks & Levine, 1977) when staff hold them to high standards for behavior and achievement. Also, cooperative learning (Johnson & Johnson, 1991; Slavin, 1983) has demonstrated great value for directly increasing student outcomes and indirectly advancing the organizational teamwork of employees. Furthermore, nonacademic factors (e.g., conduct codes, school symbols, activities) play a key role in a quality school. There needs to be a uniform, multicultural code of conduct, firm discipline, and procedures and practices that are perceived as fair by all groups (Lincoln, 1976; NIE, 1978; Pettigrew, 1975; Rist, 1978; Willie & Greenblatt, 1980). In addition, if African American students are to attend postsecondary school and gain access to job networks, they need quality counseling (McPartland & Crain, 1978). Counselors are especially critical if the education of African American students is to lead to higher education, higher-status occupations, and higher incomes. Counselors must be carefully selected and trained to be fair and not to steer low-SES youth into low-status vocational programs and high-SES youth into college preparatory and other high-status programs (Cole, 1978; Oakes, 1985; Rosenbaum, 1976).

Quality schools require leadership and commitment from the top. Although the principal often sets the school's tone and teacher expectations (Egerton, 1977; NIE, 1978; Noblit, 1979), he or she cannot accomplish school goals without the assistance and leadership of school staff, local associations, parents, district administration, and students. A school's and district's leadership must be socioeconomically and ethnically integrated (Willie & Greenblatt, 1980), both to provide a basis for trust on the part of the community and to provide role models for children (Cohen, 1980; Schofield, 1978).

The importance of staff development for assuring quality decisions cannot be overstated. Gay (1978), Forehand, Ragosta, and Rock (1976), and Orfield (1975) have all explained the importance of effective in-service training for teachers, administrators, school boards, and all supporting staff. Both teaching and nonteaching staff (Lincoln, 1976) need to know how to teach children who may have had inferior schooling, to teach heterogeneous groups of children, and to carry out most of the educational and institutional changes required to attain quality outcomes. Training must include:

- Self-analysis to avoid stereotyping and other kinds of discriminatory behavior of which most people are unaware (Gay, 1978; Rist, 1978)
- Substantive knowledge of different groups' histories, attitudes, behaviors, and learning systems
- Techniques for teaching heterogeneous classes
- Techniques for solving daily problems, avoiding crises, and relieving apprehensions (cf. Pettigrew, 1975)

There is as much variety in ability and learning styles in schools serving African American students as there are students. If these schools are to achieve total quality, then all programs and policies must be assessed and analyzed on how they relate to desired outcomes for individual students and for the total student population. TQM requires using tools that we know work and creating a school climate that is favorable to achievement and healthy attitudes among students of high and low social status.

Educational Reform, Effective Schools, and Total Quality Management

In this section, we argue that quality outcomes can be achieved for African American students through the implementation of organizational strategies at the school level. In effect, this approach follows the TQM strategy that urges organizations to employ Statistical Product Control (SPC) techniques. SPC is aimed at product quality control *throughout* the production process and not through postproduction inspection.

Recently, the NEA completed a national study of its members in which the relationship between teachers' perceptions about the Conditions of Teaching and Learning (CTL) in their schools and the achievement of students was examined. The questionnaire used in this national study was based upon a theoretical framework that merged organizational quality and the effective schools literature.

Quality Schools

There is currently much debate about the meaning and measurement of quality and productivity in both industry and education. Both sectors are far from having a definitive answer to the quality issue. Nevertheless, one thing is perfectly clear—that quality systems are multidimensional. A number of essential conditions are provided below. Although these were originally developed for industry (Garvin, 1984), with a little modification they are just as likely to describe high-quality schools.

- Performance: Students demonstrate knowledge acquisition and application.
- Transferability: Students translate what they learn to solving other problems.
- Reliability: Students use what they have learned from one instance to the next.
- Equity: All students (not just a few) demonstrate high-quality work.
- Durability: Students gain lasting skills and competencies, which enable them to flourish after the formal schooling experience.
- Serviceability: What students need to know and how students learn are constantly assessed and updated for a future in which change is the only constant.
- Aesthetics: All participants (e.g., students, parents, and all school staff) are pleased with the school life and the educational experiences provided by the school.
- Perception: The school has a reputation for quality within and beyond its walls.

If a school does not reach a high rank on each of these essential conditions, it cannot be considered to have achieved total quality.

Organizational Patterns of Quality Schools

Bidwell (1965) pioneered the notion of viewing schools as systems that could exert education effects net of other factors. Since then, the education world has been massaging the concept. In the early 1970s, this idea emerged as "effective schools."

Effective schools research can be seen as a real departure from earlier education theory, which hypothesized that the problems of schooling in the United States could be solved by spending more money, by perfecting new curricula that could be made to work under any conditions (and would, thus, be both "student and teacher proof"), or by changing the student socioeconomic status ratio (e.g., busing). Instead, effective schools research (Brookover et al., 1978; Edmonds, 1982; Lezotte, 1990) found that all academic learning takes place within an organizational, social psychological context. It defines that context as having:

- A productive school climate and culture emphasizing the importance of learning, high expectations about student achievement, high expectations about teacher quality, and a general problem-solving orientation
- A strong leadership guiding the instructional program, with a continual striving by teachers and administrators to improve instructional effectiveness
- A focus on student acquisition of central learning skills, with curriculum based on clear goals and objectives
- A grouping of students to promote effective appropriate instruction with heterogeneity in required courses and enriched learning as the norm
- A school day in which time is used for learning activities
- A learning process that is both pleasant and closely monitored
- An orderly environment in which discipline is firm and consistent
- A positive relationship between the community and the school

Research has documented that many of these conditions (as well as others—e.g., shared high expectations, high efficacy, broad cooperation, a clear sense of purpose) are related to student achievement (Brookover & Schneider, 1975; Rosenholtz, 1989). There are, however, three important problems with the research to date about the traits of quality schools that effective schools research has thus far identified. First, it fails to address how one gains and maintains commitment from school participants. Second, it fails to address how one monitors such a system. Third, the guiding principles are so broadly stated that confusing, contradictory, and educationally ineffective behaviors have been described as effective schools practices. The first two problems can be easily addressed by applying the SPC techniques advocated in the TQM approach.

Total Quality Management and Statistical Product Control

SPC is based on the fundamental premise that all workers participate in the decision-making process. First, such participation tends to increase workers' commitment. Second, SPC is used to maximize product quality through control of work processes rather than through postproduction inspection. SPC uses graphical tools to monitor and improve the system (Ishikawa, 1982; Messina, 1987). These graphic tools are used in combination with group problem-solving methods (e.g., brainstorming) and nominal group interview techniques (e.g., focus groups) to statistically "control" processes through the identification and removal of common and specific causes that take a system out of stability. Once a process has attained a state of statistical control, it is expected to consistently provide defect-free products or services. Producing products and services without defects eliminates waste and rework costs and minimizes inspection costs; this ultimately leads to increased productivity. We have, of course, simplified the description of SPC. For elaboration, see Deming (1988), Ishikawa (1982), and Messina (1987). However, if this body of research can be summarized in a short phrase, it would be: the making of good decisions, greater worker involvement in decision making, and a focus on the system rather than on individuals.

TQM is an organizational philosophy that grew out of SPC techniques. It was used in the defense industry to maximize product quality during World War II. Decreases in demand after the war led to diminished use of SPC techniques by U.S. industry. After the war, W. Edwards Deming took TQM organizational principles to Japan and turned around that economy. Today, the Deming Prize is one of the most coveted industrial prizes in Japan. In recent years, the United States has rediscovered Deming and his 14 organizational principles, which prescribe that productive organizations must do the following:

1. Have a constancy of purpose
2. Only accept high-quality work and never accept negativism
3. Never practice mass inspection but constantly analyze all results
4. Base decisions on an analysis of quality, not upon cost
5. Constantly and forever improve production and service through teamwork and analysis
6. Constantly train and retrain
7. Have leadership that helps people do a better job and that learns by objective methods who is in need of individual help
8. Make sure that employees feel secure to ask questions or take a position
9. Never have barriers between staff areas, using teams to solve or foresee problems
10. Never use slogans, exhortations, and targets without a method of reaching results
11. Never use numerical quotas, because numbers do not equal quality
12. Eliminate all barriers to pride of workmanship
13. Educate all staff about new methods, including teamwork and statistical techniques
14. Demonstrate commitment from the top

A growing and impressive body of research shows that SPC principles can increase the quality of schools. However, like the effective schools traits, TQM principles are so broadly defined that they allow interpretations with negative organizational and educational consequences. This is especially important for African American students; it will take more than minor tinkering at the edges for quality and change to alter power structures and attitudes (Cohen, 1980) that are the vestige of the historic inequities and discriminatory practices of de facto and de jure dual school systems.

The Conditions of Teaching and Learning (CTL) Project

In 1988, the National Education Association undertook a project on the working conditions of teachers. After reviewing both the effective schools and the TQM literatures, the CTL study team decided that an excellent framework would involve a melding of these education and productivity theories. As a starting point, the CTL team translated the Deming principles for quality organizations and the effective schools traits into 11 Educational Quality Points (EQPs). These points served as the basis for a national survey of how a school's conditions of teaching and learning define a quality educational environment for all students. These 11 EQPs were not intended to be a direct translation of effective schools traits or TQM principles but rather were to focus on the essences of each. They were to be inclusive of all essential elements that can be used in creating quality schools. The following are the CTL educational quality points.

1. There is a shared understanding about achievable educational outcomes.
2. All school-community groups are involved in improving education.
3. Everyone believes that all students can achieve under the right conditions.
4. Everyone is consistently involved in identifying and remedying barriers.
5. Barriers are eliminated through a cooperative problem-solving process.
6. Assessments of work and progress toward goals are performed daily by everyone.
7. Programs, not individuals, are assessed.
8. Assessment results are actually used in making decisions.
9. All decisions on the selection of programs and materials are based on their quality and appropriateness for student outcomes.
10. There is ongoing, consistent quality staff development.
11. There is consistent, two-way, nonthreatening communication.

Methodology

Respondents for the CTL study were gathered from a national randomly stratified sample of NEA teacher members. The stratifying factor was NEA region. In total, 1,583 fully completed responses were gathered for analysis. Three kinds of school-quality scales were developed for the CTL study. The first was an overall school quality index. The second was the set of 11 EQPs. The third comprised 35 quality educational tools that a school could implement in order to improve its educational environment.

The Total Quality Index (TQI): The Total Quality Index (TQI) is simply a linear combination of the 11 EQPs:

$$TQI = \Sigma EQP_i \ (i = 1 \text{ to } 11)$$

where TQI = total quality index, EQP_i = educational quality points. The alpha reliability for TQI is .81. Using this scale, we have been able to develop a single assessment of school quality.

Educational Quality Points (EQPs): The 11 educational quality points were constructed originally from the 11 education points used in the CTL questionnaire. For each EQP, a number of questions were asked of respondents. Each set of items was then factor analyzed (common factor analysis with orthogonal rotation). The 11 EQP scales were then constructed by factor scaling, for example, linear combinations of the items weighted by their factor score. There were only two EQPs for which this procedure was not used, because only one or two items emerged from the factor analysis:

$$EQP_i = \Sigma EQP_{ij} \ (i = 1 \dots 11, j = 1 \dots k)$$

where k varies by the EQP concept.

Educational Quality Tools (EQTs): We factor analyzed items for each of the 11 EQPs. Most of the 11 EQPs consist of three or more questions, with the exception of "Assessment results are actually used in making decisions," which consists of only two questions. Consequently, this was not subjected to factor analysis. The remaining 10 EQPs were factor analyzed (varimax factor analysis with orthogonal rotation), which produced 35 independent organizational tools that schools can use to build and maintain quality outcomes. We then analyzed how well the existence or lack of existence of these tools predict student achievement, which was measured by asking teachers to rate the level of academic achievement of students in their schools. This included both overall student achievement, as well as African American and other nonwhite student achievement. The options were:

Primarily low achieving = 1
Primarily average achieving = 2
Primarily high achieving = 3

Table 8.1 displays the 35 educational quality tools.

Table 8.1   The 35 Educational Quality Tools (EQTs)

1.1 Parents and school employees are commited to long-range continuous improvements.
1.2 School administrators are commited to long-range continuous improvements.
1.3 Everyone shares a clear explicit goal.
2.0 All school community groups are involved in improving education.
3.1 Teachers, students, and parents believe that all students can learn.
3.2 School and district administration believe that all students can learn.
3.3 School has adequate space.
3.4 School has adequate supplies.
3.5 School has adequate support personnel.
3.6 School has available Psychological and Social Work services.
3.7 School is a learning environment for both employees and students.
4.1 Everyone seeks barriers to quality.
4.2 There is a general willingness to remove barriers to learning.
4.3 The educational personnel work to remove barriers to learning.
4.4 The students and parents work to remove barriers to learning.
4.5 The school and district administration works to remove barriers to learning.
5.0 Barriers to learning are removed through a cooperative problem-solving process.
6.1 There is daily assessment of students for learning by teachers.
6.2 There is daily assessment of students for learning by administrators.
6.3 Assessments use teacher-designed tests.
6.4 Assessments use oral classroom activities.
6.5 Assessments use exhibitions.
6.6 Assessments use student background information.
7.1 Programs are assessed every day.
7.2 Teachers consistently rate program quality.
8.0 Assessment results are actually used in making decisions.
9.1 Materials are selected based on their quality.
9.2 Materials are selected based on their appropriateness to student needs.
9.3 Materials are not selected based on their cost.
10.1 There is ongoing, consistent, quality staff development on teamwork, on teaching techniques, and on school-community group involvement.
10.2 There is ongoing, consistent, quality staff development that is a high-quality, state-of-the-art, practical experience for all school employees.
11.1 There is constant, two-way, nonthreatening communication between school employees and school administration.
11.2 There is constant, two-way, nonthreatening communication between the school and district administration.
11.3 There is constant, two-way, nonthreatening communication among teachers.
11.4 All communication takes place within a climate for innovation.

Results

Two models will be described in this section. The first one examined the effects of the EQPs on student achievement, both overall student achievement and African American and other nonwhite student achievement. The second model looked at the effects of the EQT on students overall and on African American and other nonwhite students.

The Educational Quality Points Model

The results of this analysis can be found in Table 8.2.

Overall Student Achievement. Of the 15 items (11 EQPs plus 4 control items) in the EQP model for overall student achievement, 7 emerged as important predictors. Among the control items, the percentage of African American and/or nonwhite students tended to reduce overall student achievement, whereas parental SES increased overall student achievement. In this case, it appears that because African American and/or nonwhite student achievement tends to be lower than the achievement of whites, the effect is to reduce overall student achievement.

Of the 11 EQPs, 5 emerged as important predictors of overall student achievement. The only negative effect on overall student achievement was exerted by ongoing, consistent staff development. The explanation we offer is that very little staff development occurs and only in high SES schools and in those that are already experiencing substantial problems. Thus by controlling for SES, we are finding the negative relationship.

The remaining quality points exerting significant effects were positively related to overall student achievement. These items were the following:

- Assessment results are actually used in making decisions.
- Everyone believes that all students can achieve under the right conditions.
- Barriers are eliminated through a cooperative problem-solving process.
- There is a shared understanding about achievable educational outcomes.

African American and Nonwhite Student Achievement. For African American and other nonwhite students, nine items emerged as important predictors. In terms of control items, four items were important predictors. First, African American and other nonwhite students in middle and elementary schools had lower achievements than their counterparts in high schools. These

Table 8.2   OLS Estimates of Models of Student Achievement (Betas): The EQP Model

Predictor		All Students	African American and Other Nonwhite Students
EQP1	There is a shared understanding about achievable educational outcomes	.0698**	−.0024
EQP2	All school-community groups are involved in improving education	.0383	.0166
EQP3	Everyone believes that all students can achieve under the right conditions	.0971*	.0736*
EQP4	Everyone is consistently involved in identifying and remedying barriers	.0753*	.0736*
EQP5	Barriers are eliminated through a cooperative problem-solving process	.0246	.0663*
EQP6	Assessments of work and progress toward goals are performed daily by everyone	.0114	.0603**
EQP7	Programs, not individuals, are assessed	.0203	−.0200
EQP8	Assessment results are actually used in making decisions	.0409**	.0277
EQP9	All decisions on the selection of programs and materials are based on their quality and appropriateness for student outcomes	−.0474	−.0588**
EQP10	There is ongoing, consistent quality staff development	−.0504**	−.0345
EQP11	There is consistent, two-way, nonthreatening communication	−.0149	−.0284
SES		.3557*	.2082*
Percentage African American and other nonwhite		−.2046*	−.1915*
Elementary School		.0361	−.0544**
Middle School		−.0056	−.0596**
Adjusted R^2		.30	.15

$*p < .05; **p < .10.$
OLS = ordinary least squares.

results suggest to us that there may be a major weeding-out effect operating here among African American and/or nonwhite students. That is, those who make it into high schools are those who have been best able to survive academically. This, of course, reinforces the importance of early intervention strategies. Second, the percentage of the student body that is African

American and/or nonwhite exerted a negative effect on the achievements of African American and nonwhite students. In contrast, parental SES, as we expected, positively enhanced the academic achievement of African American and nonwhite students.

In terms of our EQPs, five items emerged as important predictors of African American and other nonwhite student achievement. Only the selection process used in selecting resources and materials had a negative effect on the achievement of African American and other nonwhite students. In predominantly African American schools, the selection criteria are too often the cost of the material and too infrequently its appropriateness to student needs. The remainder of those quality points emerging as important predictors of African American and nonwhite student achievement were positively related to achievement:

- Barriers are eliminated through a cooperative problem-solving process.
- Assessments of work and progress toward goals are performed daily by everyone.
- Everyone believes that all students can achieve under the right conditions.

Educational Quality Tools Model

The results of this analysis can be found in Table 8.3.

Overall Student Achievement. Among the control items, parental SES and percentage of the students who are African American and/or nonwhite exert important effects on overall student achievement. As was expected, whereas parental SES positively enhances overall student achievement, the percentage of African American and nonwhite students tends to reduce it. Again, we suspect that because African American and other nonwhite student achievement tends to be lower, it tends to lower assessments of the achievements of all students.

Of the educational quality tools, eight emerge as important predictors of overall student achievement. Three of these items exert negative effects on overall student achievement.

- Barriers to quality are sought by everyone.
- Programs are assessed every day.
- Assessment results are actually used in making decisions.

Table 8.3   OLS Estimates, Expanded Model: Student Achievement: The EQT Model

Predictor		Overall Students	African American and Other Nonwhite Students
EQP1.1	Parents and school employees are commited to long-range continuous improvements	.0520**	−.0118
EQP1.2	School administrators are committed to long-range continuous improvements	.0325	−.0108
EQP1.3	Everyone shares a clear explicit goal	−.0465	−.0514
EQP2	All school community groups are involved in improving education	.0215	.0042
EQP3.1	Teachers, students, and parents believe that all students can learn	.0410	.1080*
EQP3.2	School and district administration believe that all students can learn	.0269	−.0154
EQP3.3	School has adequate space	.0017	−.0412
EQP3.4	School has adequate supplies	.0459	.0273
EQP3.5	School has adequate support personnel	−.0410	−.0467
EQP3.6	School has available Psychological and Social Work services	−.0098	.0094
EQP3.7	School is a learning environment for both employees and students	.0253	.0469
EQP4.1	Everyone seeks barriers to quality	−.1436*	−.0505
EQP4.2	There is a general willingness to remove barriers to learning	−.0458	−.0595
EQP4.3	The educational personnel work to remove barriers to learning	.0081	−.0283
EQP4.4	The students and parents work to remove barriers to learning	.1337*	.0934*
EQP4.5	The school and district administration works to remove barriers to learning	.0381	.0077
EQP5	Barriers to learning are removed through a cooperative problem - solving process	.0063	.0336
EQP6.1	There is daily assessment of students for learning by teachers	−.0098	.0088
EQP6.2	There is daily assessment of students for learning by administrators	−.0155	−.0156
EQP6.3	Assessments use teacher-designed tests	.0070	−.0416
EQP6.4	Assessments use oral classroom activities	.0310	.0291
EQP6.5	Assessments use exhibitions	.0327	.0883*

(continued)

Table 8.3   Continued

Predictor		Overall Students	African American and Other Nonwhite Students
EQP6.6	Assessments use student background information	−.0285	.0333
EQP7.1	Programs are assessed every day	−.0628*	.0232
EQP7.2	Teachers consistently rate program quality	.1913*	.1389*
EQP8	Assessment results are actually used in making decisions	−.0456*	−.0400
EQP9.1	Materials are selected based on their quality	−.0095	−.0217
EQP9.2	Materials are selected based on their appropriateness to student needs	.0910*	.0010
EQP9.3	Materials are not selected based on their cost	.0536*	−.0408
EQP10.1	There is ongoing, consistent, quality staff development on teamwork, on teaching techniques, and on school-community group involvement	−.0341	−.0473**
EQP10.2	There is ongoing, consistent, quality staff development that is a high-quality, state-of-the-art, practical experience for all school employees	−.0341	.0101
EQP11.1	There is constant, two-way, nonthreatening communication between school employees and school administration	−.0095	.0063
EQP11.2	There is constant, two-way, nonthreatening communication between the school and district administration	−.0020	−.0242
EQP11.3	There is constant, two-way, nonthreatening communication among teachers	.0074	−.0162
EQP11.4	All communication takes place within a climate for innovation	.0029	.0487
SES		.1303*	.1716*
Percentage African American and other nonwhite		−.1922*	−.1912*
Elementary School		.0111	−.0814*
Middle School		−.0045	−.0658*
Adjusted R^2		.33	.18

*$p < .05$; **$p < .10$.
OLS = ordinary least squares.

Quality tools exerting positive effects on overall student achievement include:

- Commitment to long-range, continuous improvement by parents and school employees
- Materials are selected based on their appropriateness to student needs.
- Materials are not selected based on their cost.
- Students and parents work to remove barriers to learning.
- Teacher rating of program quality is high.

African American and Nonwhite Student Achievement. In estimating the effects of our educational quality tools on African American and other nonwhite students, all the control items exerted significant effects. Of these items, percentage of students who are African American and other nonwhite and middle and elementary school environments had negative effects. As was to be expected, parental SES had a positive effect on the academic achievement of African American and other nonwhite students.

Of the five educational quality tools significantly affecting African American and/or nonwhite student achievement, only ongoing, consistent staff development on teamwork, on teaching techniques, and on school-community group involvement negatively affected achievement. It may be that given the extremely rare occurrence of this training, these programs are in place only in schools with substantial problems.

The remaining four educational quality tools had positive effects on the academic achievement of minority students:

- Teachers, students, and parents believe that all students can learn.
- Assessments use exhibitions.
- The students and parents work to remove barriers to learning.
- Teachers consistently rate program quality.

Summary/Conclusion

We began this chapter by noting the failure of past desegregation efforts to create equitable educational opportunities for African American students. We point out that it might be more meaningful to devise plans to improve the quality of schools that African American students attend. This, it appears to us, is the rationale for looking at the effective schools literature. But, although the effective schools literature has been instrumental in advancing our knowledge about quality schools, it seems to have suffered from at least two major problems. First, it was difficult to assess the success of various quality school proposals because adequate assessments were rarely in place. Second, such programs rarely obtained the sustained commitment from all interested parties, for example, education employees, parents, and students.

A major clue as to how these proposals can be shored up comes from the business sector's discussions of SPC, especially the writings of the late W. Edwards Deming. In 1988, the NEA began a study to identify quality schools. In identifying these qualities, the NEA study team on the Conditions of Teaching and Learning was organized and began merging the major concepts from both the SPC and effective schools literatures. The result was 11 EQPs. From these points, a national survey instrument was constructed and used among a national, randomly stratified sample of NEA teacher members.

In this chapter, we have attempted to examine the academic achievement of African American students. However, because we lack direct measures of such achievement, we estimated two models of achievement: overall student achievement and African American and nonwhite student achievement.

Our results indicate two things to us. First, although not all of our school-quality items exert significant effects on student achievement, both overall and among African and nonwhite students, enough points emerged as important predictors to warrant great optimism on our part. Second, as has been the case in previous research, we found substantial differences between white and African American and nonwhite groups in how the model operated. That is, the same items in the model did not predict student achievement similarly. Also, we found that, generally, the models did a better job of predicting the achievement of all students rather than African American and nonwhite students.

Although we acknowledge that there is substantial work to be done, we are heartened by our results and feel we are moving in the right direction: increasing the educational achievement of African American students is best done by improving the quality of their schools, rather than through the demographic manipulation of populations.

References

Armor, D. (1972). The evidence on busing. *The Public Interest, 28*, 90-126.
Armor, D. (1978). *White flight, demographic transition, and the future of school desegregation.* Santa Monica, CA: Rand.

Bidwell, C. E. (1965). The school as a formal organization. In J. G. March (Ed.), *Handbook of organizations* (pp. 972-1019). Chicago: Rand McNally.

Bradley v. Milliken, 1418 U.S. 7171 (1974).

Bradley v. Milliken II, 433 U.S. 267 (1977).

Bradley, L., & Bradley, G. (1977). The academic achievement of black students in desegregated schools. *Review of Educational Research, 47,* 399-449.

Bridge, R. G., Judd, C. M., & Moock, P. R. (1979). *The determinants of educational outcomes: The impact of families, peers, teachers, and schools.* Cambridge, MA: Ballinger.

Brookover, W. B., & Schneider, J. M. (1975). Academic environments and elementary school achievement. *Journal of Research and Development in Education, 9*(1), 82-91.

Brookover, W. B., Schweitzer, J. W., Schneider, J. M., Beady, C., Flood, P., & Wisenbaker, J. (1978). Elementary school social climate and school achievement. *American Educational Research Journal, 15*(2), 301-318.

Bryk, A. S., Lee, V. E., & Holland, P. B. (1993). *Catholic schools and the common good.* Cambridge, MA: Harvard University Press.

Cohen, E. (1980). Design and redesign of the desegregated school: Problems of status, power, and conflict. In W. G. Stephan & J. R. Feagin (Eds.), *School desegregation: Past, present, and future* (pp. 251-280). New York: Plenum.

Cole, K. (1978). Guidance and counseling in the desegregated school. *Theory Into Practice, 17,* 183-186.

Coleman, J. S. (1966). *Equality of educational opportunity.* Washington, DC: Government Printing Office.

Crain, R., & Mahard, R. (1978). Desegregation and black achievement. *Law and Contemporary Problems, 42,* 17-56.

Deming, W. E. (1988). Improvement of quality and productivity through action by management. *National Productivity Review, 1,* 12-22.

Edmonds, R. (1982, December). Programs of school improvement: An overview. *Educational Leadership,* pp. 4-11.

Egerton, J. (1977). *Education and desegregation in eight schools.* Amherst, MA: Center for Equal Education.

Eubanks, E., & Levine, D. (1977). Jesse Jackson's PUSH program for excellence in big-city schools. In D. Levine & R. Havinghurst (Eds.), *The future of big city schools: Desegregation policies and magnet alternatives* (pp. 218-234). Berkeley, CA: McCutchan.

Evans v. Buchanan, 447 F. Supp. 982 (D. Del., 1978).

Forehand, G. A., Ragosta, M., & Rock, D. A. (1976). *Conditions and processes of effective school desegregation.* Princeton, NJ: Educational Testing Service.

Garvin, D. A. (1984). What does "product quality" really mean? *Sloan Management Review, 26*(1), 25-43.

Gay, G. (1978). Multicultural preparation and teacher effectiveness in desegregated schools. *Theory Into Practice, 17,* 149-156.

Ishikawa, K. (1982). *Guide to quality control.* Tokyo: Asian Productivity Organization.

Johnson, D. W., & Johnson, R. (1991). *Learning together and alone: Cooperative, competitive, and individualistic learning* (3rd ed.). Englewood Cliffs, NJ: Prentice Hall.

Krol, R. A. (1980). A meta-analysis of the effects of desegregation on academic achievement. *Urban Review, 12,* 211-224.

Lezotte, L. W. (1990). Lessons learned. In B. Taylor (Ed.), *Case studies in effective schools research* (pp. 115-188). Dubuque, IA: Kendall/Hunt.

Lincoln, W. (1976). *A transferable process for the prevention and resolution of racial conflict in public secondary schools.* Washington, DC: National Institute of Education.

Luster, R., & McAdoo, H. P. (1994). Factors related to the achievement and adjustment of young African American children. *Child Development, 65,* 1080-1094.

McPartland, J., & Crain, R. (1978). *Discrimination, segregation, and minority social mobility processes.* Paper prepared for the National Academy of Sciences.

Messina, W. S. (1987). *Statistical quality control for manufacturing managers.* New York: John Wiley.

National Institute of Education. (1978). *Violent schools—safe schools: Volume 1.* Washington DC: Author.

National Institute of Education. (1984). *School desegregation and black achievement* (unpublished report). Washington, DC: Author. (ERIC No. 242 671)

Noblit, G. (1979). Patience and prudence in a southern high school. In R. Rist (Ed.), *Desegregated schools* (pp. 65-88). New York: Academic Press.

Oakes, J. (1985). *Keeping track: How schools structure inequality.* New Haven, CT: Yale University Press.

Orfield, G. (1975). How to make desegregation work. *Law and Contemporary Problems, 39,* 314-340.

Pettigrew, T. (1975). The cold structural inducements to integration. *Urban Review, 8,* 137-144.

Pollard, D. S. (1989). Against the odds: A profile of academic achievers from the urban underclass. *Journal of Negro Education, 58,* 297-308.

Reed v. Rhodes, 455 F. Supp. 569 (N.D. Ohio, 1978).

Rist, R. (1978). *The invisible children.* Cambridge, MA: Harvard University Press.

Rosenbaum, J. (1976). *Making inequality.* New York: John Wiley.

Rosenholtz, S. J. (1989). *Teachers' workplace: The social organization of schools.* New York: Longman.

Rosenthal, R., & Jacobsen, L. (1968). *Pygmalion in the classroom.* New York: Holt, Rinehart & Winston.

Schofield, J. (1978). *The impact of positively structured schooling on intergroup behavior.* Washington, DC: National Institute of Education.

Slavin, R. E. (1983). *Cooperative learning.* New York: Longman.

St. John, N. (1975). *School desegregation.* New York: John Wiley.

Today's news. (1989, February 3). *USA Today,* p. 7A.

Verdugo, R. R. (1981). *Race, powerlessness, and the status attainment process: Evidence from the 1960s and early 1970s.* Unpublished doctoral dissertation. Department of Sociology, University of Southern California.

Walton, M. (1986). *The Deming management method.* New York: Putnam.

Weinberg, M. (1975). The relationship between school desegregation and academic achievement. *Law and Contemporary Problems, 39,* 240-270.

Weinberg, M. (1977). *The role of the community in the school desegregation problem.* Washington, DC: National Institute of Education.

Willie, C. (1976). Racial balance or quality education. *School Review, 84,* 313-325.

Willie, C. (1978). *Sociology of education.* Lexington, MA: Lexington Books.

Willie, C., & Greenblatt, S. (1980). *Community policies and educational change: Ten school systems under court order.* New York: Longman.

Wortman, P. M. (1982). *School desegregation and black achievement: An integrative review.* Ann Arbor: University of Michigan.

9

African American Student Leadership
Implications for Quality in
College Achievement in the 21st Century

CAROLYN J. THOMPSON

The year 1994 was a landmark one; it marked three decades since the passage of the 1964 Civil Rights Act, which, according to its Title VI, prohibits institutions that receive federal funds from discriminating against students on the basis of their race, color, national origin, sex, handicap, or age (U.S. Bureau of National Affairs, 1964). Thirty years ago, more than 40% of baccalaureate degrees earned by African Americans were conferred by historically black colleges and universities (HBCUs) (Carter-Williams, 1984). These numbers are substantial, given that HBCUs represent 3.5% of the nation's colleges and universities and enroll about one fifth of the African Americans in college (Garibaldi, 1984). HBCUs have a history of admitting students whose levels of high school academic preparation range from well-prepared to marginally prepared for college-level studies. Yet, despite the wide range of students' preparation levels, HBCUs have histori- cally graduated the majority of students they admitted, although more recent graduation rates have regressed (Trent, 1991). Even with these high success rates, many college-bound African Americans did not have access to HBCUs, because the majority are located in southern and border states, and many African Americans seeking college admission are not. In addition, many students seeking public higher education in locations that did not have HBCUs experienced discriminatory admissions practices at institutions where they applied.

Title VI of the 1964 Civil Rights Act brought greater access to all types of colleges and universities for African Americans, and along with access came the promise of degrees to be received as well. Today, the majority of African Americans who attend college enroll in historically, predominantly white institutions (Trent, 1991). Yet these institutions have not enjoyed the same success in graduating African Americans that was experienced by HBCUs, or that equal their recruitment and enrollment efforts. Some institutional retention rates for African Americans are as low as 20%, indicating that nearly 80% who enroll are not able to obtain their degrees from these institutions, or at all. Predominantly white institutions are and have been "at risk" of losing the majority of African American (and other underrepresented and underserved) students who enroll. And despite the threat of maintaining the racial distinctiveness of HBCUs,[1] they still award approximately one third of the baccalaureate degrees earned by African Americans each year (Roebuck & Murty, 1993).

African American student leaders have been identified as having characteristics that facilitate their ability to negotiate at-risk college and university environments and persist to degree completion; they have higher rates of retention and graduation from predominantly white colleges and universities than other African American students (Sedlacek, 1987; Thompson, 1990; Tracey & Sedlacek, 1984). Research on African American student leaders is quite limited, however, and little is known that would help explain their greater success in college than other African American students. Moreover, research has indicated that a significant number of African American students with high academic abilities leave predominantly white institutions while an equal number, some of average ability, remain (Astin, 1982). Providing leadership opportunities for African American students in the college setting may be the key for at-risk colleges and universities to increase their now-discouraging retention rates, particularly because research suggests that the students' experiences in college rather than their precollegiate experiences contribute to their ability to remain in and complete college (Kuh, Schuh, Whitt, & Associates, 1991; Thompson, 1990; Thompson, Ward, & Lewis, 1991).

Predominantly white institutions enroll the majority of African Americans who attend college. Given their current trend of not retaining and graduating them, it is important for both these institutions and members of the African American target population to identify means of obtaining greater levels of educational achievement. This chapter explores the potential for improving the retention rates of African American college and university students by focusing on student leaders. The purpose is to understand the successful negotiation of college environments by African American student leaders as a way of understanding potential ways of empowering other students in similar campus settings. This is not to suggest that campus environments are not in need of improvements in order to meet the needs of the 21st-century student populations. It is to suggest that understanding the resilience of a population rather than its failures is a way of preparing for the future success of this college population. To understand the emerging African American college population of the 21st century, the pipeline of potential college students will be explored. This will be followed by a discussion of trends in educational attainment levels of African Americans from high school through postgraduate degrees, based on a study of African American college student leaders.

The Pipeline

Over the last 10 years, the size of high school graduating classes, along with the size of the overall high school population, has decreased. Because this is the principal market for college recruitment, the size of the overall college-going population is decreasing as well. Even with the decreasing high school population, the American Council on Education (1995) reported that over the past decade, the rate of African Americans graduating from high school has increased slightly. The report revealed further that although African Americans have experienced little improvement in college participation rates since 1990 (when their college participation was at 33%) among African American males, 2% more attended college in 1993 than 3 years earlier. Although underrepresented populations (mainly African American and Latina/Latino) have not been the principal market for college recruitment, by the year 2000 colleges and universities will be looking to these populations, along with the general adult population, to sustain their enrollments. By the year 2003, postsecondary enrollments are expected to have increased to 16.1 million, nearly 2 million more students than the 14.2 million students enrolled in 1991 (National Center for Education Statistics, 1993). It is expected that more than three quarters of the students will enroll in public institutions, increasing public enrollments by over 30%. One quarter of the traditional college-age population are expected to be from underrepresented groups, and 15% are

Table 9.1   Households With Children Who Will Be College Age by the Year 2000 for
             African American and White Freshmen

| | Percentage of Households With Children Under Age 18 | | | |
Race	Female-Headed	Male-Headed	Total Single-Parent	Two-Parent
African American	46.5	5.3	51.8	45.6
White American	13.9	3.6	17.5	82.3

SOURCE: 1992 U.S. Bureau of the Census.

expected to be African Americans, who will matriculate mainly in public
colleges and universities (U.S. Bureau of the Census, 1990).

21st-Century College-Age Youth

An examination of data from the 1990 U.S. Census reveals that of
current households that have children who will be college age by the year
2000, African American youth are three times as likely as white youth to
come from single-parent households (see Table 9.1). Nearly 52% of African
American youths reside in single-parent households, compared to roughly
18% of white youths. This poses serious concerns of college affordability
for the large number of African American youth who will be of college age.
Given the inequitable earning power of women when compared to men,
the concern for African American youth is even greater. Whereas roughly
14% of white youth are in female-headed households, the corresponding
figure for African American youth is nearly 47%, more than three times
greater.

Further concerns are raised when comparing the backgrounds of recent
entering college freshmen. An examination of these characteristics by Astin
(1990) reveals that African American students are disadvantaged by a
number of nonacademic factors (see Table 9.2). They are more than twice
as likely as their white counterparts to have one or both parents deceased
(10.1% and 4.4%, respectively), or to have divorced parents (44.3% and
20.4%, respectively). They are also more than twice as likely to have either
parent with less than a high school education, and three times as likely to
have an unemployed father, or parents whose annual income is less than
$20,000 a year.

Table 9.2   Background Characteristics of African American and White Freshmen (Fall 1989)

	Percentage Among	
Background Characteristic	*African American Freshmen*	*White Freshmen*
Parents divorced or separated	44.3	20.4
One or both parents deceased	10.1	4.4
Parents alive and living together	45.6	75.2
Father is not a high school graduate	19.6	8.8
Mother is not a high school graduate	14.7	6.1
Father is unemployed	5.8	1.9
Mother is unemployed[a]	8.0	5.1
Parental income below $20,000	37.6	12.4

SOURCE: Astin, 1990. Adapted with permission from the Higher Education Research Institute, from *The Black Undergraduate* (1990).
a. Not the same as being a full-time homemaker.

College Enrollments and Educational Attainment

Table 9.3 presents postsecondary enrollment trends by race and gender for the 15-year period from 1976 to 1991. It reveals that gains in college enrollments were marginal for African Americans, and that for African American men, there has been a decline in the number entering college (3.9% in 1991, down from 4.6% at the undergraduate level in 1976). Moreover, this decline is evident for African American males at all degree levels. Although the changes are small, they are not encouraging, given that fewer than 4% of African American males are enrolling in college at any level.

Educational Progression From High School

The National Center for Education Statistics (NCES) (1993) reports the levels of educational attainment for students 6 years after their senior year of high school. A review of the data by race (see Table 9.4) indicates that African Americans, like Latina/Latino Americans and Native Americans, are more likely to have attained only a high school diploma (69%, 70%, and 61%, respectively) or a 2-year license or degree (19%, 21%, 28%, respectively). African Americans and Latina/Latino Americans have the highest percentage of their populations not progressing beyond a high school diploma 6 years after high school. The percentages of all populations

Table 9.3   1976 to 1991 Enrollment in Higher Education by Level, Race, and Gender

	Percentage by Gender					
	1976		1986		1991	
Race	Male	Female	Male	Female	Male	Female
Undergraduate Enrollment						
African American	4.6	5.5	3.8	5.6	3.9	6.2
Latina/Latino American	2.1	1.7	2.5	2.8	3.0	3.6
Native American, Eskimo, Aleut	0.4	0.4	0.3	0.4	0.4	0.5
Asian/Pacific Islander American	1.0	0.8	2.0	1.8	2.3	2.3
European/White American	43.7	39.8	37.5	43.2	35.0	42.9
Graduate Enrollment						
African American	2.6	3.7	2.0	3.5	2.1	4.0
Latina/Latino American	1.2	0.9	1.6	1.9	1.5	2.0
Native American, Eskimo, Aleut	0.2	0.2	0.2	0.2	0.2	0.3
Asian/Pacific Islander American	1.2	0.8	2.0	1.4	2.2	1.8
European/White American	47.1	42.1	40.0	47.2	37.7	48.4
First Professional Degree Enrollment						
African American	3.0	1.6	2.8	2.5	2.9	3.4
Latina/Latino American	1.5	0.4	2.1	1.3	2.4	1.7
Native American, Eskimo, Aleut	0.4	0.1	0.2	0.2	0.3	0.2
Asian/Pacific Islander American	1.2	0.5	2.6	1.6	4.3	3.2
European/White American	71.5	19.7	56.4	30.2	50.4	31.1

SOURCE: U.S. Department of Education, National Center for Education Statistics (1993).

attaining a 2-year license or degree are comparable, with the exception of Native Americans (where approximately one third more acquire these certificates). However, those who have acquired at least a 4-year degree 6 years after high school are not comparable. Some students who reported having only acquired a high school diploma may be among the college-going population working toward a baccalaureate degree. However, African Americans are still half as likely as whites, and one third as likely as Asian Americans, to have acquired a 4-year or graduate degree.

Examination of levels of educational attainment by socioeconomic status (an NCES composite measure of parental education, family income, father's occupation, and household characteristics) reveals findings that are even more disturbing (see Table 9.5). Even African Americans in the upper-SES level lag behind their white and Asian counterparts in the attainment of baccalaureate degrees: roughly 13% behind whites and 15% behind Asians at the baccalaureate level. Moreover, for those in the middle-income levels, the

Table 9.4   Level of Education Attained by 1986 of 1980 High School Seniors by Race

Race	*Percentage by Levels of Educational Attainment*					
	No HS Diploma	*HS Diploma*	*License*	*Associate Degree*	*Bachelor's Degree*	*Graduate/ Profess- ional Degree*
African American	1.2	69.4	13.9	5.3	9.9	0.2
Latina/Latino American	1.7	70.2	13.8	7.3	6.8	0.1
Native American, Eskimo, Aleut	<0.05	61.3	18.6	9.3	10.8	<0.05
Asian/Pacific Islander American	<0.05	49.6	12.6	8.7	27.3	1.7
European/White American	0.8	60.0	11.5	6.6	20.2	0.9

SOURCE: U.S. Department of Education, National Center for Education Statistics (1993).

Table 9.5   Level of Education Attained by Spring 1986 of 1980 High School Seniors by Socioeconomic Status (SES) and Race

Race and 1980 SES[a]	*Highest Level of Educational Attainment*					
	No HS Diploma[b]	*HS Diploma*	*License*	*Associate Degree*	*Bachelor's Degree*	*Graduate/ Profess- ional Degree*
African American						
Lower 25 percent	1.4	73.0	12.7	5.1	7.7	0.1
Middle 50 percent	0.3	67.5	14.7	6.5	10.7	0.3
Upper 25 percent	<0.05	56.3	12.4	5.4	25.5	0.4
Latina/Latino American						
Lower 25 percent	1.6	73.9	11.8	7.8	4.9	<0.05
Middle 50 percent	1.0	67.0	14.7	6.5	10.7	0.2
Upper 25 percent	0.3	60.0	11.4	9.6	18.0	0.07
Asian/Pacific Islander American						
Lower 25 percent	<0.05	53.4	17.3	15.7	12.0	1.6
Middle 50 percent	<0.05	51.1	11.7	11.1	26.1	<0.05
Upper 25 percent	<0.05	42.9	6.5	4.8	40.0	5.9
European/White American						
Lower 25 percent	0.9	75.1	12.2	5.0	6.6	0.3
Middle 50 percent	0.3	62.0	13.0	8.0	16.3	0.4
Upper 25 percent	<0.05	44.9	8.6	6.2	38.2	2.2

SOURCE: U.S. Department of Education, National Center for Education Statistics (1993).
a. Socioeconomic staus (SES) is a composite score measuring parental education, family income, father's occupation, and household characteristics in 1980.
b. Seniors who had dropped out of high school after Spring 1980 and had not completed high school by 1986.

comparable attainment at the baccalaureate level trails 5% behind whites and 15% behind Asians. Thus, greater attention needs to be given to increasing these levels of degree attainment among African Americans in all SES groups.

College Student Leaders

In spite of the bleak college enrollment and degree attainment trends for African Americans over the past two decades, African American college students who have leadership potential and experiences are significantly represented among the students who do well and eventually graduate. A review of research on African American students attending predominantly white institutions (Sedlacek, 1987) reveals several points that provide insight into the experiences of college student leaders. First, their leadership ability is often demonstrated in what are considered to be nontraditional ways while they are attending college (when compared to other students attending predominantly white institutions). They are more likely to hold off-campus leadership appointments in their communities or churches, whereas their on-campus leadership experiences are more likely to take place in race-oriented channels (e.g., African American student organizations, sororities, or fraternities) rather than in student government or on faculty committees. Moreover, African American students tend to develop their own leadership styles rather than look to white faculty and staff as role models. The result is that during their college years, there are noted differences in the manner in which African American students are able to demonstrate their leadership abilities. The combination of different leadership styles and the nature of the organizations in which African American students hold appointments is such that their leadership ability is less likely to be validated by white faculty, college personnel, and other students (Sedlacek, 1987). Consequently, with the exception of race-oriented organizations, many African American students remain outsiders to the college environment, possibly without the full range of opportunities to become fully integrated into the campus culture.

Some African American students are able to involve themselves in both race-oriented organizations and those of the larger student body. Racial enclaves on predominantly white campuses have been criticized as selective resegregation. However, many African American students find that they have several roles to play based on who they are, the nature of the college environment, the nature of the organizations in which they participate, and their fit with their own ethnic culture (Loo & Rolison, 1986). Racial identity, for African American students, is as important for their adjustment to college as their fit with the overall college community. The racial enclave may serve to facilitate the integration of African American students into the larger college culture while also providing opportunities for them to hold leadership appointments that might not otherwise be available to them.

Student leadership has additional benefits that should excite educators concerned about the academic development of students. First is the positive correlation of leadership experience to grades as evidenced by students' "scores on the leadership portion of the American College Testing Program's student profile section" (Sedlacek, 1987, p. 489). Yet college and university admissions offices continue to rely heavily on standardized tests scores, along with high school grades (sometimes using only the grades from the more difficult courses), to predict the first-year retention and academic progress of the students they admit (Bailey, 1978). Arguments against this academic prediction model are (a) that educational systems should seek to develop more than just academic ability, (b) that socially useful talents involve more than tested ability, and (c) that academic indicators such as grades are not adequate predictors of real life or job success (Bailey, 1978). Moreover, African American students generally get lower scores on standardized tests than other college populations, thereby limiting their potential for admission to selective institutions. Although the causal relationship of leadership experience to grades has not yet been determined, leadership experience among African American students (even leadership in gangs), as well as high grades in college, are both associated with student retention in and graduation from college (Tracey & Sedlacek, 1984). Leadership is also a socially useful talent that may be related to later success in life.

How African American students are able to interact with their own cultural community, as well as the larger campus community, should interest educators. The role of leadership requires interacting with others and, along with others, influencing campus culture. Campus involvement has been demonstrated to be a key element in the development of student talents (Astin, 1977, 1985). Students who invest their time and energy studying while on campus, participating in student organizations and interacting with faculty and peers, are more likely to become integrated into the campus culture, get higher grades, and complete their bachelor's degrees (Astin, 1977, 1985; Bean & Kuh, 1984; Tinto, 1993). Thus, better understanding the involvement of African American student leaders is a way of understanding how to promote the interaction of students with others in culturally diverse college environments.

In addition to the literature that provides insight into the experiences of college student leaders, several observations based on personal interactions with administrators at predominantly white institutions need to be highlighted. First is a concern expressed by some white administrators that African American students who involve themselves in activities in African American communities are more likely to drop out of college. Their expressed need to discourage these types of activities among African American college students is particularly disturbing. Recent discussions on the development of civic responsibility have centered around having students devote time to community endeavors while they attend college. Such activities are seen as both philanthropic and valuable to student development, when they involve white students trying to uplift communities of those seen as less fortunate than they. Negative views of African American student involvement in their communities not only inhibits student development, but also ignores the value of future community leaders using their own community as a training ground for the development of their leadership potentials. Perhaps, then, the emphasis of campus cultural diversity efforts should be on respecting and welcoming population differences rather than merely acknowledging and "celebrating" them.

The dearth of research on African American student leaders in educational settings limits education personnel from understanding the true value of fostering leadership development in their student populations. In a quasi-experimental study using a secondary school population of African American student leaders, Nichols (1985) demonstrated the utility of the school setting for student leaders when they were compared to a sample of the school's general student population. The study evidenced that over time, student leaders perceived themselves as having a greater ability to positively affect the school culture and to influence what happened to themselves in the school environment. Their complacency and, sometimes, victimization was replaced with empowerment. Part of the importance of this study is that the sample included students who had engaged in counterproductive academic and social behaviors prior to their participation in the project; some were active in gangs. The relationship of gang leadership to college retention and graduation has been demonstrated in previous studies (Sedlacek, 1987; Tracey & Sedlacek, 1984).

Aside from studies that identify previous leadership experience in gangs among successfully college-retained African American students, studies have not identified this population as part of their college student samples. Students whose leadership experiences include off-campus appointments in community organizations and churches also have not been identified in the research. Such research not only would contribute to the knowledge base that guides college and university efforts to retain African American students, but also would provide a greater understanding of some of the unidentified values that this student population holds that contribute to their resilience in educational settings. Studying any population of African American student leaders attending predominantly white colleges and universities would, therefore, facilitate greater understanding of how African American students become integrated into college environments. This is the intent of the study discussed in the next section.

African American College Student Leaders: A Study

Methodology

Descriptive statistics are used to present a profile of the characteristics, skills, and experiences of African American student leaders.[2] The data are then compared to results from two national studies of college students, the National Study of Black College Students, conducted by Walter Allen (1987), and *The Black Undergraduate,* conducted by Alexander Astin (1990). Without an understanding of student leadership in the context of national data, the study's findings would be of limited generalizability. Thus, a comparison of African American student leaders with these national populations allows for a context in which to understand African American student leadership characteristics.

The sample of student leaders consists of 318 African American college students who held leadership positions in campus organizations—student government and race-oriented student organizations (sororities, fraternities, and other African American student organizations). Data on student leaders were collected prior to their attending a Big Eight student leadership conference. Student leaders were surveyed using the questionnaire developed by Walter Allen for the National Study of Black College Students (NSBCS). The NSBCS survey instrument consisted of approximately 60 open- and closed-ended items that provided information on student demographics, precollegiate academic experiences and accomplishments, and college experiences. Students in the NSBCS study attended 16 campuses nationally, of which 8 were large, comprehensive, public, predominantly white universities. With the exception of regional differences, the predominantly white institutions attended by NSBCS students were similar to those attended by student leaders. Students in *The Black Undergraduate* study

Table 9.6   Comparison of Student Leaders With Other African American College
            Populations (in percent)

Variables	NSBCS[a] (N = 283)	Student Leaders (N = 318)	1989 Freshmen[b] (N = 16,000-20,000)
Background Characteristics			
Sex: male	35.0	32.0	NA
Sex: female	65.0	68.0	NA
Religious preference:			
Baptist	43.0	62.9	54.2
Catholic	11.0	6.3	9.2
Methodist	12.0	7.9	9.2
Church of God	NA	7.9	NA
Other	NA	2.2	15.0
Father is a college graduate[c]	37.0	27.7	25.5
Father is not a high school graduate[c]	13.0	10.7	19.6
Mother is a college graduate[c]		26.0	27.2
Mother is not a high school graduate[c]		10.1	14.7
Sibling is a college graduate	29.0	22.8	NA
Sibling has some college	40.0	36.2	NA
Sibling is a high school graduate	16.0	9.2	NA
Parental income below $21,000	NA	33.9	37.6
Parental income below $25,000	45.0	37.8	NA
Parental income $60,000 or above[d]	NA	8.2	19.0
A or A– grades in high school	NA	17.5	10.5
C+ or lower grades in high school	NA	20.0	32.0

attended approximately 600 colleges and universities of all types nationally.
Between 16,000 and 20,000 African American students participated in this
study (Astin, 1990).

In the second phase of the study, data on African American student
leaders only were used. Factor analysis was conducted on variables that
represent areas of student interactions within the college environment.
Results showed several involvement constructs, one of which was used as a
dependent variable in the regression analysis: involvement in studies. The
two additional dependent variables used for regression analyses are student-faculty interaction and college grades.[3] The remaining constructs
resulting from the factor analysis—extracurricular involvement, social involvement, interactions with African Americans, and interactions with

Table 9.6   Continued

Variables	NSBCS[a] (N = 283)	1989 Freshmen[b] Student Leaders (N = 318)	(N = 16,000- 20,000)
College Experiences			
Highest degree planned:			
Doctorate or advanced professional			
degree (Ph.D., Ed.D., M.D., J.D.)	35.0	27.3	30.0
Master's	51.0	35.0	37.7
Bachelor's	13.0	34.9	25.7
Less than a bachelor's	1.0	0.3	4.7
Attending their first-choice college	NA	59.4	53.0
Living in college residential housing	NA	47.9	64.6
College classification:			
Freshman	27.0	29.8	100.0
Sophomore	23.0	26.7	0.0
Junior	24.0	20.3	0.0
Senior	25.0	17.5	0.0
Other	0.0	5.7	0.0
Considered leaving college	33.0	41.6	NA
Feel "somewhat" or "considerably"			
a part of campus life	38.0	63.1	NA

NOTE: NA means the information was not available.
a. National Study of Black College Students (NSBCS). Sources: Walter Allen (1987), Allen et al. (1989).
b. SOURCE: Astin (1990).
c. The NSBCS combined parents' educational characteristics.
d. The NSBCS gave figures for income over $75,000.

others—were used, along with other variables, as independent variables in the regression analyses.

Results

Parental Education

Comparisons of the three populations of African American students are presented in Table 9.6. Similarities and differences between student leaders and each of the two national samples are evident. The level of parental education of the student leaders compares favorably to those of African American students nationally. The percentage of fathers who had attained at least a bachelor's degree is 28% for student leaders and 26% for the 1989 freshmen. The corresponding figures for the mothers are 26% and 27%, respectively. However, the percentage of parents who did not complete high school is lower for the student leaders. Whereas nearly 11% of the fathers and 10% of the mothers of student leaders did not graduate from high school, the corresponding figures for the 1989 freshmen are 20% for fathers and 15% for mothers. The proportion of parents who completed college is about equal, but the parents of the student leaders were more likely to have at least completed high school. For students in the NSBCS sample, the educational attainment of the parents is combined. These figures indicate that a smaller percentage of parents of NSBCS students were college graduates (37%), compared to 54% of combined parents of student leaders and 53% of combined parents of 1989 freshmen. Fewer of the NSBCS students' parents did not complete high school, 13% compared to 21% and 34% for the leaders and 1989 freshmen, respectively.

Parental Income

A look at parental income indicates that fewer families of student leaders are in either the lowest or the highest income brackets, compared to African American students nationally. About 34% of the student leaders, compared to 38% of the 1989 freshmen, had parents who earned less than $21,000 annually. About 45% of the NSBCS students, and 39% of the parents of student leaders, earned less than $25,000 annually. More than twice as many parents of 1989 freshmen, compared to those of student leaders, earned more than $60,000 (19% compared to 8%, respectively). The median combined income of parents of student leaders is between $25,000 and $28,000, whereas the mean income is between $40,000 and $50,000 annually.

Sibling Education

Turning to the level of educational attainment of siblings, fewer student leaders had brothers and sisters who were either college graduates, completed some college, or who were high school graduates, compared to NSBCS students. However, more than half of each of these two populations had siblings who had completed at least some college. One factor determining the level of education attained by siblings is birth order. Among the student leaders, 57% were either first (34%) or second (23%) born, and they were, therefore, less likely to have brothers or sisters with more education than they had. What is most significant here is that in both populations, students were from families where education appears to be highly valued and where they had role models who had successfully negotiated a college environment.

Precollege Education

Based on self-reported grades of all three populations, the student leaders were almost twice as likely to have earned As in high school as African American students nationally (18% compared to 11% of the 1989 freshmen), and they were less likely to have earned grades lower than C+ (20% compared to 32% of the 1989 freshmen). The majority of the student leaders had B averages in high school (63%), and those with less than a C average constituted less than 1% of our sample.

All of the student leaders entered college between 1976 and 1986. Thus, they would have started kindergarten between the mid-1960s and the mid-1970s, a time when options for attending integrated/desegregated schools were greater. About 46% of the sample indicated that they had attended integrated/desegregated schools for all 13 of their grade school years, from kindergarten through 12th grade. The majority of the student leaders (77%) attended high schools that were fairly well integrated/desegregated, whereas only 2% indicated that they had never attended an integrated/desegregated school.

Educational Aspirations

In comparing the educational aspirations of the three populations, fewer student leaders aspired to attain graduate degrees than the students in either national population. One would expect the aspirations of the students who are likely to be successful as undergraduates (the leaders) to be higher. Also, research has indicated that students who make realistic self-appraisals and students who prefer long-range to short-range goals are more likely to complete bachelor's degrees (Tracey & Sedlacek, 1984). The fact that a larger percentage of student leaders aspire to only a bachelor's degree may be an indication that long-range goals of shorter duration appear to be more attainable to students.

Unhappy College Experiences

Students were asked about the unhappy experiences, both academic and personal, that they experienced while in college. Over half of the students (53%) reported an academic problem—poor grades—whereas problems of personal adjustment were noted by one fifth of the student leaders. The findings also indicated that when academic or personal problems arose, student leaders usually sought support for resolving their concerns.

Institutional Commitment

Even the student leaders who were not attending their first-choice institution were committed to their present university. This commitment is important: according to Tinto's theory (1993), it tends to facilitate student integration into the academic and social systems of the institution.

Both student leaders and NSBCS students were asked if they had ever considered leaving the college in which they were currently enrolled. Although student leaders seemed more likely to have considered leaving college, they were also more likely (25% more than NSBCS students) to indicate that they felt somewhat or considerably a part of the general campus life.

Campus Race Relations

Although student leaders indicated that they felt somewhat or considerably a part of campus life more frequently than their African American peers nationally, they were not exempt from experiences of discrimination. The majority (60%) said they had experienced discrimination, and about half said they experienced discrimination frequently, as opposed to hardly ever or seldom. The male students were more likely to report experiencing discrimination than the female students; most experienced discrimination only on occasion. The types of discrimination reported usually were intentional derogatory remarks and subtle discriminatory acts; other students were the most likely discriminators, followed by faculty. When discriminatory experiences were examined by class level, it appeared that the longer a student stayed in college, the greater was his or her chances of experiencing discrimination. About 44% of the freshmen indicated that they had experienced discrimination, compared to 65% of the sophomores and 63% of the juniors. Seniors and those classified as others reported experiencing discrimination at 75% and 72%, respectively.

Students who serve in leadership roles on campus apparently do experience discrimination. Yet they also feel more a part of campus life than African

American students generally. Although student leaders considered leaving college more frequently than their comparison group of NSBCS students, discrimination was generally not the reason given; rather, financial hardship seems to be the cause. These students appear to have the necessary knowledge and social skills to deal with racism, skills needed by African American students who attend predominantly white institutions (Tracey & Sedlacek, 1984).

Predicting College Involvement

A comparison of the predictors of the three outcome measures of students' academic experiences in college reveals that, with the exception of high school GPA predicting college GPA, the involvement of student leaders in the college's academic system was a function of their college experiences (see Table 9.7). There were no common predictors for all three outcome measures. However, several variables served as common predictors of two dependent variables. One of the most striking was the negative relationship of the students' opinions that African American and white students have similar problems to both involvement in studies and college grades. Student leaders who recognized some of their differences tended to invest more time in studies and get higher grades.

Social involvement served as a common predictor of involvement in studies and student-faculty interaction. Although social involvement was a measure of participation in non-campus organized activities, its presence as a predictor suggests that becoming involved socially may facilitate academic integration. This is consistent with Tinto's (1993) longitudinal model of academic and social integration, which shows a reciprocal relationship between the two types of integration. Extracurricular involvement, which is a measure of participation in and feelings about campus-organized activities, serves to negatively predict student-faculty interaction, while it also positively predicts college grades. Students who feel a part of campus life and who participate in extracurricular activities get high grades, yet they interact less frequently with faculty.

Conclusions and Recommendations

The information provided from this study indicates that in terms of family background characteristics, student leaders were not from the most

Table 9.7   Comparison of the Three Regression Models

	Dependent Variables					
	Involvement in Studies		Student-Faculty Interaction		Average College Grades	
		final		final		final
Variable	r	beta	r	beta	r	beta
Precollege Experiences						
High school grades	.10	.0591	−.02	−.0223	.31	.2690*
Self-rating: High school teachers' evaluation of you[a]	.14	.0632	−.02	−.0227	.16	.0127
College Experiences						
Self-rating: Type of person you feel you are[a]	.22	.1750*	.07	.0537	.07	−.0152
Self-rating: Professors' evaluation of you[a]	.13	.0614	.05	.0764	.22	.1524*
Quality of educational experiences	.04	.0326	.10	.1212*	−.04	−.0885
Feelings about the intensity of academic competition on campus[b]	.18	.1545*	−.04	−.0061	.03	−.0055
Perceived intensity of academic competition on campus[b]	.22	.1597*	.04	.0424	−.05	−.1196*
Opinion: African American and White students have similar problems[c]	−.13	−.1150*	.01	.0242	−.21	−.1974*
Hours per week spent in student organizational meetings	.11	.0802	.06	.1159*	.11	.0602
Social involvement	.15	.1380*	.16	.1511*	−.07	−.0987
Extracurricular involvement	.05	.0232	−.19	−.2353*	.15	.1083*
Involvement in studies	DV[d]		.04	.0151	.19	.1328*
	(R = .38)		(R = .30)		(R = .46)	

a. Self-rating variables are coded on a scale of 1 to 4, with 1 = *below average* and 4 = *highest*.
b. Intensity of academic competition on campus variables is coded on a scale of 1 to 5, with 1 = *very negative/not at all intense* and 5 = *very positive/extremely intense*.
c. Similarity of problems of African American and white students is coded on a scale of 1 to 4, with 1 = *strongly disagree* and 4 = *strongly agree*.
d. DV = Dependent Variable.
*p < .05.

affluent families nor were they from the least affluent. They were quite similar to their peers nationally in terms of family background. They performed well academically in high school, with more student leaders than African American students nationally earning A averages and fewer earning grades lower than C+. Data for comparison on high school performance were only available for the 1989 freshmen sample, which also included students in 2-year and 4-year colleges—students who traditionally have different academic profiles. The high school academic performance of student leaders was better than that of African American students in all types of colleges and universities nationally, but it may be comparable to their peers in universities. Educational aspirations of student leaders, on the other hand, tended to be lower; more student leaders than African American students nationally aspired only to earn a bachelor's degree. Among African American student leaders, more considered leaving their university; at the same time, a larger percentage also felt a part of the general campus life. Although they were active in the academic and social systems of the university, and although the majority tended to feel a part of campus life, they were not exempt from experiences of discrimination. Perhaps it is these experiences that help them to recognize the differences in their problems from those of white students. Their positive experiences on campus, however, may offset any unpleasant experiences. At the same time, their recognition of differences, along with their positive self-concepts, which positively predict involvement in studies, may provide the internal motivation for them to perform well.

Student leaders recognized their differences and their strengths. They were involved in the campus social and academic systems and they sought help, usually within the university, when problems arose. Their integration into the campus environment was, however, a function of college experiences rather than precollege experiences. Implications for practice suggest, therefore, that colleges and universities should work to provide activities for students with various backgrounds and interests, based on their individual and cultural values, thereby encouraging their active participation in campus-organized activities. In addition, responsibility for providing outlets that appeal to diverse student bodies should not be assigned solely to the students.

In terms of future research, the importance of developing studies that include students in nontraditional, off-campus leadership roles must be emphasized. Such studies are central to facilitating an understanding of the more complete picture of the relationship of leadership experience to academic achievement and degree attainment. More important, the role of the African American community in nurturing the leadership potential of African American youths, thereby contributing to their future educational achievements, needs to be understood. Better understanding this contribution is the best way of providing and strengthening available opportunities for the development of tomorrow's college graduates and community and civic leaders.

Notes

1. See the cases of United States, Petitioner, v. Kirk Fordice, Governor of Mississippi, et al.; and Jake Ayers et al., Petitioners, v. Kirk Fordice, Governor of Mississippi, et al., case numbers 90-1205 and 90-6588, argued Nov. 13, 1991, and decided June 26, 1992.
2. Parts of this study were previously reported by Thompson et al. (1991). They are used here with permission from the *UCLA Journal of Education*.
3. For comprehensive details of the research methodology, see Thompson et al. (1991).

References

Allen, W. R. (1985). Black students, white campuses: Structural, interpersonal, and psychological correlates of success. *Journal of Negro Education, 54*(2), 134-147.
Allen, W. R. (1987). Black colleges vs. white colleges: The fork in the road for black students. *Change Magazine, 9*(3), 28-31, 34.
Allen, W. R., Montoya, R., de Britto, A. M., Presley, C., Drummond, C., & Scott, A. (1989). *Preliminary report: 1985 survey of undergraduate students attending predominantly white, public universities.* Ann Arbor, MI: Center for Afro-American and African Studies.
American Council on Education, Commission on Minorities in Higher Education. (1995). *Fourteenth annual status report: Minorities in higher education.* Washington, DC: Author.
Astin, A. W. (1977). *Four critical years.* San Francisco: Jossey-Bass.
Astin, A. W. (1982). *Minorities in American higher education.* San Francisco: Jossey-Bass.
Astin, A. W. (1985). *Achieving educational excellence.* San Francisco: Jossey-Bass.
Astin, A. W. (1990). *The black undergraduate: Current status and trends in the characteristics of freshmen.* Los Angeles: UCLA, Higher Education Research Institute.
Bailey, R. L. (1978). *Minority admissions.* Lexington, MA: Lexington Books.
Bean, J. P., & Kuh, G. D. (1984). The reciprocity between student-faculty informal contact and academic performance of university undergraduate students. *Research in Higher Education, 21*(4), 461-477.
Carter-Williams, M. (1984). Student enrollment trends in black colleges: Past, current, and future perspectives. In A. Garibaldi (Ed.), *Black colleges and universities: Challenges for the future.* New York: Praeger.
Garibaldi, A. (1984). Black colleges: An overview. In A. Garibaldi (Ed.), *Black colleges and universities: Challenges for the future.* New York: Praeger.
Kuh, G., Schuh, J., Whitt, E., & Associates. (1991). *Involving colleges: Successful approaches to fostering student learning and development outside the classroom.* San Francisco: Jossey-Bass.

Loo, C., & Rolison, G. (1986). Alienation of ethnic minority students at a predominantly white university. *Journal of Higher Education, 57*(1), 58-77.

National Center for Education Statistics. (1993). *Projections of education statistics to 2003.* Washington, DC: U.S. Department of Education, Office of Educational Research and Improvement.

Nichols, B. (1985). *Self-perceptions of control and esteem as related to participation in a leadership training program.* Unpublished doctoral dissertation, University of California, Los Angeles.

Orfield, G. (1993). *The growth of segregation in American schools: Changing patterns of separation and poverty since 1968.* Cambridge, MA: Harvard Project on School Desegregation.

Roebuck, J. B., & Murty, K. S. (1993). *Historically black colleges and universities: Their place in American higher education.* Westport, CT: Praeger.

Sedlacek, W. (1987). Black students on white campuses: 20 years of research. *Journal of College Student Personnel, 28*(6), 484-495.

Thompson, C. J. (1990). *Predicting involvement and educational attainment: A comparative study of black and white college students.* Unpublished Ph.D. dissertation, UCLA.

Thompson, C. J., Ward, W., & Lewis, L. (1991). Characteristics of the successful college student: A profile of African American student leaders. *UCLA Journal of Education, 5*(1), 101-124.

Tinto, V. (1987). *Leaving college: Rethinking the causes and cures of student attrition.* Chicago: University of Chicago Press.

Tracey, T., & Sedlacek, W. (1984). Noncognitive variables in predicting academic success by race. *Measurement and Evaluation in Guidance, 16,* 171-178.

Trent, W. (1991). Focus on equity: Race and gender differences in degree attainment, 1975-76: 1980-81. In W. Allen et al. (Eds.), *College in black and white: African American students in predominantly white and in historically black public universities* (pp. 41-59). Albany: State University of New York Press.

U.S. Bureau of the Census. (1992). *1990 census of population: General population characteristics, United States.* Washington, DC: Government Printing Office.

U.S. Bureau of National Affairs. (1964). *Civil Rights Act of 1964, with explanation as passed by the Congress and sent to the President.* Chicago: Commerce Clearing House.

◪ P A R T   I V ◪

Quality Schooling for African Americans
Visions Beyond Desegregation

INTRODUCTION

Mwalimu J. Shujaa

In this concluding section, we take another look at school desegregation in order to look beyond it. Chapter 10, the first of the three chapters in the section, is by Emilie V. Siddle Walker, who elaborates on her notion of institutional caring. She describes institutional caring as an attribute of the culture within many historically segregated schools for African Americans. Walker argues that the value placed on caring about students in these segregated schools is largely nonexistent in the majority of desegregated schools. She advocates segregation as a context for school reform, focusing on the ways in which many historically segregated schools demonstrated their commitment to and cared for African American children.

In Chapter 11, Christine J. Faltz and Donald O. Leake ask whether the all-black school is inherently unequal or a culture-based alternative. They challenge assumptions about the efficacy of school desegregation and offer the example of African American immersion schools in Milwaukee's public school system as a viable strategy for providing quality schooling. Ultimately, Faltz and Leake reject the idea that it is necessary to desegregate all black schools if they are culturally relevant, developmentally appropriate, and institutionally strong.

In the final chapter, Hannibal T. Afrik and I profile the Council of Independent Black Institutions (CIBI). This organization represents a different ideological stream in the history of African people who left Africa in captivity than that which guided the integrationist approaches to school desegregation. We tell a largely untold story about the emergence of an organization through which many of the leading thinkers in the contemporary education of African Americans have passed.

10

Can Institutions Care?
Evidence From the Segregated
Schooling of African American Children

EMILIE V. SIDDLE WALKER

In the tradition of educational researchers who use the narrative as a way of knowing, this discussion begins with a story. This particular story is not part of the research base; in fact, the information was obtained coincidentally when a young African American male, after viewing a documentary about a historically segregated school, began to share with me his view of the school he attended. His description provides a perspective that forms the backdrop for this discussion.

The 16-year-old with whom I talked—"Man" is what he likes to be called—thinks of school as a place where he encounters enemies. He does not have good relationships with most of his teachers; his perception is

AUTHOR'S NOTE: Portions of this article have been presented previously in talks given at the Asa Spaulding Lecture at the University of North Carolina at Chapel Hill and the American Educational Research Association meeting in New Orleans, 1994. The author wishes to thank the Spencer Foundation, Graduate School of Education at the University of Pennsylvania, and the Emory University Research Committee for financial support for the project. Research assistants Trudy Blackwell and Evelyn Lavizzo provided invaluable assistance in conducting and transcribing interviews.

centered on the fact that he doesn't feel they like him. He does not participate in any school activities. He says they're just for the smart students and
that school personnel think "black people are too dumb to be in their
clubs."[1] This feeling was confirmed for him when one of his friends tried
to become part of a performing arts club and was turned away because, as
he was told, he wasn't "cooperative enough." Man is seldom given the
opportunity to witness performances or speakers at school assemblies;
according to him, they only happen "once in a blue moon." Moreover, he
has never had the opportunity to participate in one.

What the students did do in school last year was to take a field trip to
the local jail.[2] This trip was not part of any class, and Man is unsure why he
was chosen. Once there, he witnessed male and female classmates being
solicited by inmates and watched several classmates get locked up after they
misbehaved. One was forced to remain in the cell while the rest of the
students went to lunch. He also saw friends' mug shots and fingerprints
taken. Although some of the students volunteered for these activities, others
were picked by the police officers after being told: "You look like you will
get in trouble, so we'll see you again."

Man's description of his life in school, along with additional examples
and commentary about the roles of the principal and teachers, was first told
to me in spring 1993 and retold in a formal open-ended interview the
following September. On the surface, his negative perceptions would seem
to have little relationship to a historical research project that has focused
on understanding the legalized segregated schooling of African American
children in the southern United States. A closer look, however, suggests this
student's story may provide a focal point for raising questions about the
significance of past experiences.

This discussion stresses the importance of studying the segregated
schooling of African American children. It is, however, more than a trek
down nostalgia lane. I argue that an understanding of segregated schooling
serves several important functions in the educational literature; among
them are providing a historically accurate and balanced portrayal of African
American schooling and offering an opportunity to provide context for
discussions of school reform. I consider the case of one particular segregated school, discussing both the methodology used to uncover the themes
that characterized the schooling and some of the evidence that explains the
emergence of a particular theme, institutional caring. Finally, I consider the
questions raised when this theme is juxtaposed with Man's story of his
current school experiences.

Segregation Revisited

Conversations about the legalized segregated schooling of African American children have traditionally focused on the dominant images of inferior facilities, secondhand books and materials, and poorly paid and undereducated teachers. Historical assessments chronicle the dispropor-tionate allocations in pupil-teacher ratio, the length of the school day, the supplemental services provided, and the expenditure per pupil in average daily attendance (Ashmore, 1954; Bullock, 1967; Harlan, 1958; Kluger, 1977; Woodward, 1974). In North Carolina in 1945-1946, for example, the value of school property per pupil enrolled was $217 for white students and $70 for African American children ("Why the South," 1949). Such discrep-ancies were common throughout the South (Ashmore, 1954).

Although this portrait of segregated schooling is accurate in its recount-ing of the inequities in facilities and resources, it is incomplete in that it focuses on only one dimension of segregated schools. Indeed, inequities were a fact of segregated school life. This truth must not be ignored. Yet evidence exists to indicate that African American teachers, principals, and parents were able to create learning environments that were valued by those who participated in these schools, in spite of the inequalities imposed upon them by white school boards. Most notably, these environments have been documented in the earlier scholarship of Jones (1981), Sowell (1976), and Irvine and Irvine (1983).

In one of the earliest accountings, by Sowell (1976), the schools are remembered as having atmospheres where "support, encouragement, and rigid standards" combined to enhance student self-worth and increase aspirations to achieve. In Sowell's description of six "excellent" black schools, students describe teachers and principals who would not let them "go wrong," teachers who were well-trained, dedicated, and demanding and who "took a personal interest in them," even if it meant devoting personal money and time outside of the school day (pp. 31, 47, 51).

In the first book-length manuscript describing the good in segregated schools, Jones (1981) provides a portrait of one of the two well-known Dunbar High Schools. According to her survey results, teachers didn't give students a choice between "learning and not learning"; to fail to learn was "unacceptable to teachers, family, peers, and the community. The choice was how much one would learn, and what subjects would be mastered" (p. 3).

Moreover, in these and other, later descriptions, the segregated school is most often compared with a family, where teachers and principal, with parentlike authority, exercised almost complete autonomy in shaping student learning and ensuring student discipline. Also playing an active role were parents, who are remembered for the monetary and nonmonetary contributions they made to the education of African American children (Clark, 1965; Delpit, 1992; Foster, 1990, 1991a; Irvine, 1990; Irvine & Irvine, 1983).

The findings from these earlier studies have been confirmed by more recent research (Cecelski, 1994; Dempsey & Noblit, 1993; Foster, 1990, 1991b), all of which provides evidence of the nurturing provided by teachers and principals as part of the school experience, by the high standards to which students were held, and by the positive support of the community.

The positive portrait painted of the schools in these studies, however, has been little understood and seldom referenced. Much remains to be explained about school climate, methods of motivating students, parental interactions, and other variables influencing student success. Without research into such questions, African American children are treated as though they have no history of success in school, and the principals and teachers who taught them are deemed to have no particular expertise worth passing on to future generations. Equally important, the omission contributes to a historically inaccurate portrayal of segregated schooling, relegating it to the simplistic summation that the schools were without resources and therefore unequivocally inferior.

Looking in depth at segregated schooling is also important for another reason. Many well-meaning change efforts lack a context of successful African American students, teaching, and communities, a context that would facilitate the implementation of meaningful reform. Consider an example I have elaborated upon elsewhere (Walker, 1993a). In my experience, a question frequently posed as the beginning point to address school reform is, How do we get these parents (usually African Americans) to become interested in their children's schooling? Such a question assumes parents are uninterested and that the reform effort must begin by generating an interest. Yet even a cursory understanding of African American history demonstrates that many African American parents have traditionally valued education and have played supportive roles in their children's schooling. The reform question might thus better be phrased: Are there barriers existing in schools that prohibit African American parents from participating in the supportive manner in which some have traditionally functioned and what can schools do to eliminate these barriers? The different phrasing of the question will elicit very different answers. In one scenario, the problem focuses on parents; in the other, the problem focuses on schools. Only by asking and answering the right questions are we likely to generate reform that will have a lasting influence on improving African American schooling.

This *re*-view of segregated schools, then, will contribute to a fuller understanding of them as educational institutions. It embraces an educator's analysis—of curriculum, learning, relationships, and so on—to understand the strengths and limitations of the schooling offered to African American children during an era of legalized separation. As such, it neither discredits nor discounts the legal and political analyses documenting the detriments inherent in the inequality of resources that resulted in such a system; however, it does provide an additional lens by which the schooling of African American children during the period of legal segregation may be viewed. In addition, this discussion provides the context needed as we proceed with the complex task of reform.

Setting and Methodology

The case study that provides the data point for this discussion has focused on reconstructing the nature of schooling in a historically segregated school for African American children that was, by community standards, defined as a "good" school.[3] The research looks at one particular elementary/high school that existed in the North Carolina between 1933 and 1969, the Caswell County Training School.[4] Situated in the middle of rural Caswell County in a small county seat called Yanceyville, the school provided the only place in the county where African American children could receive a high school education. Its earliest recorded history documents the purchase of a first school building, an old two-story house, by African American parents, after the Ku Klux Klan murdered its white owner. By the time court-ordered desegregation occurred in 1969, the facilities included a three-story brick building, a gymnasium, and an auditorium. Indeed, in part because of the large numbers of African American children enrolled, it was the largest school in the county system.[5]

The principal received his master's degree in education from the University of Michigan and was frequently in attendance and on the program at state and national educational meetings. Dorothy Zimmerman, a retired white supervisor, said whenever she wanted to know anything about trends in education, she went to Professor Dillard, because he was going to those meetings "long before the rest of us."

With educational aspirations similar to the principals, over 50% of the teachers were involved in graduate training by 1953, and all were members of their professional organization. After salary equalization reform in North Carolina in 1944-1945, the teachers' salaries exceeded the salaries of the white teachers because of their additional training and experience ("Local School Group, 1957; "N.C. Negro Teacher," 1960). Throughout the school's history, many parents provided financial and other types of support.

Perhaps most significant, this segregated school was fully accredited by the Southern Association of Schools and Colleges in 1953; the area high school for white children was not. Thus, when desegregation began in fall 1969, African American children left their accredited segregated school to be desegregated into an unaccredited white school.

To reconstruct the events in this environment as they held meaning for the participants, I used historical ethnography as the method of inquiry.[6] Consistent with the tradition of historians, the methodology focuses on reconstructing events in the school between the years of 1933 and 1969. Unlike historical research, however, and more in the form of ethnography, I sought not simply to recreate a chronology of events, but to understand the significance of those events as they held value to the participants.

Collection of data covered a 6-year period and consisted of three overlapping phases. In the first phase, open-ended interviews generated a number of themes valued by the participants, and historical documents were used to confirm the presence of those themes during the actual time of the events. In the second phase, more focused interviews and document review were used to assess the parameters of the themes, for example, establishing for whom the schooling was good and under what circumstances. In the final phase, the good was situated in the context of the problems and confirmed through continued focused questioning and document review.

The database has over 100 open-ended and focused interviews with former teachers, students, parents, and administrators. The interviewees range from those who were part of the school in the early 1930s to those who were present at its closing as a segregated school in 1969. They include those who, through length of stay or participation in events, may be deemed to have had a close relationship with the school, students who were not successful in school by academic standards, and teachers who were part of the school for only brief periods. Likewise, we have sought out parents who maintained a visible presence in the school and those who did not.

The document collection encompassed school board minutes (1928-1969), yearbooks (1949-1969), newspaper accounts (1926-1969), principals' reports (1934-1969), pictures (1934-1969), Southern Association evaluation materials, and other miscellaneous student newspaper accounts, report cards, books, and so on. Throughout, interviews were triangulated with other interviews and with documents from the era to ensure accuracy of portrayal; in particular, data were cross-referenced to account for the influence of nostalgia.[7]

Overview of Findings

To be sure, the data have revealed the inequalities that existed in this environment with regard to resources. Parents had to buy a bus and give it to the school board in 1935 in order to get state-supported transportation for their children to high school. The story is frequently told among older informants of how parents and students chopped trees to build a new high school and hauled them to the site of the school, only to have them taken by the white school board and used to build a white school. For most of its history, the school was not a priority in the distribution of resources by the school board and it had an extremely poor facility until 1951.

In spite of these inequities, the principal, parents, and teachers forged a system of education for children that has been documented to have been highly valued by those who were participants. Parents are shown not just as silent victims of an oppressive system, but as instrumental supporters who supplied the financial needs of the school when the county would not. In addition, they functioned as advocates who frequently appeared before the local school board and the state board of education to make financial requests. Parents thus worked in partnership with the school to supply for the children what the professional educators could not.

In turn, the teachers and principal broadened teaching to include both the transmission of subject matter and a focusing on the needs of the "whole child." In their approach to teaching and in their extra-classroom commitments of time and money to students, the teachers sought to prepare their students to excel in the segregated world in which they would graduate. In effect, the teachers and principal functioned as parents of the students— giving students the experiences many of their parents could not provide— and the parents functioned as parents of the school. Teachers and principal thus worked together to create the caring environment that nurtured African American children in spite of the inequality in distribution of resources.

The caring at the root of the schools' practices seems to provide the most suitable explanation for the relationships between teachers, principal, students, and parents. Frequently remembered in studies that document the segregated schooling of African American children (Foster, 1990, 1991a; Irvine & Irvine, 1983; Jones, 1981; Sowell, 1976; Walker, 1993b), this is the type of caring I label *interpersonal caring* because it documents evidence of an individual, or individuals, who provide direct attention to meeting the psychological, sociological, and/or academic needs of another individual or individuals within the school environment. By definition, it resembles the work on caring by Noddings (1984, 1986) and Gilligan (1982), but it is more aptly characterized by Ladson-Billings (1995) at the conclusion of her study on effective teachers of African American students:

> Their common thread of caring was their concern for the implications their work had on their students lives, the welfare of the community, and unjust social arrangements. Thus, rather than the idiosyncratic caring for individual students (for whom they did seem to care), the teachers spoke of the import of their work for preparing the students for confronting inequitable and undemocratic social structures. (p. 474)

Although CCTS methods of teaching students how to function in the larger democratic society differ from Ladson-Billings' teachers, in that the curriculum was more overtly accepting of the importance of participating in mainstream culture, the beliefs about the role of a caring teacher and principal are similar.

These and other findings are elaborated upon elsewhere (Walker, 1996). For purposes of this conversation, one small component of the larger whole I refer to as *institutional caring* is briefly reviewed.

Institutional Caring at CCTS

In addition to the relationships between teachers, students, principal, and parents, caring at CCTS also operated within an institutional structure that supported the interpersonal messages of caring. That is, like an individual seeking to meet the academic, psychological, and sociological needs of students, the institution also overtly sought to provide structures that would facilitate the meeting of student needs.

I label this type of caring *institutional caring* because it combines the presence of interpersonal relationships with a supportive school structure. That is, the school as an institution identified the academic, social, or psychological needs of students (much as a caring individual teacher might) and through its policy arranged for those needs to be met. Caring thus was personal, relational, and situational, and it was concurrently supported by the structured response of the institution to the needs of students.

CCTS exhibits at least two characteristics that suggest that the institution was exhibiting caring in its institutional policies. First, it demonstrated an awareness of student needs and explicitly accepted the meeting of those needs as part of the school's responsibility. Second, it implemented school structures aimed at meeting student needs.

Student Needs and School Responsibility

In the early 1950s, the students at CCTS were the products of 39 rural schools, 15 of which were one-teacher and 19 of which were two-teacher; in 1954, the largest had only four teachers. With a low county per-capita income and few industries available in the largely farming community, the students were perceived by school personnel as having few opportunities to participate in many forms of cultural activities. The students, the principal records in a handwritten observation, "lack [an] appreciation of aesthetic values (music, art, literature)." He further describes the county as having "no museums, no forums or lyceums, no plays, no recreational facilities (except a wildlife reserve), and only two motion picture theaters." Other than church, the only forms of entertainment came from "certain night clubs, cafes, and two pool rooms."

The identification by the institution of the cultural needs of the students was accompanied by an institutional acceptance of responsibility for meeting those needs. The principal wrote, for example, that the lack of museums, forums, and plays and their "being located in a rural area [meant] that recreational activities [were] at present centered around churches," then added with an arrow: "and schools." He further observed that "the lack of recreational activity impose[d] upon [the] school the responsibility of providing areas in which [the] student might have opportunity to develop" (School Evaluative Criteria, 1953, pp. 32-33). A version of the school philosophy also demonstrates awareness of need and assumption of responsibility to meet the need: "The school realizes the significance of its rural setting. However, the school feels it has the responsibility of providing the type of curriculum that will stimulate its pupils to make satisfactory life adjustments."

The text goes on to enumerate some fundamental concepts to which the faculty adhered and provides additional statements in the areas of curriculum, pupil activities, library service, guidance, instruction, outcomes, staff, plant, and administration. Of the 32 statements of belief outlined in these categories, 22 centered directly on the needs of pupils; 3

implicitly referred to pupils. In particular, the items listed under the heading "Guidance" demonstrated the centrality of the needs of students to the operation of the school. The secondary school's goal, the authors wrote, is to "discover . . . the needs of the pupil and decide specific experiences to be provided." The school has the responsibility to eliminate "conditions which make pupil adjustment difficult." Finally, "the secondary school *should assume responsibility* [italics added] for assisting pupils in all phases of personal adjustment" (CCTS School Philosophy, circa 1954).

Although the wording varies in other versions of the philosophy, the thrust of the text remains unchanged. The goal of the schooling was to accept the children where they were and to help them reach, as the teachers termed it in their interviews, their "highest potential." According to David Wiley, who headed the accreditation team and participated in the revisions over the years, the written philosophies were more than just words to please an evaluation committee. Wiley recalled, "We had a committee to write the philosophy. . . . This was a committee of teachers and everyone voted for it. The philosophy reflected what we did and what we believed. It was not just nice words on paper."

School Structures Designed to Meet Student Needs

In addition to identifying student needs and making a commitment to meet those needs, the faculty and principal at CCTS also provided a variety of ways to address the lack of cultural opportunities available to their students. One of these was the activity program.

According to the principal's master's degree thesis (Dillard, 1942), the goal of the program was to develop self-esteem, involve as many students as possible in activities they were interested in, and give students opportunities to develop leadership skills. All of these goals were significant for a farming community where, outside of the school, the students would have little opportunity to fulfill these goals.

To ensure that the goals would be met within the school, a pupil activity program was implemented that had several components. The rationale for the components is most aptly provided by Dillard (1992); it is briefly summarized here. To ensure participation, clubs met during the school day so that transportation problems would be eliminated. Moreover, the clubs did not collect activity fees, so that no students were eliminated because they lacked financial resources. To help students identify interests and be exposed to many different areas in which they might excel, a variety of clubs were offered, and students could choose among them.

Over the course of the school's history, as many as 53 different types of clubs were offered. Some of these were academically focused clubs such as history, science, and future teachers; some were hobby-oriented, such as handicraft or lens and shutter; others focused on life skills, such as debating, courtesy, and so on. To extend students' knowledge of particular areas, all clubs regularly planned topic-related conversations during meetings.

The building of leadership qualities was addressed through the officers. With an average of 15 to 20 clubs per year and 4 specified leadership roles, about 60 to 80 leadership slots were available for students per year. This number does not count students who participated as committee chairs or committee members. Of these opportunities, former student Yvonne Byrd commented, "The different clubs gave different opportunities for leadership. If you couldn't be president of the student council, you could be president of the Future Teachers of America if you wanted to be a leader."

Assessment of the pupil activity program based on involvement indicates that the program was effective. In 1934-1935, for example, when the high school had four teachers and 143 students, 137 students were involved in the club program, including 25 in the Glee Club, 35 in the drama club, and 47 in the literacy club (Dillard, 1935).[8] In 1966-1967, 25 different clubs were listed with 88.5% student participation (Dillard, 1967). During the intervening years, the number and type of clubs varied, based on the interests and needs of the students.

The success of the program in meeting the needs the school identified is also corroborated by the report of an evaluation team of the Southern Association of Schools and Colleges. In 1954, they "highly commend" the program—referring in one place to its "outstanding characteristics"—and list 12 points of evidence to support their evaluation, including the opportunities provided to develop leadership skills and the use of clubs that met the needs and interests of the students (Southern Association Report, 1954). They record that the "principal and teachers seem to be deeply concerned about the development of curricula that will meet the needs and interests of the pupils" (p. 2).

Perhaps the most revealing evaluation of the importance of the activity program is the comments of students. In interviews, students gave the clubs the credit for helping them develop self-esteem and for providing more opportunities for them to interact with their teachers, particularly to "model" them in areas of common interest. Sally Totten recalled that clubs gave students opportunities to participate in activities beyond the classroom. "If you had a talent," she concluded, "there was something for you."

In memories and school documentation, teachers and principal articulate clearly their belief that the extracurricular program was central for
addressing the needs of their students. Research then and now confirms the
truth of this perspective. Smylie, Yowell, and Kahne (1995) provide a
summary of the research in this area:

> Research has shown a positive relationship between participation in
> cocurricular programs and the development of a student's educational
> aspirations, especially for low-achieving students. Other research indi-
> cates that students who participate in these programs report a greater
> identification with their school, are more happy with their school expe-
> riences, and take more initiative in their work than students who do not
> participate in these programs. Further, participation fosters greater op-
> portunities for student contact and social development with teachers and
> other adults in nonclassroom settings. Participation has been related
> positively to adult socializing patterns, greater social integration, and
> lower senses of self-estrangement and powerlessness as long as 15 years
> after high school graduation. (pp. 219-220)

Clubs at CCTS thus provided a tangible way to meet the needs CCTS
faculty perceived their students as having. Although the idea of clubs was
not novel, the consistent presence of the activity program from the schools
earliest days as a high school in 1933-1934 provides some insight on the
importance of the programs in African American schools (Dillard, 1942)
and stands in stark contrast to the early descriptions of one historian, who
concluded that "interest in extracurricular activities [among African Ameri-
cans] ha[d] barely been aroused" (Long, 1932, p. 176).

Related to the use of clubs, and demonstrating the institution's policy
of caring for the needs of its students, is the Chapel program. Chapel was
not a school form of church, although it did include definite religious
practices, such as prayer and religious songs. More accurately characterized,
however, Chapel was a weekly gathering of students, teachers, and principal—an assembly, to use more contemporary language. Several functions
of this assembly have been identified.

First, the gathering provided an audience for the presentations that all
clubs were required to make at some point during the year. As such, it was
an extension of the activity program, in that it provided a focal point for
club planning and gave students the opportunity to demonstrate their
interests and exercise their talents before other students. Presentations
included such activities as square dancing, dramatic performances, musical

programs, and public debate and involved all segments of the student body, including the elementary department. In 1953-1954, 36 regular assemblies were planned, each lasting 30 to 45 minutes; others were added as "occasions and events warrant[ed]" (CCTS, 1950, p. 197).

Chapel was also a teaching situation for the principal. He used it as an opportunity to do group teaching about appropriate behavior, relationships, and the importance of education. Although his tone and words were sometimes admonishing, such as expressing his dismay over someone writing on the bathroom walls, he also often used the opportunity to inspire. "The best equipment may be across the way [at the white school]," he is reported to have said, "but the best minds are right here in this school." He talked to students about how they had to be extra good to make it in the world and told them they could be anything they wanted to be if they tried hard enough. He gave lectures on appropriate behavior, college, and relationships. Although the substance of his comments could be compared to the black preacher, who was known for undertaking any subject for discussion, his method of presentation differed from the preacher's oratorical style. One student recalled, "he just talked to you."

Chapel thus became, according to teacher Paul Robinson, a group learning situation. During the assemblies, students could be taught how to behave as listeners and how to appreciate certain types of talents. Moreover, as teacher Lucille Richmond noted, Chapel gave children the opportunity to capitalize on their own abilities to speak, sing, dance, and so on before an appreciative audience.

This dual focus of Chapel—to provide opportunities for student talent to be highlighted and appreciated and to provide opportunities for students to be exposed to ideas they might not otherwise hear in a group setting—fit needs the school identified its students as having. The opportunities to participate in and see performances fulfilled the need for exposure articulated in the school's philosophy and personal faculty statements; the opportunities to hear talks was another way of broadening the students' knowledge base.

Another institutional policy designed to meet the needs of students—to have close interactions with adults who could motivate them to have high aspirations—was the homeroom program. In this program, four or more teachers were assigned to act as homeroom teachers for an entering class of freshman students. In these individual homeroom classes, all plans or activities relating to freshmen were orchestrated; student Ann Parker, a 1956 graduate, recalled that they "talked and planned projects" during the time together. Students likewise received information relating to their class schedules and the principal's expectations during this period. At the end of the freshman year, the teachers assigned to them rotated up one grade along with the class. This rotation upward continued each year—with teachers assisting with the requisite responsibilities of particular years, such as the junior-senior prom and the class production of the senior yearbook—until the students graduated. After serving as senior class advisers, the teachers were reassigned to an incoming freshman class, and the process began again.

This homeroom plan was an important mechanism for facilitating interpersonal relationships between teachers and students. Teacher David Wiley talked about how in following a class for 4 years, "you get to know the student well. You had to accept them and love them." Judy Mitchell, a student who began in 1954, remembered the personal attention students received in homeroom: "It was like that group of teachers had a lot of concern and care and looked out after us for those 4 years. And it became like a family. They were like a family to us." As with other institutional structures, this one also is reported to have been deliberately conceived to meet the needs CCTS students had in the school environment.

In each of these examples of institutional structures, and in the other undiscussed examples that were evident in the school (e.g., teacher-planned trips to churches to talk with parents about the drop-out problem, institutional policies on grouping), the institution sent messages consistent with the messages sent during interpersonal interactions. In short, the school structure did not blame students for what they did not know as a result of their lack of exposure at home. Rather, it embraced strategies designed to help the students. Thus the mere presence of an activity program or Chapel program was not the basis of the institutional caring; many schools had, and continue to have, elaborate club and assembly programs. What is significant is that the policies were clearly correlated to address the perceived needs of the poor African American students they served. You can succeed and we will help you succeed: this was a dominant message of the school. This message was communicated to students, both in the interpersonal interactions they had with teachers and principal and in the institutional structures created to help them succeed. The institutional policies thus expanded and reinforced the interpersonal relationships.

Using Segregated Schooling to Pose Questions for Reform

One of the reasons the segregated schooling of African American children was valued, according to this research and previous research on the environment of segregated schools, was the way it demonstrated its commitment to, and caring about, children. Remarkably, in an era when African American children received external societal messages suggesting their lack of intellectual ability, the school provided internal opportunities that allowed large numbers of students to experience public success, to achieve self-esteem as a result of their success, to be motivated to believe in what they were capable of achieving, and to demonstrate they were competent in a variety of areas. As such, the school's planned programs were able to militate against the negative effects of the larger society and the lack of experiences students brought with them to school.

But what, if anything, does this have to do with Man? After all, this school represents an era far removed from the complexities of his high school. Except for the racial background of some of the students, no similarities exist in time frame, school type, geographic region, or other student body characteristics. Yet, Man's experiences raise some important questions that should not be ignored. Man is a student who is neither on drugs nor in a gang but who is not part of any activities in his school. He perceives that he and others of his race are not wanted. Man seldom gets to be present in school assemblies and has never been part of a program presented at one, thus having been denied the learning either experience could afford. He has been taken on a field trip to jail.

The question must be raised as to what types of messages are being sent by the institution to this student. What is he being implicitly told about his abilities and about the expectations the school has for him? How significant are these institutional messages in his development? If the school does "want" him to be part of it and he has somehow received the wrong message, then the even larger question must be addressed: Why and how were such perceptions created?

Man's situation as an African American student, when contrasted with the school experiences provided for students at CCTS, raises even more questions. For example, what type of institutional policies are currently in place that take into account the needs African American children bring to school and are explicitly designed to meet those needs? Do schools understand the communities from which their African American students come and, in response, develop programs to meet the students' needs? Why is it that some African American students so seldom get to showcase their talents in assemblies and clubs? Why are those students skilled with balls provided more recognition than those who can speak or act or sing? Most of all, are institutions providing opportunities that inspire African American and other children to believe in what they are capable of achieving? Do schools send messages that supersede the larger societal messages of low expectations, or do the schools, through their institutional structures, reinforce those messages?

As we focus reform on institutional changes such as decreasing class sizes, increasing mandated courses, and other forms of school change, more attention must be given to exploring the hidden messages being communicated to African American students and to considering how to reform the messages being sent. Caring interpersonal relationships between particular teachers and particular students are important, but they can be undermined if the institution sends conflicting messages. Considering this facet of reform, too, is essential if policies are to be implemented that actually address the needs of students and thereby have some hope of changing their school experiences. As for Man, the questions come too late. He has already dropped out.

Notes

1. This reference seems to refer generally to academic clubs, performing arts, and the like. He reports that black students are involved as cheerleaders or as members of the drill team.

2. Man was given the option not to go, but said he'd rather go than stay at school all day.

3. By *community standards*, I mean that the school has not been defined as good because of external documentation such as test scores, college attendance rates, or other easily verifiable external data. Instead, the research accepts the community's evaluation of its school as a good one and seeks to understand, from the perspective of the participants, why it is that the schooling was valued.

4. The *training* in the school title can be traced to the school's receipt of funds from the Rosenwald Foundation in 1926; prior to that time, it was known as the Yanceyville School. However, the term does not imply that the school had a nonacademic curriculum.

5. The total number of black children enrolled in school in the last years of segregation exceeded the enrollment of white students. However, it can also be speculated that the unusually large facilities were also due in part to the county's effort to demonstrate that it was providing an "equal" education for blacks; the new building was constructed just as *Brown v. Board of Education* was winding its way to the Supreme Court.

6. Elsewhere, I provide detail on the theoretical and practical basis of this approach (Walker, 1996).

7. A more complete description of the methodology is available in Walker, 1996.

8. Records are not available that would account for students who may have been in more than one club.

References

Ashmore, H. (1954). *The Negro and the schools.* Chapel Hill: University of North Carolina Press.

Bullock, H. (1967). *A history of Negro education in the South.* Cambridge, MA: Harvard University Press.

Cecelski, D. (1994). *Along freedom road: Hyde County, North Carolina, and the fate of black schools in the South.* Chapel Hill: University of North Carolina Press.

CCTS Faculty. (1950). *Evaluative criteria* (Washington Cooperative Study of Secondary School Standards).

CCTS School Philosophy. (circa 1954). Unpublished CCTS School document. (Available in author collection.)

Clark, K. (1965). *Dark ghetto.* New York: Harper & Row.

Delpit, L. (1992). Acquisition of literate discourse: Bowing before the master? *Theory Into Practice, 31*(4), 296-302.

Dempsey, V., & Noblit, G. (1993). The demise of caring in an African American community: One consequence of school desegregation. *Urban Review, 25,* 47-61.

Dillard, N. L. (1935). *Principal report.* Raleigh, NC: State Archives.

Dillard, N. L. (1942). *A survey of extracurricular activities in five Negro secondary schools of North Carolina.* Unpublished masters thesis, University of Michigan.

Dillard, N. L. (1967). *Principal report.* Raleigh, NC: State Archives.

Foster, M. (1990). The politics of race: Through the eyes of African American teachers. *Journal of Education, 172*(3), 123-141.

Foster, M. (1991a). Constancy, connectedness, and constraints in the lives of African American teachers. *NWSA Journal, 3*(2), 233-261.

Foster, M. (1991b). *Reclaiming silenced voices: Connectedness and constraints in the lives and careers of black teachers.* Paper presented at the National Academy of Education, Stanford University.

Gilligan, C. (1982). *In a different voice.* Cambridge, MA: Harvard University Press.

Harlan, L. (1958). *Separate and unequal: Public school campaigns and racism in the southern seaboard states, 1901-1915.* Chapel Hill: University of North Carolina Press.

Irvine, J. (1990). *Black students and school failure: Policies, practices, and prescriptions.* New York: Greenwood.

Irvine, R., & Irvine, J. (1983). The impact of the desegregation process on the education of black students: Key variables. *Journal of Negro Education, 52*(4), 410-422.

Jones, F. (1981). *A traditional model of educational excellence.* Washington, DC: Howard University Press.

Kluger, R. (1977). *Simple justice.* New York: Random House.

Ladson-Billings, G. (1991). Returning to the source: Implications for educating teachers of black students. In M. Foster (Ed.), *Qualitative investigations into schools and schooling.* New York: AMS Press.

Ladson-Billings, G. (1995). Toward a theory of culturally relevant pedagogy. *American Educational Research Journal, 32*(3), 465-491.

Local school group approves resolution on teachers' pay. (1957, March 28). *Caswell Messenger.*

Long, H. (1932). *Public secondary education for Negroes in North Carolina.* New York: Teachers College, Columbia University.

N.C. Negro teacher pay tops white. (1960, October 2). *Durham Morning Herald* (University of North Carolina Clipping File).

Noddings, N. (1984). *Caring: A feminine approach to ethics and moral education.* Berkeley: University of California Press.

Noddings, N. (1986). Fidelity in teaching, teacher education, and research for teaching. *Harvard Educational Review, 56*(4), 496-510.

School Evaluative Criteria. (1953). Washington, DC: Cooperative Study of Secondary School Standards. (Version with CCTS notes available in private author collection.)

Smylie, M. A., Yowell, C. M., & Kahne, J. (1995). Educational remedies for school segregation: A social science statement to the U.S. Supreme Court in *Missouri v. Jenkins. Urban Review, 27*(3), 207-233.

Southern Association of Schools and Colleges Evaluation. (1954). *Report.* Raleigh, NC: State Archives.

Sowell, T. (1974). Black excellence: The case of Dunbar High School. *The Public Interest, 35*, 1-21.

Sowell, T. (1976). Patterns of black excellence. *The Public Interest, 43*, 26-58.

Walker, E. (1993a). Caswell County Training School, 1933-1969: Relationships between community and school. *Harvard Educational Review, 63*(2), 161-182.

Walker, E. (1993b). Interpersonal caring in the "good" segregated schooling of African American children: Evidence from the case of Caswell County Training School. *Urban Review, 25*(1), 63-77.

Walker, V. (1996). *Their highest potential: An African American school community in the segregated South.* Chapel Hill: University of North Carolina Press.

Why the South will filibuster for the filibuster. (1949, March 12). *The Carolina Times* (Clipping File Through 1975, North Carolina Collection, UNC Library, Chapel Hill).

Woodward, C. V. (1974). *The strange career of Jim Crow* (3rd rev. ed.). New York: Oxford University Press.

11

The All-Black School
Inherently Unequal or
a Culture-Based Alternative?

CHRISTINE J. FALTZ

DONALD O. LEAKE

How does one measure "equal treatment in education"—by input or output? That is, should we focus on the means of obtaining a quality education (input), or should we direct our resources toward quality education as an end (output)? As early as 1935, W. E. B. DuBois expressed concern over impending desegregation issues. He urged blacks to focus on the educational goal, rather than the means of achieving that goal:

> Theoretically, the Negro needs neither segregated schools nor mixed schools. What he needs is education. What he must remember is that there is no magic, either in mixed schools or segregated schools. A mixed school with poor and unsympathetic teachers, with hostile public opinion, and no teaching of truth concerning black folk, is bad. A segregated school with ignorant placeholders, inadequate equipment, poor salaries . . . is equally bad. Other things being equal, the mixed school is the broader, more natural basis for the education of all youth. It gives wider contacts; it inspires greater self-confidence;

and suppresses the inferiority complex. But other things seldom are equal, and in that case, Sympathy, Knowledge, and the Truth, outweigh all that the mixed school can offer. (p. 335)

In February 1955, less than a year after *Brown v. Board of Education* (1954), DuBois warned that "at best it will be a generation before the segregated Negro school entirely disappears" (as cited in Foner, 1970, p. 283). He further believed that the elimination of the "Negro school" will change forever the content of the curriculum for African American children: He said that the "teaching of Negro history will leave the school and with it that brave story of Negro resistance" (p. 283).

Although he grossly underestimated the time frame for implementation, DuBois could not have been more prophetic in his views regarding the loss of the black experience as a subject of schooling. After 40 years of desegregation, the all-black school remains a fixture in our urban areas, but the character of these schools has changed dramatically. Bureaucratic and classroom practices persist that deny black children the necessary opportunities and resources to fulfill their potential: Arguably, these schools are not attuned to the history and personal dreams of the African American parents and children they serve.

The quest for equal educational opportunity and the corresponding need to address and eliminate the subtle nuances of discrimination in our schools is as compelling an issue today as it was on May 17, 1954. There is little doubt that *Brown* effected a radical social transformation in this country that we are still feeling more than 40 years later. But the wave of triumph that engulfed the black community in the wake of the *Brown* decision was soured by the realization that change would not occur with "all deliberate speed," as mandated by the Court (Kluger, 1975).

The purpose of this chapter is twofold: first, to examine three basic assumptions we make about the saliency of desegregation within a historical context, and second, to offer a culture-based alternative to desegregation as operationalized in Milwaukee's African American immersion schools.

The Historical Context of Desegregation

Quite possibly the most important and controversial test of the 14th Amendment began in 1895 in a Supreme Court case involving Homer Plessy, a biracial resident of Louisiana who refused to ride in the "colored" section of the train. In establishing the "separate but equal" doctrine (*Plessy v. Ferguson*, 1896), the Supreme Court ruled that segregation did not create a badge of inferiority if separate facilities were equal. This separate but equal doctrine provided the constitutional support for state laws requiring separate schools based on race.

In 1953, five cases involving school segregation were presented to the Supreme Court. Because the cases were taken in alphabetical order, *Brown v. Board of Education of Topeka, Kansas* (1954), became the first case to challenge a state law requiring the segregation of schools. In 1954, with Chief Justice Earl Warren writing for the majority, the Supreme Court unanimously rejected the Plessy court decision, ruling that separate educational facilities were inherently unequal.

Repeatedly the courts invoked *Brown*, broadening its scope to hold that all forms of segregation were discriminatory. The ripple effects of these court cases resulted in the desegregation of restaurants, buses, water fountains, and beaches, but resistance to the court-ordered mandate continued in U.S. schools (Kluger, 1975). Meanwhile, the debate that followed in the courts was centered around whether the solution to these inherently unequal schools was to be a color-blind or a color-conscious one (Walberg, 1992).

The subsequent attempts at mandatory changes in the racial composition of schools ordered by some courts seemed to go beyond the color-blind, nondiscriminatory mandate of Brown. On July 15, 1955, a district court in South Carolina acted on a school segregation case that was remanded to it by the Supreme Court—*Briggs v. Elliott*.

Circuit Court Judge John Parker wrote that there was nothing in either the U.S. Constitution or in the *Brown* decision that takes away from individuals the right to choose their school. The state could not deny access to a school on the basis of race. However, Parker argued, children of different races may voluntarily attend different schools, just as they do different churches. "The Constitution, in other words, does not require integration. It merely forbids discrimination" (*Briggs v. Elliott*, p. 777). At the time, Parker's words were used by many states to maneuver around or outright defy the court order to desegregate. Those states offered blacks freedom of choice, knowing that few blacks would have the courage to send their children to all-white schools where they were not wanted.

A few years later, in the U.S. Civil Rights Act of 1964, Congress defined desegregation as the "assignment of students to public schools without regard to their race, color, religion, or national origin, but desegregation shall not mean the assignment of students to public schools in order to overcome racial balance" (p. 246). This color-blind definition would not stand long. In 1968, in *Green v. County School Board of New Kent County,* the Supreme Court struck down the *Briggs* decision and accepted a view of the Constitution as color-conscious and of desegregation as color-conscious, involuntary changes in the racial composition of schools.

The Impact of Desegregation

Indeed, more than four decades after the court issued its implementation decree, the impact of the *Brown* decision as an instrument of educational reform as well as social change has been unprecedented (Green, 1984). However, research findings assessing the effectiveness of desegregation strategies on the achievement of African American[1] children have been inconclusive and mixed at best. Although it avoids issues related to the constitutionality of desegregation, Nancy St. John's analysis of over 100 social science studies conducted during the two decades following Brown concluded,

> On the basis of this evidence, biracial schooling must be judged neither a demonstrated success nor a demonstrated failure . . . as implemented to date desegregation has not rapidly closed the black-white gap in academic achievement, though it has rarely lowered and sometimes raised the scores of black children. (as cited in Bell, 1980, p. 6)

Furthermore, in his summary of 35 years of empirical research on the relationship between black students' learning and racial composition of schools, Walberg (1992) concluded that "no consistent evidence of the positive effects of school racial composition or desegregation on black learning has been forthcoming" (p. 363). Yet we continue to invest millions of dollars to desegregate. Thousands of costly buses fill the streets of our urban centers each morning, moving students across town past their neighborhood schools to racially mixed buildings, even though we cannot consistently demonstrate educational benefits.

What may have been a noble idea in 1954 never delivered on the promise of equal educational opportunity for black children. There are those in our educational community, both African American and white, who believe that desegregation is an indispensable necessity to a quality education. Many of these individuals insist that we must accept the process for its own sake, and they censure as separatists those who challenge them to look objectively at the results. On the other side, a number of individuals, both African American and white, would agree with DuBois that what black children need is a quality education regardless of the school's racial composition (Bell, 1987a, p. 137).

Proponents of his position deny that the equal educational opportunity promised by the U.S. Supreme Court requires an integrated setting and reject the notion that it is not possible to achieve academic excellence in a predominately black school environment. Furthermore, many of us are outraged by the often erroneous assumptions that pervade our society, beliefs that black children inevitably suffer intellectually when their education occurs mainly in black schools and that the motivation and achievement of African American children necessarily improves when they are enrolled in majority white schools (Busby & Barrett, 1988).

After Busing, Are Desegregated Schools Also Inherently Unequal?

An analysis of 174 desegregated districts by Meier, Stewart, and England (1989) clearly documents that since *Brown*, segregation was prohibited and mixing was encouraged, and sometimes required, but the inequity continues. The authors discuss how, in an effort to gain access to equal educational opportunities for black students, educators focused on eliminating segregated schools and gaining entry to the predominately white school systems—desegregation. But this approach ignored the inherent resistance the public had to integration and arguably led to the development of other ways to limit access. Second-generation discrimination, as defined by Meier et al. (1989), is "practices that impede the integration of schools and deny black students equal access to education" (p. 22). The authors found evidence that, by disproportionately tracking blacks into lower academic tracks and whites into higher academic tracks, and by disproportionately using disciplinary actions against black students, school systems were able to limit interracial contact and thereby reduce white flight. In the process, most blacks received lower-quality educational opportunities. Consequently, the researchers concluded, efforts to desegregate defy the intent of *Brown*, as this nation witnesses the persistence of practices that result in inherently unequal schools.

Even if we were to momentarily overlook the injustices of second-generation discrimination, we must acknowledge that massive efforts to desegregate schools all across the country have, at best, resulted in minimal mixing of black and white children. At worst, one could argue that the courts' efforts have contributed to white flight and ultimately resegregated conditions (Meier et al., 1989). More than four decades after the *Brown*

Table 11.1 Percentage of U.S. Black and Latina/o Students in Predominantly Black and
Latina/o and 90-100 Percent Black and Latina/o Schools, 1968-1992

	Predominantly Black and Latina/o		90%-100% Black and Latina/o	
	Blacks	Latina/os	Blacks	Latina/os
1968-1969	76.6	54.8	64.3	23.1
1972-1973	63.6	56.6	38.7	23.3
1980-1981	62.9	68.1	33.2	28.8
1986-1987	63.3	71.5	32.5	32.2
1991-1992	66.0	73.4	33.9	34.0

SOURCE: Orfield, 1993. Reprinted with permission of the Harvard Project on School Desegregation,
Cambridge, MA, p. 7.

decision, the enrollment in many of our large city school systems has become
predominately Black and Latina/o. In our 25 largest cities, students of color
make up more than half of the enrollment in public schools (Hodgkinson,
1985). As Table 11.1 shows, from 1986 to 1991, the proportion of black
students rose in schools that enroll more than half Black and Latina/o
students, reaching levels that had existed prior to the first court-ordered
busing decision in 1971. By 1991, approximately two thirds of all black
students and nearly three fourths of all Latina/o students attended schools
that were predominately Black and Latina/o; one third attended schools
that were more than 90% Black and Latina/o (Orfield, 1993, Table 1).

Assumptions Underlying Desegregation

In the past, three basic assumptions have impeded any frank discussion
of the desegregation ideology. First is the assumption that desegregation
"works," even in the absence of empirical evidence. In any bureaucratic
structure, there exists the danger of being victimized by institutional assumptions so familiar that they are never questioned—particularly by those
most intimately involved. Due to the sensitive nature of the topic, educators
seem reluctant to ask very basic questions about the efficacy of desegregation strategies. Questions like: Who benefits from court-mandated desegregation? or Does education improve for African American students after
districts comply with court mandates?

If the purpose of the *Brown* decision was to assure equal access to a
quality education (Kluger, 1975), then logic would suggest support for

strategies that work and abandonment of policies/strategies that are clearly unsuccessful. However, many educators tend not to be results-oriented in matters related to desegregation. Four decades of school desegregation have produced neither genuine racial desegregation of public education nor the extension of equal educational opportunity to the majority of black students in America (Busby & Barrett, 1988). Correspondingly, the educational community seems willing to ignore the growing body of empirical evidence that clearly documents second-generation discrimination (Bates, 1990; Meier et al., 1989). Educators seem reluctant to engage in any frank discussion of the desegregation ideology for fear of giving support and encouragement to those with racist agendas. Mindful of this point, the present discussion should not be interpreted as a repudiation of the integration ideology embedded in the civil rights movement. It is not. However, researchers can no longer afford to look the other way while another generation of children is miseducated because of reluctance to ask needed questions of fervent desegregationists.

The second assumption is that black parents are ardent supporters of desegregation. There is a particular mind-set among proponents of desegregation and white liberals in the educational community that the goal of black parents is to obtain an integrated educational setting for their children. The reality of the matter is that black parents want a quality education for their children (Bell, 1987a; Lightfoot, 1978). However, a number of black parents feel that the only way this can be achieved is by sending their children to predominantly white schools, a view perpetuated by the post-*Brown* philosophy (Bell, 1980).

Given the overall perception of schools in the black community, it was only natural that many black parents would "choose" to leave their "contained" environment for one that was desegregated (Fuller, 1985). Because many black parents were aware that, in many instances, their children were not receiving a quality education, and given the belief that their children's lack of achievement was directly attributable to the social/cultural deficits of their community, black people were convinced to bear a disproportionate burden for desegregation. According to Fuller (1985), it was only later that the community realized that acceptance of this burden would not automatically result in a quality education for their children.

Research suggests that if black parents can be assured of equal educational opportunities without forced busing, they would rather not have their children bused (Cuddy, 1983). When asked if they would prefer to attend their own neighborhood schools if the quality were equivalent to suburban white schools, 75% of the blacks participating in Boston's urban-to-suburban transfer program answered affirmatively. This is not to say integration is undesirable. We live in a culturally diverse society, and we should facilitate integration of our communities. But what must be emphasized then is not a forced bus ride, but rather educational excellence for students of color (Cuddy, 1983). However, as implemented, busing to desegregate seems to have discriminated against those same blacks who were supposed to benefit most.

What happens to the essential elements of parent and community involvement when the school is in a noncontiguous neighborhood? Due to the tremendous distances some parents have to travel to their child's desegregated school, it is often hard for them to establish a visible presence (Harris, 1983). Surely all black parents should have the option of sending their children to predominately white schools if they choose. However, given the uncertain educational outcome of exercising that option, black parents who prefer to send their children to all-black schools that offer equal educational opportunity ought to be encouraged, not assailed (Bell, 1987b).

The third assumption is that a quality education can only occur in a desegregated setting (Irvine, 1991). Inherent in definitions of racial balance are the erroneous assumptions that black children inevitably suffer intellectually when their education occurs in all- or predominately black schools and that the motivation and achievement of black children necessarily improve when they are enrolled in majority white schools (Scott, 1983). Court remedies seem to infer that not only can blacks not learn unless seated next to whites, but they cannot learn unless seated next to a certain percentage of whites (Bell, 1980).

The barriers of continuing resistance, a less than supportive Supreme Court, and the growing concentration of most poor blacks in large urban areas render implausible continuing efforts to achieve compliance with *Brown* through reliance on racial balance plans. Because most urban areas lack a sufficient number of white students to adequately desegregate (Hodgkinson, 1985), we must either write off the majority of urban schools or concentrate our efforts on improving the predominantly black schools. Moreover, many today are legitimately asking what demonstrated educational purpose is served when black students ride a segregated school bus for perhaps an hour across town, from a segregated neighborhood to a racially balanced school, and then back again for another hour on a segregated school bus to their segregated neighborhoods (Rabinow, 1983)?

A Study in Desegregation: Milwaukee, Wisconsin

The first assumption questions the efficacy of desegregation. What is clearly needed in any discussion regarding desegregation is a sense of proportionality, that is, how the results relate to the larger picture. If change is not proportional to the larger picture, then the relationship of the factors to the original problem remain unaffected. We must be willing to apply a proportional litmus test to any strategy that is supposed to result in a change. Arguably, in matters regarding school desegregation, the disparity in achievement between black and white students is the single most critical area in need of change. Therefore, in the context of proportionality, a strategy should be deemed effective only if it abridges the gap in student achievement. It is within this context we examine a court-ordered desegregation plan in Milwaukee, Wisconsin.

In 1976, the Milwaukee Public Schools (MPS) and suburban districts in the metropolitan area agreed to participate in a voluntary student transfer plan. The program was promoted as a magnet-school model that permitted both interdistrict and intradistrict[2] transfers if the racial balance at the receiving school was improved. The expectation was that these social rearrangements produced by desegregation[3] would result in greater educational success for all children. A substantial body of empirical data (Greater Milwaukee Education Trust, 1991; Meier et al., 1989; Milwaukee Urban League, 1988; Willie, Alves, & Hartman, 1990; Wisconsin Policy Research Institute, 1989) suggests that desegregation plans as operationalized in the MPS and elsewhere have not met the goal of open and equal access to a quality education. MPS did implement its desegregation program peacefully and met or exceeded the court-imposed desegregation goals for each year (Harris, 1983). By 1979-1980, 79% of MPS students attended racially balanced schools (Milwaukee Public Schools, 1980); nevertheless, the inner-city schools remained virtually all black (Smith, 1987). These segregated schools could have been eliminated with a plan that required 100% desegregation, but this was a politically unpopular decision that was not made by the federal judge in 1976. Segments of both the white and black communities argued against 100% desegregation—whites because it would have required mandatory busing and blacks because they wanted some all-black schools (Harris, 1983).

Also, significant demographic changes occurred in Milwaukee during the 1970s. White enrollment declined by more than 50%, whereas black enrollment grew by more than 20%. Contrary to these trends, the district

Table 11.2 Neighborhood Attendance Areas by Percent Minority, Number of Attendance Area Students, Number of School Seats Available, and Surplus (Deficit) of Seats, 1986-1987

Area	Percentage Minority	Students	Seats	Surplus (Deficit)
I	80-100	40,855	19,091	(21,765)
II	60-79.9	14,703	10,985	(3,718)
III	30-59.9	17,379	19,946	2,567
IV	15-29.9	5,084	6,978	1,894
V	1-14.9	11,351	19,168	7,817

SOURCE: Milwaukee Public Schools: 1986-87 Attendance Area/School Enrollment, The Interim Steering of the New North Division School District, Milwaukee Public Schools, 1987. Reprinted with permission.

continued to build new schools in the predominantly white neighborhoods. Furthermore, as part of the desegregation program, a number of black neighborhood schools were converted to citywide schools or closed. As a result, schools in black neighborhoods no longer had the space to accommodate area students. Literally thousands of black parents were forced to bus their children: The choice of a neighborhood school was nonexistent. To illustrate, Table 11.2 depicts the impact of this program for 1986 to 1987: In areas organized by the percentage African Americans and other non-whites, the table shows the number of students in each area, the number of available school seats, and the surplus or deficit of seats.

Roughly 53,000 of MPS's 100,000 pupils are bused each day to achieve desegregation goals: 40,000 of them within the city and 13,000 to suburban schools. However, 80% of the white pupils are not bused, whereas 80% of the black pupils are bused (Williams, 1991). When whites are bused, it is primarily to other white neighborhoods; if they are bused to the inner city, it is most often to citywide specialty schools.

To further compound the problem, rising costs associated with busing and administration have significantly reduced the instructional share of the MPS budget. Between 1976 and 1988, implementation of the desegregation program has taken dollars out of the classroom. Although the instructional budget grew (105%), it grew less than total spending (132%) and less than inflation (114%) (see Figure 11.1).[4]

Moreover, in 1975-1976, the year before the desegregation program began, the per pupil budget in MPS was $1,846. Twelve years later, in

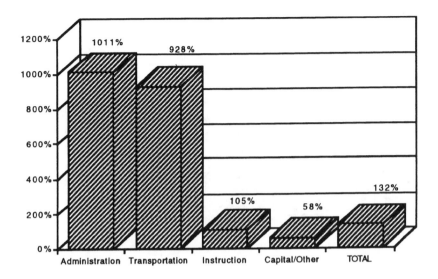

Figure 11.1. Percentage Growth in Milwaukee Public Schools by Category: From 1976 to 1988
SOURCE: Wisconsin Policy Research Institute, 1989. Reprinted with permission.

1987-1988, per pupil spending had risen 190%, to $5,351, but during the same time period, the instructional share of the budget decreased by 8% while the administration and transportation costs increased 10% and 6%, respectfully (see Figure 11.2).[5] The Wisconsin Policy Research Institute (1989) reported substantial growth in transportation costs related

> mostly to busing. . . . [It was further indicated that] a significant, but undetermined, portion of the administrative increase is due to the substantial commitment of MPS central office staff to the administration of busing contracts and the complex pupil assignment process. (p. 32)

Educational Equity in Milwaukee

The increased cost of busing would most certainly be justified if it produced a corresponding increase in academic achievement of black students and eliminated the achievement gap between black and white students. However, such results did not occur. It is difficult to compare

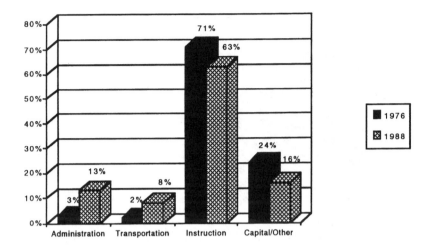

Figure 11.2. Percentage Allocation of Milwaukee Public Schools Budget Comparing Year Prior to Busing to 1988 Expenditures
SOURCE: Wisconsin Policy Research Institute, 1989. Reprinted with permission.

pre-1976 data with current data because grades and achievement scores were not maintained in a consistent format. We do know that by the 1990-1991 school year, although 78% of the black students attended deseg-regated, nonspecialty[6] schools, the following existed:

- Average grades reported for black students were D to D+. In fact, in 6 of the 10 desegregated high schools, the average grade point average (GPA) of black freshmen was below a 1.00 (see Table 11.3).
- Between 27% and 60% of the grades reported for black freshmen were F (see Table 11.3).
- At the 10th-grade level, in all but one high school, 76% or more of the black students tested below the national average in reading and mathematics (see Table 11.4).
- There were significant gaps in black and white achievement; in math and reading, the gap was more than 20 percentage points in every school (see Table 11.4).

Schools can and do make a difference in such factors as student achievement and behavior (see, for example, Rutter et al., 1979). When

The All-Black School

Table 11.3 Fall Semester Grade Point Averages (GPA), on a 4.00 scale, and Course Failure Rates, by Race, for Freshmen at Desegregated Nonspecialty High Schools (1990-1991)

High School	Grade Point Average Black	White	Failure Rate Percentage Black	White	Percentage Black Enrollment
A	1.52	1.59	27	36	74
B	.98	1.71	47	30	70
C	1.23	2.06	34	18	70
D	.98	1.77	48	24	69
E	1.23	2.33	37	15	65
F	1.27	1.97	35	17	55
G	.95	1.52	52	37	49
H	.91	1.92	48	22	47
I	.64	1.39	60	36	33
J	.87	1.16	50	43	30

SOURCE: MPS/Greater Milwaukee Trust report, April 1991. Reprinted with permission from the Milwaukee Public Schools, Milwaukee, WI.

Table 11.4 Percentage of 10th-Grade Students at or Above the National Average on the Test of Achievement and Proficiency (TAP) in Reading and Mathematics, Grade Point Averages (GPA), and Percentage Suspended, by Race, at Desegregated Nonspecialty High Schools (1990-1991)

School	Enrollment Percentage White	Black	Reading Test of Achievement and Proficiency Percentage White	Black	Math Test of Achievement and Proficiency Percentage White	Black	Grade Point Average White	Black	Percentage of Students Suspended White	Black
A	16	65	44	15	47	20	1.93	1.69	5	16
B	31	64	33	13	36	15	1.68	1.12	11	18
C	32	64	67	20	54	21	2.16	1.35	2	13
D	33	64	50	13	51	17	1.86	1.17	10	32
E	37	59	44	12	46	9	2.17	1.41	10	25
F	38	53	47	24	42	22	2.01	1.45	20	38
G	48	42	67	23	65	23	1.80	1.08	2	3
H	51	42	64	27	63	34	2.09	1.12	1	3
I	56	30	44	8	52	10	1.68	1.03	14	34
J	25	24	40	14	40	19	1.47	1.08	19	40

Source: MPS 1991 Report Card, Milwaukee Public Schools, 1991. Reprinted with permission.

Table 11.5 Percentage of Black MPS Elementary Students at or Above the National
Average on the Iowa Test of Basic Skills (ITBS): Reading, Mathematics and
Language Arts, and Suspension Rates, Categorized by the Percentage of
Black Enrollment in the School (1990-1991)

Grade 5 School Enrollment	Reading	Math	Language Arts	Percentage of Black Students Suspended
0%-24% Black	12.56	29.45	21.43	6.20
25%-65% Black	27.48	32.60	37.00	4.14
66%-89% Black	27.88	33.82	41.67	2.33
90%-100% Black	31.96	36.00	29.56	0.77

SOURCE: *MPS 1991 Report Card*, Milwaukee Public Schools, 1991. Reprinted with permission.

students are actively learning content that has personal meaning for them,
there seem to be higher achievement levels and fewer discipline problems
in schools. Managing student behavior is, however, a complex and integral
part of the teaching experience. Although the consequences for misbehav-
ior vary, any decision to remove a student from the learning environment
will obviously affect what the student is able to learn. After expulsion,
suspending a student from school is the most severe response to a violation
of school rules. Table 11.4 provides a summary of student suspensions
administered in Milwaukee's desegregated nonspecialty high schools.

The major premise underlying desegregation suggests that educational
opportunity for black students will improve in a racially mixed setting;
however, studies suggest that the education black students receive when
they attend schools with whites is usually different and inferior (Carnegie
Corporation, 1984-1985; College Board, 1985). In fact, in Milwaukee, data
indicate that in all but one category, achievement levels tended to be higher
in schools with higher percentages of black students (see Table 11.5).

As we stated previously, our intent is not to suggest that a school's
effectiveness is automatically tied to its racial composition. However, we
believe the data summarized in Table 11.5 indicate that a black student can
obtain a quality education in a predominantly black setting and is not
necessarily guaranteed one in a desegregated setting. When we compared
the numbers of students who began ninth grade in 1976, the first year of
desegregation, with the numbers who graduated 4 years later, in 1980, the
completion rate for black students was 45%, compared to a completion rate

of 61% for white students. In 1990, the high school completion rate for black students was 32%, whereas for white students, it was 56%. Thus, 14 years after the implementation of the desegregation plan, the high school completion rate for African American students had declined by 13%, compared to a 5% decline for white students (Greater Milwaukee Education Trust, 1991). The disparity between black and white high school completion rates has increased during the desegregation years.

Quality Education Versus Desegregation

In the 1970s, the overall perception of schools located in Milwaukee's black community was that the educational quality was inferior to that offered by the suburban districts. Therefore, it was understandable when many black parents opted out of their attendance area for one that was desegregated. Black parents were generally aware that, in many instances, their children were not receiving a quality education. Moreover, they were asked to believe that student underachievement was directly attributable to the social and cultural deficits of their community. Desegregation was promoted as a viable solution to ineffective schools, and blacks were asked to bear the disproportionate burden for desegregation (Fuller, 1985).

The implication that desegregation would help children "escape" from the pathological conditions of their community was not only flawed, but racist. In an effort to strike down the separate but equal model, the message became all-black institutions are inferior, and the goal of desegregation became the elimination of all-black institutions. In reality, these assumptions inherently foster low expectations for black students and have resulted in a new form of segregation and discrimination that contradicts the mandate of Brown, rather than implementing it. In point of fact, implementation of court-ordered desegregation did not result in a better education for Milwaukee's students. The racist views that were a part of this society were perpetuated and were arguably reflected in the implementation of the desegregation plans in Milwaukee and other cities (Bell, 1987b).

The Fragmented Community

According to Irvine (1991), before desegregation, the all-black school

took on uniquely stylized characteristics reflective of its members—patterns of communication, cultural preferences, and normatively diffused modes of behavior. . . . [These complex organizations were] not only educational institutions in the ordinary sense of the term but institutions that addressed the deeper psychological and sociological needs of their clients. (p. 35)

The black school was second only to the church in its importance to the black community infrastructure. Unfortunately, the desegregation movement in Milwaukee significantly contributed to the isolation between blacks and their schools. Previously, many segregated black communities functioned quite effectively to meet the needs of their residents. Many would agree it was the well-intentioned liberal social policies motivated by *Brown* that undermined the mutual support networks of the segregated black community (Irvine & Irvine, 1983; Jewell, 1988). Moreover, the neighborhood school, the institution that served as the educational and social center of the community, a source of pride to parents and students alike, and most important, the focus for individual and collective aspirations, was destroyed (Johnson, 1954).

Table 11.6 demonstrates the fragmentation that occurred in Milwaukee. It ranks the top 20 neighborhood attendance areas by the number of different schools to which children were bused in 1987-1988. The table shows the percentage of attendance area children who were black, the number who attended their neighborhood school, the number bused, and the number of schools to which they were bused.

Admittedly, a number of factors have contributed to the loss of a sense of community and positive neighborhood identification in Milwaukee's African American community; however, the implementation procedures of school desegregation have played a major role. For example, the scattering of black students throughout the city, as graphically illustrated in Figure 11.3, increased the alienation of black youths from their neighborhoods while, at the same time, reducing the ability of parents and neighbors to participate in the schools and help control the emerging problems.

Hence, the public schools in predominately African American sections of Milwaukee are no longer community institutions, have little relationship to the neighborhoods, and are impotent educational institutions (Hagedorn, 1988).

Is the neighborhood school concept a relic standing in the way of the educational progress? Or are neighborhood schools merely a diversionary tactic to avoid desegregation? The real question should be, How can we assure that all children have equal access to a quality education, even if it results in a return to neighborhood schools? In practice, neighborhood schools mean safe, quick, and inexpensive access for children, and they allow children to have classmates as afterschool playmates. When the

Table 11.6 Attendance Area Busing Pattern: Top 20 Neighborhood Attendance Areas

Attendance Area School	Percentage Black	Number Attending Area School	Number Bused	Number of Schools to Which Bused
AA	96	481	1,652	104
BB	82	474	1,014	99
CC	96	504	1,071	97
DD	86	499	983	96
EE	96	510	646	94
FF	98	585	606	94
GG	68	393	757	93
HH	97	606	657	92
II	99	733	812	91
JJ	78	505	768	91
KK	88	379	744	90
LL	64	456	612	89
MM	98	596	414	88
NN	80	471	640	88
OO	97	460	481	85
PP	81	487	401	83
QQ	99	522	391	81
RR	63	359	521	81
SS	97	501	302	79
Total		9,521	13,472	86 (average)

SOURCE: September 1988 MPS *Sending and Receiving Attendance Reports,* Milwaukee, WI, Public Schools, 1988. Reprinted with permission.

school is located close to home, parents find it easier to be involved in the schools and are more likely to participate, thus helping to increase the bond between the community's values and the school's academic and social mission (Hagedorn, 1988). In schools where this collaborative relationship does not exist, strategies should be implemented to make parental involvement a part of the school culture. From a cost-benefit perspective, investing in neighborhood schools and parental involvement makes sense.

Certainly, we would agree that those parents who choose to send their children to a desegregated school should have such an option. But for those who prefer neighborhood schools, choices should be available as well. Moreover, with the Milwaukee district currently less than 31% white, and the proportion of whites dropping every year, it is neither realistic nor

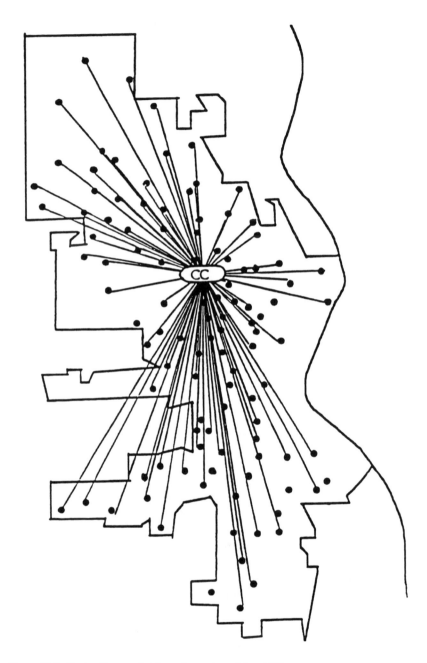

Figure 11.3. Busing Pattern for Attendance Area School CC
SOURCE: Wisconsin Policy Research Institute, 1989. Reprinted with permission.

mathematically sound to expect each of the schools to be desegregated in any meaningful way. If all-black schools are destined to exist in urban areas, it is incumbent upon us to make them work. Consequently, we should be focusing our attention and resources on strategies to make schools instructionally sound and academically effective institutions.

The current discussion raises questions about the efficacy of a strategy that uses racial balancing to improve academic achievement. Clearly this strategy has not worked in Milwaukee, and we seriously question whether it has worked elsewhere. Thus, the real issue at hand in urban districts is, Will racial balancing continue to drive our educational priorities or should we develop strategies to enhance all-black schools?

A Culture-Based Model:
The African American Immersion School

In January, 1990, the authors were part of a task force impaneled by MPS to study the district's programs and to determine how the district was serving (or failing to serve) African American males. Data generated by this task force revealed that more than 80% of the 5,716 African American males enrolled in Milwaukee high schools had GPAs below 2.0; whereas African American males made up 27.6% of all students in MPS, they accounted for 50% of the students suspended and 94% of the students expelled (African American Male Task Force, 1990).

Although the original charge was to examine the plight of African American males, the task force reviewed issues relevant to both genders and readily acknowledged the existence of parallel problems for African American females. Corollary figures on the educational experiences of female African American students further substantiated the necessity for immediate substantive changes in MPS policies and practices as they affected African American students of both genders.

The task force recommended that two African American immersion school (AAIS) sites be selected from 19 schools in the Milwaukee district that had a 90% or greater concentration of African American students. Some highly respected educators continue to challenge the AAIS concept based upon the belief that it promotes resegregation and countermands the *Brown* decision, which struck down separate but equal facilities almost four decades ago. However, the AAIS concept specifically addresses the educational challenges of districts in which African American students make up the majority. In Milwaukee, the AAIS model is perceived as encompassing concepts, content, themes, perspectives, and pedagogy reflective of the African/African American ontology. In a theoretical sense, this model provides a framework for the development of a total learning environment designed to fit the needs and draw upon the strengths of African American students. More specifically, the immersion-school model is helping students acquire competence in social skills, communication, problem solving, critical thinking, effective citizenship, self-actualization, and male and female identity development, particularly as these competencies relate to ethnicity.

In Milwaukee, the African American immersion schools are coeducational neighborhood schools, located in all-black communities. Because the two schools previously had an existing population of predominantly black students, the immersion school plan did not necessitate the deliberate or artificial creation of racially identifiable schools. However, the two immersion schools do challenge the old, unstated assumption that African American children can learn best when they are sent to schools with large nonminority populations.

Although the immersion schools adhere to the district's nondiscriminatory enrollment policy, when parents make the choice to send their children to these schools, they are informed that an intense sensitivity to African and African American perspectives will guide decisions regarding curricular content, instructional strategies, and additional school programming. The premise of these unique schools is to lay the foundation for a realistic historical and political analysis of African Americans in our society. These schools are child-centered: They are educational settings where instructional strategies that complement the culture and learning styles of black children can be developed and implemented (African American Male Task Force, 1990). The walls, halls, and classrooms reflect the heritage of the children.

In most urban schools, minority students are expected to exist in an environment that negates their language, denies their historical existence, and demeans their culture. In addition, current practice in desegregated settings effectively excludes African American males from the mainstream culture. Arguably, the "traditional curriculum" is too narrow. It tends to have a Eurocentric content and philosophical core that presents a view of the world as seen through the eyes of white males and supports the adoption of that view for all students, regardless of culture (Asante, 1987). Conversely, the curriculum of the AAIS is broad based and multicultural; designed to fit the educational needs and draw upon the strengths of African American students; and intended to prepare students to learn, live, and work in a culturally diverse society. Although a multicultural curriculum is the ultimate goal, the focus of the program evolves from the life experiences of the students and clearly embraces the heritage of Africans and African Americans. The intent is to infuse the curriculum with specific content about black people.

The program draws upon community resources. The school day is structured to create an expanded school family that involves

- A strong sense of community among teachers, parents, and home
- Community members who have established long-term commitments and mentoring relationships with students (For example, all fifth-grade students have an adult mentor from the community with whom they meet regularly.)
- Teachers who have long-term commitments with groups of students; that is, teachers are assigned to a group of students for multiple years
- A requirement that teachers make 18 home visits each semester
- A variety of instructional experiences beyond the school walls
- An evolving sense of community values and responsible citizenship (Students perform community service activities, such as neighborhood cleanups and recycling drives.)
- A proactive role in the educational process for parents and guardians (Through outside funding, both schools have established on-site Parent Involvement Centers.)

These schools have as their primary focus the nurturing of black children and serve to affirm and build positive self-images through in-school experiences.

In any setting, the success of school reform depends a great deal on the commitment, experience, and competence of the professional staff. Reading, writing, and arithmetic do not take place within a value-free situation. One must read about something, and the content of that something is determined by the values of those in authority (Freire, 1985; Rabinow, 1983). Major concerns for the immersion schools included,

1. Who are the role models?
2. What are the success stories being taught?
3. What are the histories, attitudes, and generalizations pervasive within the educational structure?

Beginning with the principal, the entire staff of the immersion school consists of professionals who specifically requested placement in that setting.

Particular attention was given to recruiting African American professionals and paraprofessionals, not because white teachers are inherently less effective, but because of the urgent need to provide role models for nonwhite students. In point of fact, all students need exposure to successful teachers of other races; however, according to the National Education Association's 1991-1992 report, more than 86% of the teaching force will be white, serving a student population that is becoming increasingly nonwhite (Meier et al., 1989; NEA, 1992). Therefore, although raising the African American and other nonwhite teacher representation in all schools is critical, the selection of teachers for the immersion schools was based more on experience and teacher interest, rather than on race or gender.

Milwaukee's African American Immersion Schools:
An Evaluation in Progress

In any major reform effort, it is unreasonable to expect immediate results. However, although the elementary immersion school has only been in operation for 3 years, and the middle school for 2 years, there are numerous reasons for optimism. Patience is our watchword. The African American Immersion Schools Evaluation Project is an independent endeavor under the direction of Drs. Pollard and Ajirotutu from the University of Wisconsin-Milwaukee. The evaluation project's aims include providing feedback to school staffs, researchers, and practitioners regarding the implementation and outcomes; identifying effective strategies for African American students that can be replicated elsewhere; and informing the educational community regarding effective strategies for educating African American children. Both qualitative and quantitative data are being employed to document and evaluate these schools, using a holistic and participatory model.

The AAIS Evaluation Project reports that "both schools have demonstrated significant progress in transforming their cultural milieu from a Eurocentric to an Afrocentric orientation" (Pollard & Ajirotutu, 1994, p. 1). Thus far, there is evidence that the curriculum in each school is being infused with African and African American history and culture. There is progress with ongoing staff development at both schools, which requires that each teacher complete additional coursework in African and African American history and culture. Organizationally, both schools have made progress toward the development of a greater sense of community, including school-within-school groups, families, and uniform adoption for students. In addition, there is evidence of increased community and parent involvement.

Evidence of student growth is being documented in several areas, including self-image, social behavior, and academic performance. Both schools have evidenced more positive social behavior. Furthermore, in its third year, the elementary school has showed evidence of dramatic academic gains (Pollard & Ajirotutu, 1994). For example, in April 1994, all third-grade public school students in the state of Wisconsin were given a reading comprehension test. When the results of this standardized test were disaggregated by school district, 78% of all MPS third graders scored above the standard, 10% of the scores were inconclusive, and 12% scored below the standard. For black third-grade students in the district, 72% scored above the standard, whereas 15% scored below the standard. However, in the African American immersion elementary school, 87% of third-grade pupils scored above the standard, and only 6% scored below the standard (Milwaukee Public Schools, 1994).

Moreover, although strides toward improved achievement have been made districtwide in MPS, the immersion school's success surpassed district averages. When the 110 MPS elementary schools were ranked by average scores over the past 3 years, the immersion school ranked 85th; however, in 1994, the third year of implementation, it soared to 34th place (of 110 schools).

Summary

The purpose of this chapter was to discuss the limitations of desegregation as implemented under *Brown* and to promote, as an alternative, a strategy that will improve urban schools: culture-based education. Milwaukee has been criticized by education's bastions of integration for approving plans to develop two African American immersion schools. Perhaps these critics should be forced to walk in the shoes of Milwaukee's black children, who have borne the disproportionate burden of desegregation for the past 18 years, before they cast the next stone. These African American immersion schools were not proposed as a knee-jerk reaction or as "an act of desperation," as some have suggested. Neither are they a token attempt at political correctness. Rather, this is an issue of justice. Children need to see themselves in the learning process. Furthermore, it is not just a matter of increasing the self-esteem of African American children: These children must learn how to read, write, compute, and problem-solve to be successful adults. Therefore, these schools were conceived by a predominantly black task force of Milwaukee's educational, community, and business leaders as a response to the economic, political, and social realities affecting the life chances of the African Americans in Milwaukee.

When critics warn that African American students in general, and black males in particular, could be "stigmatized" by the separation of the immersion school setting, we are compelled to challenge that they may already be stigmatized by the disproportionate share of the burden for busing that they bear. This pattern could very well send the message to the African American child that "if I don't sit next to a white person, I can't learn." Other factors could also have stigmatizing effects on African American students, such as their dismal academic achievement, suspension, or expulsion records, or the nightly news, which is a constant reminder that more black males are in prison in this country than in college (Hodgkinson, 1985).

After nearly 20 years of implementing busing as a strategy to achieve desegregation in Milwaukee, the expected achievement gains for black children have not been realized. The paradox is that the nurturing environment necessary for such achievement has been undermined by the very process designed to facilitate the desired educational benefits. Therefore we offer as an alternative the AAIS model.

Are these all-black immersion schools inherently unequal? We argue that they are not. These schools are culturally relevant, developmentally appropriate, and instructionally strong. As our society continues to work toward the goal of full integration, our schools should focus on providing high-quality education for students wherever they are.

Notes

1. Please note that we have chosen to use the terms *black* and *African American* interchangeably to represent American individuals from the Negroid race of African ancestry.

2. Transfers of students within MPS are intradistrict transfers. Transfers between MPS and suburban districts are interdistrict transfers.

3. MPS defines desegregation as occurring when a school has a black enrollment of between 25% and 65%. By this standard, in 1991, 101 of the system's 140 schools were desegregated. The primary method of achieving desegregation was busing. Before 1976, 14 of 158 schools were desegregated, using the then-standard of black enrollment of 25% to 45%. Of the remainder, 37 were mostly black, and 107 were mostly white (Wisconsin Policy Research Institute, 1989).

4. Total increase in inflation from 1976 to 1988 was 114%, as measured by the Consumer Price Index for Milwaukee Urban Consumers (1976 = 167.1; 1988 = 358), as determined by the Metropolitan Milwaukee Association of Commerce per U.S. Department of Labor, Bureau of Labor Statistics.

5. Per pupil spending is based on total expenditures, from MPS annual financial reports, divided by "actual head-count enrollments" (less transfers to suburbs), from the 1987-1988 School/Student Statistical Profile.

6. As part of the desegregation program, MPS set up certain elementary, middle, and high schools as citywide specialty or magnet schools, with programs such as gifted and talented, Montessori, trade and technical, the arts, etc. These schools do not have neighborhood attendance areas.

References

African American Male Task Force. (1990). *Educating African American males: A dream deferred.* Milwaukee, WI: Milwaukee Public Schools.

Asante, M. K. (1987). *The Afrocentric idea.* Philadelphia: Temple University Press.

Bates, P. (1990). Desegregation: Can we get there from here? *Phi Delta Kappan, 72*(1), 8-17.

Bell, D. (1980). *Shades of* Brown: *New perspectives on school desegregation.* New York: Teachers College Press.

Bell, D. (1987a). *And we are not saved: The elusive quest for racial justice.* New York: Basic Books.

Bell, D. (1987b). The case for a separate black school system. *Urban League Review, 11*(1-2), 136-145.

Briggs v. Elliott, 926 F. Supp. 36 (1955).

Brown v. Board of Education of Topeka, Kansas, 347 US 483 (1954).

Busby, D. A., & Barrett, C. A. (1988). Impact of integrated education on blacks in the South. *Equity and Excellence, 23*(4), 57-62.

Carnegie Corporation of New York. (1984-1985). Renegotiating society's contract with the public schools. *Carnegie Quarterly, 29-30*(1-4), 6-11.

College Board. (1985). *Equality and excellence: The educational status of Black Americans.* New York: Carnegie Corporation.

Cuddy, D. L. (1983). A proposal to achieve desegregation through free choice. *American Education, 19*(4), 25-31.

DuBois, W. E. B. (1935). Does the Negro need separate schools? *Journal of Negro Education, 4*(328).

Foner, P. S. (Ed.). (1970). *W. E. B. DuBois speaks: Speeches and addresses 1920-1963.* New York: Pathfinder.

Freire, P. (1985). *The politics of education: Culture, power, and liberation.* New York: Bergin & Garvey.

Fuller, H. (1985). *The impact of the Milwaukee Public School System's desegregation on black students and the black community.* Unpublished doctoral dissertation, Marquette University, WI.

Greater Milwaukee Education Trust. (1991). *Our schools, our future: A community call to action* (A report from the Greater Milwaukee Education Trust and the Milwaukee Public Schools on the state of education in Milwaukee). Milwaukee, WI: Author.

Green, M. (1984). Thinking realistically about integration. *New Perspectives, 35-36.*

Green v. County School Board of New Kent County. 391 U.S. 430 (1968).

Hagedorn, J. (1988). *People and folks: Gangs, crime, and the underclass in a rustbelt city.* Chicago: Lake View Press.

Harris, I. M. (1983). The inequalities of Milwaukee's plan. *Integrated Education, 21*(1-6), 173-177.

Hodgkinson, H. (1985). *All one system: Demographics of education, kindergarten through graduate school.* Washington, DC: The Institute for Educational Leadership.

Irvine, J. J. (1991). *Black students and school failure: Policies, practices, and prescriptions.* New York: Praeger.

Irvine, R. W., & Irvine, J. J. (1983). The impact of the desegregation process on the education process of black students. *The Journal of Negro Education, 52*(4), 410-422.

Jewell, K. S. (1988). *Survival of the black family.* New York: Praeger.

Johnson, C. S. (1954). Some significant social and educational implications of the U. S. Supreme Court's decision. *The Journal of Negro Education, 23,* 364-371.

Kluger, R. (1975). *Simple justice: The history of Brown v. Board of Education and black America's struggle for equality.* New York: Vintage.

Lightfoot, S. L. (1978). *Worlds apart: Relationships between families and schools.* New York: Basic Books.

Meier, K. J., Stewart, J., & England, R. E. (1989). *Race, class, and education: The politics of second-generation discrimination.* Madison: University of Wisconsin Press.

Milwaukee Public Schools. (1980, August). *Reflections on the Milwaukee desegregation experience.* Milwaukee, WI: Author.

Milwaukee Public Schools. (1987). *1986-1987 attendance area/school enrollment.* Milwaukee, WI: Author.

Milwaukee Public Schools. (1988). *Sending and receiving attendance reports.* Milwaukee, WI: Author.

Milwaukee Public Schools. (1991). *MPS 1991 report card.* Milwaukee, WI: Author.

Milwaukee Public Schools. (1994). *Report of MPS results: Wisconsin grade three reading test.* Milwaukee, WI: Author.

Milwaukee Urban League. (1988). *Milwaukee today: A racial gap study.* Milwaukee, WI: Author.

Orfield, G. (1993). *The growth of segregation in American schools: Changing patterns of separation and poverty since 1968.* Cambridge, MA: Harvard Project on School Desegregation.

Plessy v. Ferguson, 163 U.S. 537 (1896).

Pollard, D. S., & Ajirotutu, C. (1994). *Documenting the African American immersion schools: A work in progress.* Milwaukee: University of Wisconsin.

Rabinow, K. L. E. (1983). Propositional paper: School desegregation and human capital. *Urban Education, 17*(4), 439-456.

Rutter, M., Maughan, B., Mortimer, P., & Ouston, J. (1979). *Fifteen-thousand hours: Secondary schools and their effect on children.* Cambridge, MA: Harvard University Press.

Scott, H. J. (1983). Desegregation in Nashville: Conflicts and contradictions in preserving schools in black communities. *Education and Urban Society, 15*(2), 235-244.

Smith, M. (1987). The creation of an inner city district for inner city residents: A commentary. *Metropolitan Education, 5,* 1-6.

U.S. Civil Rights Act, Public Law 88-352 (1964).

Walberg, H. J. (1992). Involuntary school desegregation versus effective education. In J. Lynch, C. Modgil, & S. Modgil (Eds.), *Cultural diversity and the schools: Prejudice or progress?* (Vol. 2). Bristol, PA: Falmer.

Williams, A. P. (1991, February 20). Keynote address presented at the American Legislation Exchange Council Conference, Milwaukee, WI.

Willie, C. V., Alves, M. J., & Hartman, D. J. (1990). *Long-range educational equity plan for Milwaukee Public Schools.* Milwaukee, WI: Milwaukee Public Schools.

Wisconsin Policy Research Institute. (1989). *An evaluation of state-financed school integration in metropolitan Milwaukee* (Vol. 2, No. 5). Milwaukee, WI: Author.

12

School Desegregation, the Politics
of Culture, and the Council
of Independent Black Institutions

MWALIMU J. SHUJAA

HANNIBAL T. AFRIK

> Negro communities, Negro private schools, Negro colleges will and must
> be supported. This racial organization will be voluntary and not compul-
> sory . . . voluntary organization for great ends is far different from com-
> pulsory segregation for evil purposes.
>
> W. E. B. DuBois, 1960

This chapter is about the politics of education and the relationships of
power involved in the societal and cultural contexts of schooling and
education. Power is defined by Nobles and Goddard (1984) as "the ability
to define reality and to have other people respond to your definition as if it
were their own" (p. 107). In the context of the politics of education, Spring
(1990) defines power as the "ability to control the actions of others and the
ability to escape the control of others" (p. 45). For our purposes, we are
concerned with the power to define and control education and schooling.

For all its legal brilliance, school desegregation as a strategy to achieve
quality education for African Americans has been impotent to effect changes
in the power relationships of schooling and education. Power relationships
that existed prior to the U.S. Supreme Court's decisions on the constitutionality of school segregation were essentially unchanged by those decisions.
Thus, although the NAACP legal strategists systematically eroded the

253

"separate but equal" doctrine, the "integration" without power that resulted left the same authorities who managed school segregation to manage
school desegregation. These authorities made the decisions about which
schools would be closed, which teachers would be released, what schools
children would attend, and at what pace the changes would take place.

The Council of Independent Black Institutions (CIBI) was founded in
1972 as a national organization to unify a far-flung, rapidly developing
movement of Pan-Africanist-oriented independent schools in the United
States. CIBI's founding represented the implementation of ideas from a
different ideological stream than that which guided integrationist strategies
that swept African American communities during the period leading up to
and following the Supreme Court's *Brown v. Board of Education* decision.
In this chapter, we use the emergence of CIBI to illustrate how concepts of
quality education for African Americans extend beyond school desegregation when the power to define and control education is contested. A case
analysis of CIBI's activities during its early years is used to explain some of
the ways in which this organization sought to define and organize control
of education. We conclude with a discussion of the politics of culture in the
context of education and schooling.

The Emergence of CIBI: Context and Concept

The community control of public schools movement was an attempt
by African Americans in cities such as New York City, Chicago, Los Angeles,
Boston, and Washington, D.C., to obtain power over schools in African
American communities. It marked a watershed period in African American
strategies to obtain quality education by forcing confrontation over the
issue of power. In her analysis of the community control of public schools
movement of the late 1960s, Gittell (1969) surmised that the school desegregation movement provided African Americans "with insights into their
exclusion from the school decision-making process" (p. 365). She points
out further that the struggle for school desegregation highlighted both the
educational and political failure of big city school districts and the unwill-
ingness of the whites who controlled those districts to concede power. These
struggles over control of schools in settings such as the Ocean Hill-Brownsville
Experimental School District in New York City brought the power of whites
to control African American schooling into clear focus.

Claims by African Americans to the right to control the public schools
their children attended were met by organized opposition from politicians

and schooling professionals. Clearly, the opposition to community control was led by whites; however, when some African American teachers became convinced that their professional interests were threatened by community control, the movement to seize control of public schools was defeated. This led some African Americans in the community control movement to take the position that the *Brown* decision not only had contributed little to African American political power over schooling, it had actually created conditions that deepened class contradictions among African Americans. In the Ocean Hill-Brownsville case, some African American teachers refused to support the local governing board's efforts to transfer what it had determined to be "uncooperative" teachers and to install African American supervisors. In 1968, Leslie Campbell (later to become Jitu Weusi), a teacher in the Ocean Hill-Brownsville district and advocate of community control, wrote:

> Suddenly along comes the "revolution" and the establishment is forced to "integrate" to try to appease the rebellious black masses. The Negro professional is catapulted into positions of relative importance and wealth. . . . The creation of a schism between the Negro professional and black masses is the last remaining weapon of the Establishment in its effort to maintain white supremacy. (1970b, p. 26)

The attack on the community control of the schools movement further sharpened many African American activists' understandings of the politics of education and the dynamics of power. Several independent black schools were formed as a result. Leslie Campbell, who by then had changed his name to Jitu Weusi, left the public schools altogether and organized the Uhuru Sasa Shule (Freedom Now School) in Brooklyn in 1970. A skillful and astute organizer, Weusi was also part of the leadership of the African American Teachers Association in Brooklyn. From this point, we will trace some of the events that led to CIBI's founding.

The echoing cry of "Black Power" became the vital spirit of the emerging independent black school movement. Five black power conferences were held between 1966 and 1970. Writing in the *Afro-American Teachers Forum* in 1967, after the Second National Conference on Black Power held in Newark from July 20-23, Jitu Weusi (Leslie Campbell) expressed the fervor of many who attended those meetings.

> The dream that was born of this convention was the idea of black nationhood (here in North America) and self-determination for black

people. The ideas and resolutions adopted by the conference all
project toward that day when the black population of North America
can say proudly, "I don't want to be part of yours, I have my own." If
black power has one common meaning, it most certainly means that
black people have a right to and must rule and control their destinies
here in America. (1970a, p. 23)

The California Association for Afro-American Education and Nairobi
College jointly sponsored a conference from August 17 to 19, 1970, in East
Palo Alto, California. The aims of the conference were to set up criteria for
the evaluation of independent black schools and to facilitate communications between such schools. It was here that these schools were identified
as "Independent Black Institutions" (IBIs). They represented an "organized, revolutionary approach by black people to control the development
of the minds and consciousness of our community through the self-reliant
process of [building] progressive educational institutions" (Afrik, 1981, p.
14). The conference produced six fundamental concepts that characterized
an IBI (Afrik, 1981, pp. 14-15). These were commitments to the following:

1. Communalism—the antithesis of competitive individualism
2. Decolonization—the acquisition of ownership and control by African people of the political, economic, social, and educational institutions that are rightfully their own
3. African Personality—a set of attitudes, values, and behaviors necessary for the development and maintenance of African people throughout the world
4. Humanism—an attitudinal and behavioral perspective that stresses
   distinctively human rather than material and profit concerns
5. Harmony—the synchronous relationship between the individual
   and his/her environment
6. Nation building—the use of human and material resources for
   community development, service, ownership, and control, which,
   in reality, is survival

These concepts reflect the awareness that existed of the relationship
between culture and worldview. The movement to control African American education was taking shape around the development of institutions that
would rest on values meant to sustain positive development among African
people. Reflected in these concepts is an understanding of the need to

deconstruct ways of thinking born out of racist hegemony and an optimism about the possibilities of personal transformation toward becoming "new African" women and men. Additional evidence of how well the role of culture in power relationships was understood is the conference report's inclusion of the Nguzo Saba (The Seven Principles of Blackness), developed by Maulana Karenga in 1965, at the head of the list of goals identified for a proposed nationwide system of IBIs. The Nguzo Saba were intended by Karenga to be the "central focus and sine qua non of an internal black value system" (Karenga, 1977, p. 21).

Shortly after the California meeting, the first Congress of African People was convened in Atlanta, Georgia, on September 3 to 7, 1970. This meeting was actually the fifth Black Power Conference. The name was changed to illustrate that the scope of the conference was broader than the African American context (Ploski & Williams, 1990). We will have more to say about the significance of conceptualizing African identity in historical and cultural contexts that are distinct from and unlimited by the boundaries of the United States as a nation-state in our concluding section. What is relevant here is the identification by the organizers of the continuity between the condition of African people in the United States and the nationalist struggles against colonialism waged by African people on the continent and in the Caribbean. The Education and Black Students Workshop chaired by Preston Wilcox was one of 11 convened at the Congress. Within this workshop alone, there were 10 working sessions; one of these was on Independent Black Educational Institutions. Two reports on this working session were published. The first, edited by Preston Wilcox (1970), was *Workshop on Education and Black Students, Congress of African People, Summary Report*. The second report, edited by Frank J. Satterwhite (1971), was later published as a booklet titled *Planning an Independent Black Educational Institution*.

The charge given this working session was to "develop plans for establishing a parallel school system incorporating all legally, physically, and psychologically independent schools at every educational level into a national Pan African School System" (Satterwhite, 1971, p. 2).

Although it appears that the participants in the working session were of one mind on the need to control the educational institutions that African people attended, there were two schools of thought about the most appropriate strategy to take. One avenue was to continue to pursue community control of public schools serving large populations of children of African descent. These schools, once under the control of the African community, would be converted to IBIs. The second strategy was either to establish new independent institutions or to strengthen existing ones. It was the latter strategy that received the most attention.

A general approach to the politics of education throughout the overall workshop emphasized both the lack of power and need for power by African people over their own education. Satterwhite (1971, p. 6) lists four axiomatic assumptions that guided all of the discussions.

1. All black educators (teachers, students, parents, administrators, and community residents) must be held accountable to the black community.

2. The education of black people must be controlled by black people, whether it takes place within a white setting or within a black setting.

3. Education is a political act; its goals are people building, community building, nation building. It must be directed towards the transmission of skills, knowledge, culture, and values designed to produce a New African Man [and Woman].

4. Education must be applied as a tool in the nation-building process.

In his discussion of this working session, Haki R. Madhubuti, in his 1973 book *From Plan to Planet*, concluded that "it is unrealistic to talk about change if you are not moving to control the instruments of change in your community" (p. 41). The above assumptions reflect analyses of the ways in which power has been successfully used against African people throughout the world. The only logical course of action perceived to be available to African people was to organize for power over their lives.

From April 21 to 23, 1972, the New York African-American Teachers Association, an organization that propagated the concept of community control of schools, convened a meeting that planted the seed for a national black education system (Afrik, 1981). From the earnest discussions of those 28 people representing 14 independent schools across the country came a mandate to form an organization whose purpose would be to produce a uniform pattern of educational achievement. Moreover, this organization would be devoted to liberating political objectives and dedicated to excellence.

John Churchville, founder of Freedom Library Day School, one of the first new independent schools to emerge during the era of the black power conferences, was an invited guest at that meeting. From Churchville's (1973) account of the meeting, we gain a picture of the divided loyalties between public school reform and building independent institutions.

They had a two-section conference. On one side, they had black teachers in the public schools in New York concerned about survival in the public schools. Then they had other people coming to that conference who were concerned about alternative systems, and setting up methods for that. (p. 56)

Churchville, Jitu Weusi, and others already involved in building independent institutions were frustrated by the group's inability to develop a consensus around a plan of action. A caucus of the independent school representatives was convened during the meeting to discuss what should be done. A decision was arrived at swiftly, according to Churchville's (1973) description: "We got in a room and after 15 minutes we came out of that room with a Council of Independent Black Institutions. Our concern was to share information, materials, and curriculum and to have a material unity" (p. 57).

A national work meeting was held in Frogmore, South Carolina, from June 29 to July 3, 1972, to confirm the initial mandate from the independent school caucus at the African American Teachers Association conference. The participants in this meeting determined the principles, policies, and programs of the organization and set up a national structure to carry out its objectives. It was at this point that the national Council of Independent Black Institutions (CIBI) began to function and take form. The original statement of purpose provided that CIBI must

be the political vehicle through which a qualitatively different people is produced . . . a people committed to truth—in practice as well as in principle—and dedicated to excellence . . . a people who can be trusted to struggle uncompromisingly for the liberation of all African people everywhere. (CIBI, 1972, p. 2)

It went on to state,

The Independent Black Institution is charged with the responsibility of developing the moral character of its students and staff, and of providing the clear, sane, and well-reasoned leadership which is imperative to a correct struggle for freedom and internal community development. (CIBI, 1972, p. 2)

The formation of independent African American schools was not a new phenomenon. The historical record shows that African people have been creating their own schools in the United States since the 1790s (Ratteray, 1990; Ratteray & Shujaa, 1988). The founding of CIBI and the movement it characterizes are historically significant to African people throughout the world for at least two reasons that are relevant to the present discussion.

First, we witness the employment of institution building as a strategy for cultural liberation. CIBI's strategic use of institution building for the independent education of African people at a time when so many other African American institutions were caught in the maelstrom of school desegregation has to be respected. Institution building among CIBI's members was clearly organized resistance against the European-centered cultural hegemony and intellectual control that shrouded school desegregation. Furthermore, although it was undertaken to lay a foundation for national liberation and self-determination, institution building became a means of establishing "liberated zones" or "free spaces" where the process of education would be insulated from the cultural assault of Western hegemony.

Second, we see the emergence of a network of schools for people of African descent in which there is a shift in the cultural orientation of curriculum. The efforts undertaken by the schools that formed CIBI to deconstruct European views of the world while reclaiming, recovering, and reconstructing an African worldview and, most important, to codify this process in their curricula are invaluable contributions. CIBI helped to lay a path that had been pursued earlier by Marcus Garvey's Universal Negro Improvement Association and the Nation of Islam under the Honorable Elijah Muhammad (Essien-Udom, 1962; Martin, 1976; Ratteray, 1990). This attention to the cultural context of schooling was largely missing in the school desegregation movement. DuBois (1960) notes that many in the African American community feared that the study of African cultural history as distinct from European cultural history would set back school desegregation.

CIBI's Program

In the more than 20 years since its founding, CIBI has advocated institution-building strategies on a variety of fronts. It is instructive to discuss some of these efforts here. First, CIBI schools incorporate a Pan-African philosophy of education based on a cultural value system (the Nguzo Saba). Second, CIBI schools represent organized partnerships of parents, educators, and community residents who are collectively engaged in building and maintaining institutions of learning. Third, CIBI has produced instructional resources for classroom and home use. Fourth, CIBI has provided examples of positive educational outcomes for African American youth both academically, as demonstrated by the cognitive achievements of students and the instructional accomplishments of teachers, and culturally, by helping to popularize African-centered observances such as African Liberation Day, the birthdays of Malcolm X, Marcus Garvey, and others, and adolescent rites-of-passage programs. Fifth, CIBI has maintained standards of self-governance pending national liberation. Although not all of the initiatives have been sustained, it is important to take note of CIBI's consistent efforts to address education as a cultural issue that cannot be divorced from family, community, and racial imperatives.

Teacher Training

Top priority was given to the establishment of a teacher training agency. CIBI organized its first national Teacher Training Institute in Philadelphia, Pennsylvania, from July 23 to August 13, 1972. The 15 graduates completed the first step in qualifying for appointment to the African Teachers Corps. Since that time, CIBI has continued to sponsor national, regional, and local teacher training institutes to develop qualified teachers for IBIs.

In recent years, CIBI's Teacher Training Institutes have also included teachers and administrators on the faculties of public or private schools, undergraduate and graduate students who may or may not be in teacher preparation studies, and other members of the African American community who are interested in teaching in independent black institutions, or who want to learn the teaching methods used in these schools.

Film Production

In February 1973, CIBI completed its first film, *It's a New Day.* This 30-minute black-and-white film focused on the founding and developing of black educational institutions. *It's a New Day* became a cornerstone in CIBI's public relations and provided inspiration for the development of a number of African-centered, community-based institutions.

Parent Organizing

On May 5, 1973, and June 30, 1973, the first and second National Black Parents Conventions were held in Brooklyn, New York, and East Palo

Alto, California, respectively. About 1,000 people attended these meetings, which resulted in the creation of the National Black Parents Organization, dedicated to strengthening the black family and providing educational excellence for our children.

Family Learning

A Black Family Learning Festival was held on November 16, 1974, at the New York City Community College, with Dr. Frances Cress Welsing as featured speaker. Workshops were held to discuss African-centered literature and educational materials, parental involvement in private and public schools, new methods of teaching, and the propagation of traditional family values.

Black Manhood

Over 100 serious-minded black men attended a 3-day conclave in Philadelphia from May 2 to 4, 1975. This gathering was described as a "national work meeting in an environment conducive to an honest assessment of ourselves and our relationships to our wives, children, and community; an opportunity to reorder our priorities and make personal changes" (CIBI, 1975).

At the conclusion of the meeting, the participants formed an organization called the Black Man Secretariat. This organization sponsored an additional meeting on June 27, 1975, in Cairo, Illinois.

Speakers' Bureau

The CIBI Speakers' Bureau and Consultant Service was formed to offer advice, assistance, recommendations, references, and research in areas related to African American education. The membership of this select group of educators generally consists of individuals who have demonstrated the skills and expertise necessary to start and sustain community-based educational programs.

Science Expositions

An outgrowth of the 1976 Teacher Training Institute was the formation of a Pan-African Science Committee. This committee organized the first national science exhibition in April 1977 at Uhuru Sasa Shule in Brooklyn,

New York. Since then, each year in a different city, more than 100 children of all ages participate in the only scientific exhibition of its kind in the United States.

The broad objective of the Science Expo is to provide an opportunity for our children to demonstrate their knowledge of scientific, mathematical, and technical concepts. The students prepare projects that are evaluated according to African criteria based on the Nguzo Saba.

In order to ensure the continued success of its national Science Expo, CIBI established the IMHOTEP Science Fund in 1990. The fund provides financial assistance to CIBI students traveling to and displaying their projects at the national exhibition.

Outdoor Education Leadership Skills

The National Survival Training Committee was organized in 1977 to provide skills in coping with rural and urban emergency situations. Since its inception, a leadership cadre has conducted weekend encampments in California, Michigan, Ohio, Virginia, and Illinois. The program engages individuals or families in a deeper cultural reverence that combines traditional heritage with self-disciplined behavioral skills. Designed for both youth and adults, the training program includes four proficiency levels. Included in the training are exercises in map and compass reading, establishment of campsites, water purification, first aid, martial arts, wild food foraging, nature hikes, and physical development. Practical exercises are conducted during 1- to 3-day outdoor camping excursions or in classroom demonstrations.

Community Outreach

CIBI's newsletter, *FUNDISHA: Teach!* serves as a medium for the exchange of information and opinion on various aspects of black education. Begun in 1974 and now published semiannually, it is distributed nationally through individuals and member institutions.

CIBI has also published a variety of pamphlets and monographs dealing with issues relating to African-centered education. In 1990, *Positive Afrikan Images for Children,* a CIBI social studies curriculum guide, was published in book form. Designed to be used by teachers and parents, *Positive African Images* represents the cumulative classroom experiences in African-centered education compiled by some of CIBI's most accomplished instructors. Molefi Kete Asante gave it the following endorsement:

I find the curriculum guide conceptually Afrocentric and exciting. Indeed the work in this guide is the result of years of practice and research. What we have come to learn over the last few years is that African-American children do learn effectively from culturally consistent models of education. That is the way all children learn. This guide should influence the discussion of the proper education of children well into the next millennium. (CIBI, 1990, back cover)

Afrikan Youth Organization

Since 1977, the Afrikan Youth Organization (AYO), created by the Nation House Positive Action Center in Washington, D.C., has provided a variety of character-building experiences for young people, promoting African-centered values and appreciation of African history and culture. AYO began its rural summer camp, Heritage Village Encampment, in 1982 on the Black Star Estates land cooperative near Mineral, Virginia. The annual encampment is structured around the three major themes of nature studies, physical development, and cultural awareness/personal development.

Through CIBI's program, we see the functional relationship between independent black institutions and their communities. Theoretically, IBIs exist to meet community needs by assisting in the development of community resources. Since the community is the powerbase for an IBI, its effectiveness in serving that community is the primary factor for its legitimization. IBIs have been found to be important models within the African American community for several reasons. They demonstrate that African American people can effectively educate their own children. They provide inspiration for committed parents and teachers who are involved in public schools. Moreover, it is felt that the IBI is a valuable model in terms of institutional development within the African American community (Brookins, 1984; Lomotey & Brookins, 1988).

The goals of committed African American teachers, both in public schools and independent institutions, are often the same in terms of wanting to provide quality education for African American children. A former CIBI National Executive Officer, Kofi Lomotey, writing with Craig Brookins (1988), acknowledges that African American teachers working in different institutional contexts may share the same commitment to African American children, but they also emphasize the priority that teachers in CIBI are expected to give to institution building: "The ultimate objective is the creation of permanent African American institutions, families, and individuals whose priorities and energies ensure the achievement of the goals of independence, self-determination, and dignity for African people the world over" (p. 180).

Many of the institutions founded prior to and since CIBI's inception no longer exist. It is no easy task to confront authority or to challenge anti-African, racialized power relations that have existed for centuries. Nor is it easy to transform the effects of social institutions that have continually asserted and reasserted cultural hegemony over the thinking of African people. CIBI has endeavored to stand as an example of academic and cultural achievement for the African American community. Lee (1992) argues that the question to be asked about CIBI is whether its institutions "represent bastions of narrow, separatist, anti-American instruction or whether they offer some promise of hope for public education" (p. 174). As a founder in 1972 of the New Concept Development Center, an IBI in Chicago, when Lee speaks of hope for public education, she is arguing for an ideal circumstance in which the pedagogies and cultural environments of New Concept Development Center and other successful IBIs are experienced by all African children. In response to the question she poses, Lee argues that the "proof is in the pudding" and points to the intellectual and cultural successes of many of the students who have graduated from IBIs as proof of the vital role their work has played for the uplift of people of African descent.

The Politics of Culture

As we conclude, we feel it is important to restate that our concern is with the politics of education and the relationships of power involved in the societal and cultural contexts of schooling and education. Our analysis of CIBI's emergence as a national organization and description of its program are meant to provide a way of looking theoretically and practically at a strategy for quality African American education and schooling that differs from school desegregation in its ideological assumptions. The major issue is how power relations are addressed. School desegregation as a strategy does not challenge in any fundamental way the cultural and political authority of the ruling elite in the United States over the schooling and education of people of African descent. The African-centered institution-building model that has evolved in CIBI clearly does so by seeking power over education and schooling.

In order to understand the historicity of what CIBI represents in the context of the global struggles of African people on and off the continent against invasion, enslavement, colonialism, neocolonialism, and cultural hegemony, the realities of culture and power must be taken into account. The failure to take into account differing cultural orientations and unequal power relations among groups that share membership in a society effectively obscures the contradictions inherent in assuming that education and schooling worked out in accordance with the needs of politically and culturally privileged groups will also serve the interests of groups disadvantaged within the social order. This is the reason that education and schooling do not necessarily occupy the same space at the same time (see Shujaa, 1994). The cultural identity of people of African descent in the United States has been and continues to be influenced by the U.S. social context. It is essential to note, however, that the African cultural orientation also represents an experiential context in its own right. Thus, although African Americans exist within the U.S. social context, they also exist within the continuity of African cultural history. This continuum has existed since antiquity. Thus, it existed before the U.S. social context and any influences it has imposed upon African people and will continue to exist whether the nation-state and social arrangements rise or fall. If education is understood as the process of transmitting from one generation to the next knowledge, values, aesthetics, spiritual beliefs, and all things that give a particular culture orientation its uniqueness, then CIBI's efforts to seize and maintain political and cultural power over the education of African people are acts of cultural responsibility. The only other option is cultural surrender, perhaps gradual, but surrender nonetheless.

When the existence of competing interests is discussed as an aspect of the politics of education, the approach is generally one of managing the impact of such conflict on the existing order or system (Wong, 1992). This reduction of conflict to a problem of management is a view that reflects a perspective taken from the vantage point of those who perceive themselves to be empowered, at least for the moment, by the status quo arrangements. Predictions are made about the potential impact the conflict may have on the system or order. These are couched in terms that estimate the threat to existing power relations posed by the range of possible outcomes related to the conflict. This is the domain of the politics of education. Most people who do this kind of work submit their findings and reports to people who hold power within the existing order or system and want to maintain their positions relative to those who contest their use of power.

The thing about systems is that change is acceptable to those who wield power within them only if it can be managed in a way that does not disrupt the systems' workings and extant power relationships. School desegregation was intended by the U.S. Supreme Court to be—and has been implemented as—a form of managed change within the general social system and its subsystems. The discussion of power relations in U.S. schooling, when it occurs, is likely to treat African Americans as one interest group among others to be taken into account when calculating demands on the system (Wirt & Kirst, 1989). We take exception to such treatment. In our view, this is an assumption of cultural neutrality in schooling. More precisely, however, it is the veiled cultural hegemony of the politically and culturally dominant elites in U.S. society.

It is important to keep in mind that school systems are linked to other societal systems and that changes affecting school systems also must be managed in other contexts of the social order. The use of power to influence action on such a broad level finds its license within the cultural orientations of the ruling elite. Parsons's (1966) action theory of the social system places beliefs held about ultimate reality in the apex of a hierarchy of controlling factors over human social behavior. Beliefs about ultimate reality are part of the deep structure of culture. The cultural beliefs about ultimate reality that were shared by the ruling elites who formed the United States and that led to its construction as a "white nation" are reflected in the credo of manifest destiny as pretext for attempted genocide and the invention of the "negro" as a race cursed by God to help justify enslavement. Such culturally linked racial beliefs have influenced the use of political power to control social relations, including those related to schooling and education throughout the history of the United States. This racialization of power relations in U.S. society should force serious scholars to address the cultural centering of schooling as a contested area.

References

Afrik, H. T. (1981). *Education for self-reliance, idealism to reality: An analysis of the independent black school movement.* Stanford, CA: Council of Independent Black Institutions.

Brookins, C. (1984). *A descriptive analysis of ten independent black educational models.* Master's thesis, Department of Psychology, Michigan State University.

Campbell, L. (1970a). The black teacher and black power. In N. Wright, Jr. (Ed.), *What black educators are saying* (pp. 23-24). New York: Hawthorn.

Campbell, L. (1970b). The difference. In N. Wright, Jr. (Ed.), *What black educators are saying* (pp. 25-26). New York: Hawthorn.

Churchville, J. (1973). Freedom Library Day School. In Black Child Development Institute (Ed.), *Curriculum approaches from a black perspective* (pp. 45-64). Atlanta, GA: Author.

Council of Independent Black Institutions. (1972). Summary from first work meeting, June 30 to July 3, Frogmore, SC. Unpublished document, 28 pages.

Council of Independent Black Institutions. (1975). *Directory handbook.* New York: Author.

Council of Independent Black Institutions. (1990). *Positive Afrikan images for children.* Trenton, NJ: Red Sea Press.

DuBois, W. E. B. (1960). Whither now and why. *Quarterly Review of Higher Education Among Negroes, 28,* 135-141.

Essien-Udom, E. U. (1962). *Black nationalism: A search for an identity in America.* New York: Dell.

Gittell, M. (1969). Community control of education. In M. Gittell & A. G. Hevesi (Eds.), *The politics of urban education* (pp. 363-377). New York: Praeger.

Karenga, M. (1977). *Kwanzaa: Origin, concepts, practice.* Los Angeles: Kawaida.

Lee, C. D. (1992). Profile of an independent black institution: African-centered education at work. *Journal of Negro Education, 61*(2), 160-177.

Lomotey, K., & Brookins, C. (1988). Independent black institutions: A cultural perspective. In D. T. Slaughter & D. J. Johnson (Eds.), *Visible now: Blacks in private schools* (pp. 163-183). Westport, CT: Greenwood.

Madhubuti, H. R. (1973). *From plan to planet. Life studies: The need for Afrikan minds and institutions.* Chicago: Third World Press.

Martin, T. (1976). *Race first: The ideological and organizational struggles of Marcus Garvey and the Universal Negro Improvement Association.* Dover, MA: The Majority Press.

National Education Association. (1992). *Status of the American teacher.* Washington, DC: Author.

Nobles, W. W., & Goddard, L. L. (1984). *Understanding the black family: A guide for scholarship and research.* Oakland, CA: Black Family Institute.

Parsons, T. (1966). *Societies: Evolutionary and comparative perspectives.* Englewood Cliffs, NJ: Prentice Hall.

Ploski, H. A., & Williams, J. (Eds.). (1990). *Reference library of black America, Vol. 1.* Philadelphia: Afro-American Press.

Ratteray, J. D. (1990). *Center shift: An African-centered approach for the multicultural curriculum.* Washington, DC: Institute for Independent Education.

Ratteray, J. D., & Shujaa, M. J. (1988). Defining a tradition: Parental choice in independent neighborhood schools. In D. T. Slaughter & D. J. Johnson (Eds.), *Visible now: Blacks in private schools* (pp. 184-198). Westport, CT: Greenwood.

Satterwhite, F. J. (Ed.). (1971). *Planning an independent black educational institution.* Harlem, NY: MOJA.

Shujaa, M. J. (1994). Education and schooling: You can have one without the other. In M. J. Shujaa (Ed.), *Too much schooling, too little education: A paradox of black life in white societies* (pp. 13-36). Trenton, NJ: Africa World Press.

Spring, J. (1990). Knowledge and power in research into the politics of urban education. In J. G. Cibulka, R. J. Reed, & K. K. Wong (Eds.), *The politics of urban education in the United States* (pp. 45-55). Washington, DC: Falmer.

Wilcox, P. (Ed.). (1970). *Workshop on education and black students, Congress of African People, Summary Report, September 1970.* New York: AFRAM Associates.

Wirt, F., & Kirst, M. (1989). *The politics of education: Schools in conflict* (2nd ed.). Berkeley, CA: McCutchan.

Wong, K. K. (1992). The politics of urban education as a field of study: An interpretive analysis. In J. G. Cibulka, R. J. Reed, & K. K. Wong (Eds.), *The politics of urban education in the United States* (pp. 3-26). Washington, DC: Falmer.

Name Index

Subject Index

**CORWIN
PRESS**

The Corwin Press logo—a raven striding across an open book—represents the happy union of courage and learning. We are a professional-level publisher of books and journals for K-12 educators, and we are committed to creating and providing resources that embody these qualities. Corwin's motto is "Success for All Learners."